CHRONICLES OF THE BIG BEND

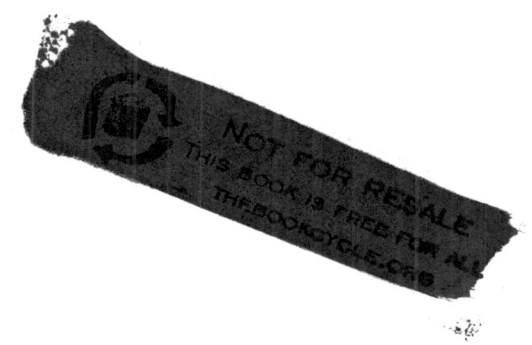

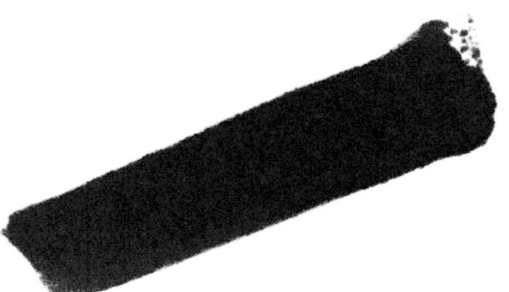

CHRONICLES
OF THE
BIG BEND

A PHOTOGRAPHIC MEMOIR OF LIFE ON THE BORDER

W. D. SMITHERS

Foreword by Kenneth B. Ragsdale

Texas State Historical Association
Austin

Library of Congress Cataloging-in-Publication Data

Smithers, W. D. (Wilfred Dudley), 1895–
    Chronicles of the Big Bend : a photographic memoir of life on the border / W. D.
Smithers; foreword by Kenneth B. Ragsdale.
        p.   cm.
    Includes bibliographical references and index.
    ISBN: 978-1-876112-61-5
        1. Big Bend Region (Tex.)—History—20th century. 2. Big Bend Region (Tex.)—
History—20th century—pictorial works. 3. Frontier and pioneer life—Texas—Big Bend Region.
4. Frontier and pioneer life—Texas—BigBend Region—Pictorial works. 5. Smithers, W. D.
(Wilfred Dudley), 1895–   6. Big Bend Region (Tex.)—Biography. I. Title

   F392.B54 S6 1999
   976.4'93—dc21
99-050158

5 4 3 2 1 99 00 01 02 03

Published by the Texas State Historical Association in cooperation with the Center for Studies in
Texas History at the University of Texas at Austin

Dustjacket design by David Timmons

Publication of this book is supported by a grant from the Erwin E. Smith Foundation

The paper used in this book meets the minimum requirements of the American National
Standard for Permanence of Paper for Printed Library Materials, Z39.48—1984

To all the characters in these chronicles,
which they themselves created.

Contents

Foreword

The Big Bend of Texas is a world unto itself, a ruggedly forbidding peninsula of land left remote and isolated by the irresponsible antics of the Rio Grande. This geologic fantasy land is the perverse creation of that mighty river as it plunges deep into Mexico and then, as if changing its mind, partially reverses its course in its search for the distant waters of the Gulf of Mexico. The land held in this embrace—the Big Bend of Texas—is one of our last frontiers.

While cities grew in other regions of the state, and railroads and highways spanned the nation, the Big Bend remained a remote hinterland—and kept its secrets well. But early in the twentieth century its primitive lure began attracting the adventurous and the inquisitive: geologists and surveyors, naturalists and folklorists, painters and journalists. Their accounts of the region's rugged beauty, forbidding flora, hostile climate, and lonely natives who still attempted to live off the crusty soil gave a measure of plausibility to the romantic legends that have always shrouded the region. While much of the romance of the Big Bend is a twentieth century phenomenon, the wellspring of the imagination is the area's more than four hundred years of recorded history.

Three quarters of a century before the Pilgrims landed at Plymouth Rock, the Big Bend area had been tentatively explored, settlements established, and travel routes surveyed; yet almost until 1900 the area remained virtually an uninhabited wasteland. This was the legacy of the Indians. The region south of the Davis Mountains and west of the Pecos River was the private bastion of marauding Apaches and Comanches. Their numerical strength ensured their supremacy and for more than three centuries the Spaniards, and later the Americans, could gain scarcely more than a tenuous foothold.

There were, however, early Anglo intrusions into the Big Bend that portended exploration and settlement, and later exploitation and development. Cabeza de Vaca entered the region in 1535 in his search for the Panuco River and became the first European to see the Big Bend. According to the historian Carlos Castañeda, the Cabeza de Vaca party pursued a southwesterly course across what is now central Brewster County and came to the outskirts of the Chisos Mountains. The Cabeza de Vaca journal describes the land and its occupants in great detail, and this profile remained current for almost three centuries: a hostile environment, unpredictable savages, vast unsettled expanses, and an unproductive arid wilderness.

In the late seventeenth century the Spanish entered the region and began a century and a half of exploration, occupation, and settlement, often interrupted by Apache and Zuma Indians. Although the Spanish traversed the area repeatedly, established settlements, and left detailed journals of their explorations, they failed to make a permanent imprint in the Big Bend. Their footprints have long since vanished from the shifting sands.

With the transfer of the lands lying north of the Rio Grande from Mexico to the United States in 1848, conditions for occupation and settlement of the Big Bend grew more favorable. Yet nearly half a century remained before the region would be thoroughly explored and its resource potential inventoried.

The late nineteenth century Big Bend settlement pattern evolved according to conditions cited by previous explorers. The prolonged Indian barrier was eliminated in the late 1880s, and the same military force that brought peace to the region also created a market for supplies and services that fostered permanent settlement. As the twentieth century dawned, cinnabar deposits that soon thrust the region to the forefront of the world quicksilver market spawned boomtowns such as Study Butte, Terlingua, and Mariposa. And along the Rio Grande both Mexican and Anglo farmers diverted precious river water to alluvial fields that produced some of the first cotton west of the Pecos.

Unique environments produced unique institutions. Early in the century, for example, there sprang up along the north bank of the Rio Grande a chain of remote stores and trading posts strung out from Boquillas to Candelaria. These emporiums, located more than one hundred miles from established distribution centers, drew customers from both sides of the river. Mexicans traveled from the interior of Chihuahua and Coahuila to make their purchases. The former owners report that while receipts ran into the tens of thousands of dollars annually, practically no money changed hands as most of the transactions were effected through barter and trade. The customers were people who lived off the land and its products were their wealth.

The livestock industry developed in proportion to the expanding population and followed largely ethnic traditions: Anglo cattlemen worked the large interior spreads along streams and watered valleys, while Mexican families watched over small herds of goats and burros along the Rio Grande, each following the cultural heritage of their ancestry. While the Big Bend economy evolved along well diversified channels—industry, mercantile trade, farming, and ranching—the wealth was highly concentrated and the dramatic extremes between affluence and poverty followed largely ethnic origins.

Lawlessness has long been a fact of border life, and in this "twilight zone" between the United States and Mexico were enacted the tragic events of man versus man that have accorded the region its highest form of human drama. The combined efforts of sheriffs, Texas Rangers, and the Border Patrol never equaled the challenge of the lawless, and when the Madero Revolution erupted into an international crisis in 1915 and 1916, the United States Army came to the aid of the local constabulary. The tragic events of the Glenn Springs raid, the Brite Ranch raid, indiscriminate banditry, and Chico Cano's reign of terror poignantly support the fact that even the military with its cavalry, mechanized support, and aerial surveillance could not conquer the Texas Big Bend.

As the century came midway in its second decade, the region, redolent in overlays of history and culture, awaited the arrival of its chronicler. On May 19, 1916, with a camera, a notepad, and an inquiring mind, Wilfred Dudley Smithers entered the Big Bend of Texas. The historical resources were vast and the recording process provided high adventure. The rest of the story is pictorial history.

I first met Bill Smithers on the morning of June 7, 1966, while in Alpine, Texas, collecting material on the Terlingua quicksilver mines. Practically everyone I interviewed in the Big Bend suggested that I "see Smithers the photographer. He's been around a long time and knows more about this country than just about anybody." The instructions were easy to follow: "Go down Holland Avenue till you come to that little house with a yard where a lot of cactus is growing. His name is on a sign on the front porch." The inscription told the whole story: W. D. Smithers, Writer-Photographer.

Smithers greeted me cordially and responded to my questions with enthusiasm; his seemingly unending storehouse of knowledge on the Big Bend confirmed what I had been told: "He . . . knows more about this country than just about anybody." But as the interview progressed, Smithers exhibited an annoying habit. Each time I quizzed him on a specific topic, he would jump up from his chair, search through stacks of boxes, and return with a handful of photographs to illustrate his answers.

Smither's thoroughness did nothing to fulfill my immediate needs. I was seeking verbal documentation, not visual illustration.

But as I bade Smithers farewell that beautiful June morning, I carried with me valuable research data, as well as the information that his photographic collection, totaling from eight thousand to ten thousand prints, was for sale. I had no way of knowing that this last bit of information was probably the most valuable research data I would ever collect.

Returning to Austin, I shared my find with University of Texas history professor and Texas State Historical Association director Joe B. Frantz, who grasped the import of the Smithers proposal, which he ushered through the university hierarchy. Seeing samples of the collection, university Chancellor Harry Ransom and associate Frances Hudspeth recognized the high quality of the collection and cleared the way to begin negotiations. Some weeks later Frantz announced casually that an airplane had been chartered to fly me and assistant association director Tuffly Ellis to Alpine to inventory Smithers's holdings and discuss acquisition of the collection.

When the transaction was completed, Joe Coltharp, university curator of photography, and I had the pleasure of delivering the first portion of the collection. On handing Smithers his first check for partial payment, I asked him, "Bill, since this is probably the most money you have ever had at one time, are you going to retire?" His answer was succinct and revealing: "Nope. I'm going to buy me a new camera."

As we drove back toward Austin that late December night, I still couldn't comprehend the true worth of the collection that the University of Texas was about to receive. But to understand better the significance of the collection, one first has to understand the man who had created it.

In retrospect, Smithers's place of birth, early acquaintances, and apprenticeships now appear as well-planned steps to a lifelong career of compiling a verbal and visual cultural history of the Texas Big Bend. Born in Mexico and reared in the strong Mexican cultural environment of San Luis Potosi, he spent his formative years in San Antonio when Mexican culture was still the dominant influence in that city. Smithers emerged from this ethnic amalgam possessing the deep sensitivity to the integrity of cultures that would win him acceptance into separate ethnic worlds.

Smithers is one of those exceptional individuals who recognized history as it was occurring and possessed the capacity to record its lessons. With an eye for detail and an uncanny memory, he preserved a graphic record of a primitive lifestyle that once existed in that "wondrous curve of the Rio Grande." He was truly an eyewitness to history; he was part of a military expeditionary force that entered a region unaccustomed to strangers and unresponsive to change. From the springseat of a military wagon, Smithers witnessed the first penetrations of the barriers to isolation. He saw the construction of some of the first roads into the Bend, and personally knew the daring young men in DeHaviland biplanes who pioneered the first aerial highways across the azure skies of the Trans-Pecos.

But then there is the unchangeable Bend, rich in legend and lore that intrusion could neither alter nor totally comprehend. Smithers is able, however, to gather peripheral knowledge of the working of the avisadores and curanderos. Yet this half-knowledge merely whets our appetites and heightens the mystique that has shrouded the region from the beginning of recorded history.

But Smithers's greatest contribution to knowledge rests primarily with his photographs, depicting an intimate view of practically every facet of life along the border. The subjects are seemingly endless: the serpent-like military wagon trains coursing rocky, winding mountain roads; a Mexican burro train loaded with chino grass fording the Rio Grande; Angora goats placidly resting in the shadow of the Chisos; the dramatic precipice of the Candelaria Rim, still forming a near-impassable barrier to both man and beast; the impending drama of Border Patrolmen waiting in ambush for liquor smugglers crossing the Rio Grande; and his infinite panoramas dwarfing man, machines, and animals, conveying an overpowering message of man's insignificance when standing amid the vastness of nature.

When Smithers accords the viewer an intimate look at the Mexican lifestyle along the border, the concept is reportorial and never maudlin. Views of the squalid interior of a Mexican hovel and the waxmaker's rock-and-stick jacal are definitive cultural statements, not social protest.

Smithers stands tallest when photographing the Mexican people, especially children. There is pathos in the photograph of the goat herder's child, bitten by a rattlesnake, being carried to a shade by his father, who is about to employ his primitive medical skills in an attempt to save his son's life; and the little Mexican girl, possessing neither toys nor dolls, lavishing her affection on her only playmate, a little burro.

Smithers witnessed the region in its primitive, unmolested state, but that was half a century ago and time has wrought its changes. The many homes he visited, both Mexican and Anglo, that once dotted the banks of the Rio Grande between Castolon and Boquillas have long since disappeared, as have the people who occupied them. The Mexican herders no longer tend their flocks and the little patches of corn, melons, chilis, and beans that once grew along Terlingua Creek have long since disappeared. The wax plant at Glenn Springs has been bulldozed off the map, as have the village and Elmo Johnson's ranch house where Smithers once lived and which was the base for much of his Big Bend research. In their places have appeared trailer parks, motels, service stations, and land developments; such "tourist traps" grow, blossom, and also eventually disappear. Yet much of the region still remains an isolated spot on a rapidly shrinking globe.

And while Smithers has, through his documentation, interpreted the region for a curious world, the Big Bend still holds many of its secrets well.

Time and experience sometimes give perspective to events that once lacked clarity and definition, and now looking back on that June morning in 1966, these events come into sharper focus. It is infinitely clear that the University of Texas has acquired one, if not *the*, truly great regional photographic collection, vast in its coverage and detailed in its interpretation. And I had discovered a devoted friend, a colleague, a sensitive artist, and a great humanitarian. His product pays eloquent tribute to its creator, the region, and the people who once made a life for themselves in the remote vastness in the Big Bend of Texas.

Kenneth Baxter Ragsdale
Austin, Texas

CHRONICLES OF THE BIG BEND

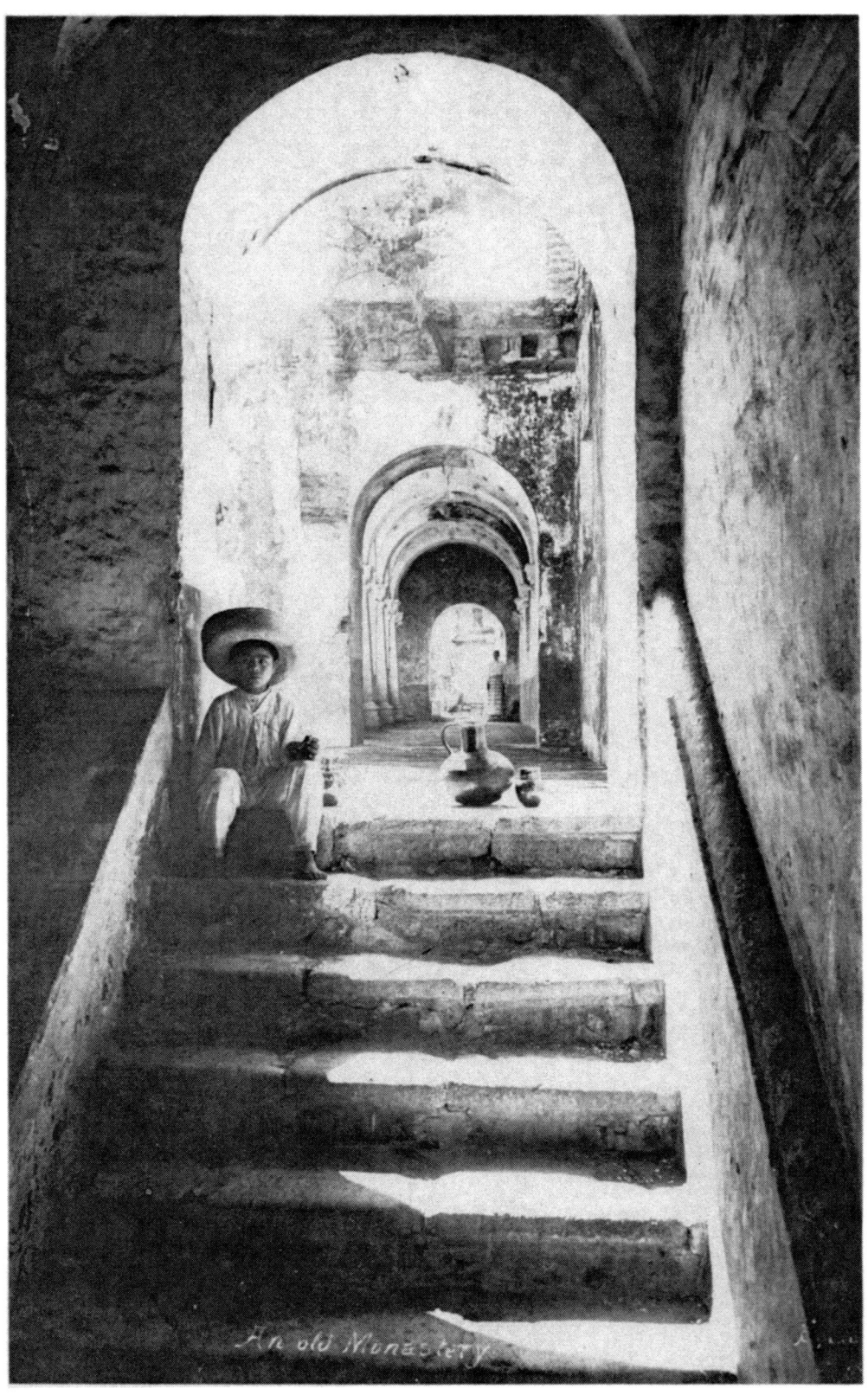

A small boy smoking in a monastery in El Desierto, 1912.

Genesis in Mexico

In a lifetime, many significant events may pass one by virtually unnoticed, their real meaning not clear until his consciousness has been enriched and his experience broadened. Too late, he may come to wish that he had been more curious, or had taken in more of the passing scene that no longer can be recalled.

In this regard I consider myself blessed, for during my lifetime I have been able to witness a number of historic events, as well as passing modes and cultures, which I was able to recognize as such at the time. My interest in history, writing, and photography led me to observe and to record many of the vanishing scenes on film. This is a story of that learning and recording process, spanning a number of subject areas and a lifetime of gathering data first-hand, as opposed to formal, directed research. In a sense, it is autobiography, for it relates my own adventure with life.

This adventure began in San Luis Potosi, Mexico, where the Smitherses numbered among the few American families. I was born there at summer's end in 1895. San Luis was a rich silver region at that time, and my father kept books for the American Smelting and Refining Company. Our years there were strongly Mexican in orientation; Mexican rural enterprise surrounded us, and many of our family habits reflected not American but Mexican tradition.

Pancho, at ten years old, was my first companion, my peer, who became much more than a friend. Teacher, adviser, and guide were three other roles I gave him—or he assumed willingly—as we embarked on an adventurous boyhood together. Pancho was a natural explorer—nearly fullblood Indian—and the things he learned in private from his father made him the perfect leader, the only leader, for this dazzled *inquisidor*. I had none of his abilities, grace, or charisma. It was always Pancho who decided where we would go, and when, and how. For all the fun and wisdom we shared, we spent a surpris-

ingly short time together—a mere two years. But those seven hundred
or so days enriched me in ways that far exceeded my schooling.

My two years with Pancho, the last two in Mexico before moving
to the United States, are still vivid, and I appreciate them now as having been instrumental in my adult decisions to return, work, and
linger in and around Mexico for much of my life. The environment
of my formative years no doubt was responsible for this affinity, for
even when we moved to San Antonio, Texas, we found it to be
strongly Mexican, of an aroma and pace foreign to what the bustling
Texas city is today.

Holidays from classes for Pancho and me seemed fully deserved
and were joyfully anticipated. School held us six days a week, from
eight to five, and vacations were sparse and short. Pancho always
knew of strange new places for us to venture to on our days off.
What great expeditions they were—and more dangerous than I then
realized. Most of his "spots" were at least five miles away, some farther, and were constantly new to us both. Although he had never
been to them, he knew their features fully, so thorough were the
teachings of his father, and so uncanny his natural talents.

Looking back on those day-long adventures, I know that, if
Pancho had not been skilled as he was, we would have been hopeless-
ly lost. But he always found our way out of the most remote forest,
calmly and confidently.

One July Sunday, we hiked to Bosque de Nopal, a large forest of
huge nopal prickly pear cactus. Each plant, twice our height, covered
as much ground as our schoolroom. The prickly pear fruit, called
tunas, and *nopalitos*, the large blades on which the tunas grow, are
prized in Mexican kitchens. From them, our mothers would make
casseroles, stews, "guacamole" salads, and many kinds of jellies and
candies. This trip to the valued prickly pear was one of our few pur-
poseful enterprises, for we returned from the trip with a flour sack
full of tunas and *nopalitos* for our families. It was one of the few
times we actually had spoils to show for our long absence and tired
feet. Our path that day stretched over twelve miles but, because we
had eaten so many tunas, we didn't need supper when we arrived
home. Although Pancho's folks never worried, mine did, and this
kind of fourteen-hour trek made them uneasy. I suppose events like
this one branded me as different from other American kids in our
part of Mexico, most noticeably from my own brothers. It seems I
was the only one truly curious about the Mexican people, and mine
was an insatiable curiosity. My desire to travel with Pancho and to
emulate him set me apart from most other boys.

The amazing thing about this journey and subsequent ones was not the time we spent or the distance covered, but Pancho's total familiarity in an area where neither of us had ever been. He recalled his father's words about the region's lands, and that was his only compass. In this sense, Pancho benefited from a double education—one in school, and one from his father. His father's lessons were much more interesting to me than the ones in classrooms: lessons in survival, geography, sorcery, and pathfinding. Pancho was taught how to observe people, plants, and animals. Girls also learned many things from their mothers, and all parent-to-child teachings seemingly were photographically retained in the youngsters' minds. Pancho became ill at ease whenever I probed the substance of his father's teachings, and my questions received only a vague response. But he could not conceal the fact that he was learning a vast number of skills that I

Main street, San Luis Potosi, 1912.

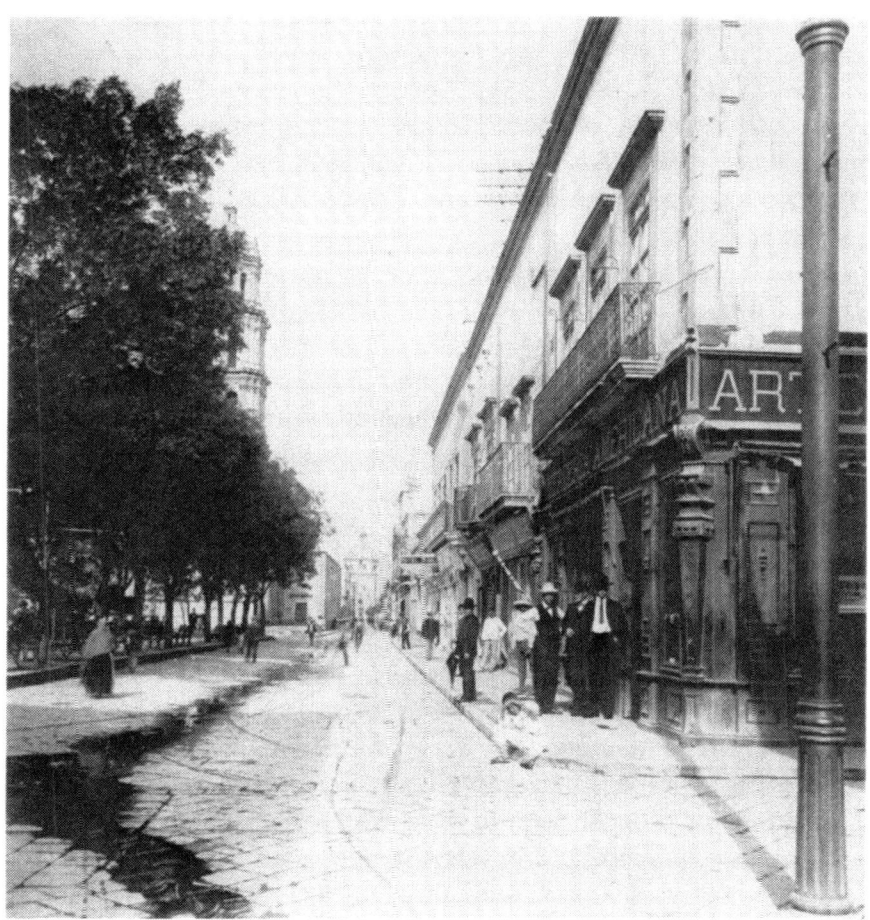

was not; his special knowledge was increasingly apparent, especially on that hot Sunday in the prickly pear forest.

While a youth in Mexico, I, as everyone else, would have fleeting encounters with two groups of legendary professionals, *avisadores* and *curanderos* (or, if female, *avisadoras* and *curanderas*), to whom I give detailed attention later in this book. The techniques of both professions are primitive, yet the underlying theories are as sophisticated as the end results are exacting.

Avisadores are message-senders; curanderos are healers and are skilled as avisadores as well. Curanderos do not achieve professional status until they reach the age of thirty, after proving their skills among their families, while an avisador can perfect his craft as a youth.

Avisar means "to give notice, to advise, to announce, to warn." The avisador sends an aviso—a message in sunlight beamed from a shiny object—a mirror, in many cases. His coded announcement or warning is flashed in all directions, to be picked up by other avisadores who may relay the message or instantly decode and disseminate it. You can see how avisadores were viewed as the protectors of villages, guardians of lives, and finders of food and water supplies. Avisadores were not, of course, completely responsible for my spending as much time in Mexico as I did, but their feats and secrets surely were among the great Mexican crafts and sciences I was determined to master.

When I was twelve, two years after we moved to San Antonio in 1905, I met an old Mexican Zapotec Indian, Juan Vargas, who gave me a striking illustration of avisadores in Mexican culture. Although Vargas never mentioned avisos to me, he referred in several fascinating stories to certain "messages" which could have been sent only by means of polished rock (or mirror) and sunlight. In 1910, he had been in San Antonio eighty years, since arriving in 1830 as a soldier in the Mexican Army. In March, 1836, he had celebrated the Texans' defeat at the Alamo.

In 1907, this 111-year-old man told me that, a month and a half after the fall of the Alamo, he and other soldiers in San Antonio had learned of Santa Anna's surrender at San Jacinto "very soon" after it happened. When I pried with "About one hour?" he avoided a direct answer in the same vague way as Pancho—a wise if, for me, aggravating evasion to protect special Mexican secrets.

A curandera brought me into the world, and a curandera saved me, with potions, prayers, and physical nourishment, from typhoid. Our family curandera, Maria, was ten times my age when I was stricken at

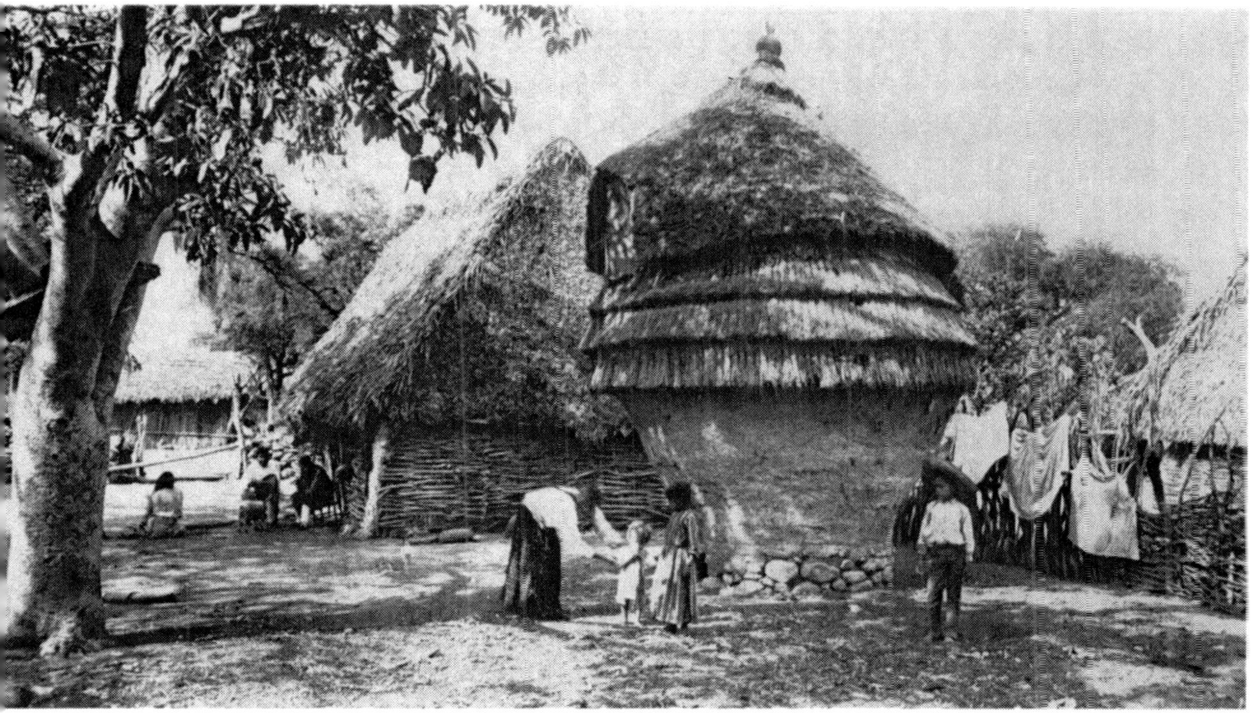

Above, a Tehuantepec mother reaches for her child before the granary where corn, beans, and other crops are stored. Near Tehuantepec, 1912. Below, Tehuantepec Indian woman wearing traditional headdress, a huipil.

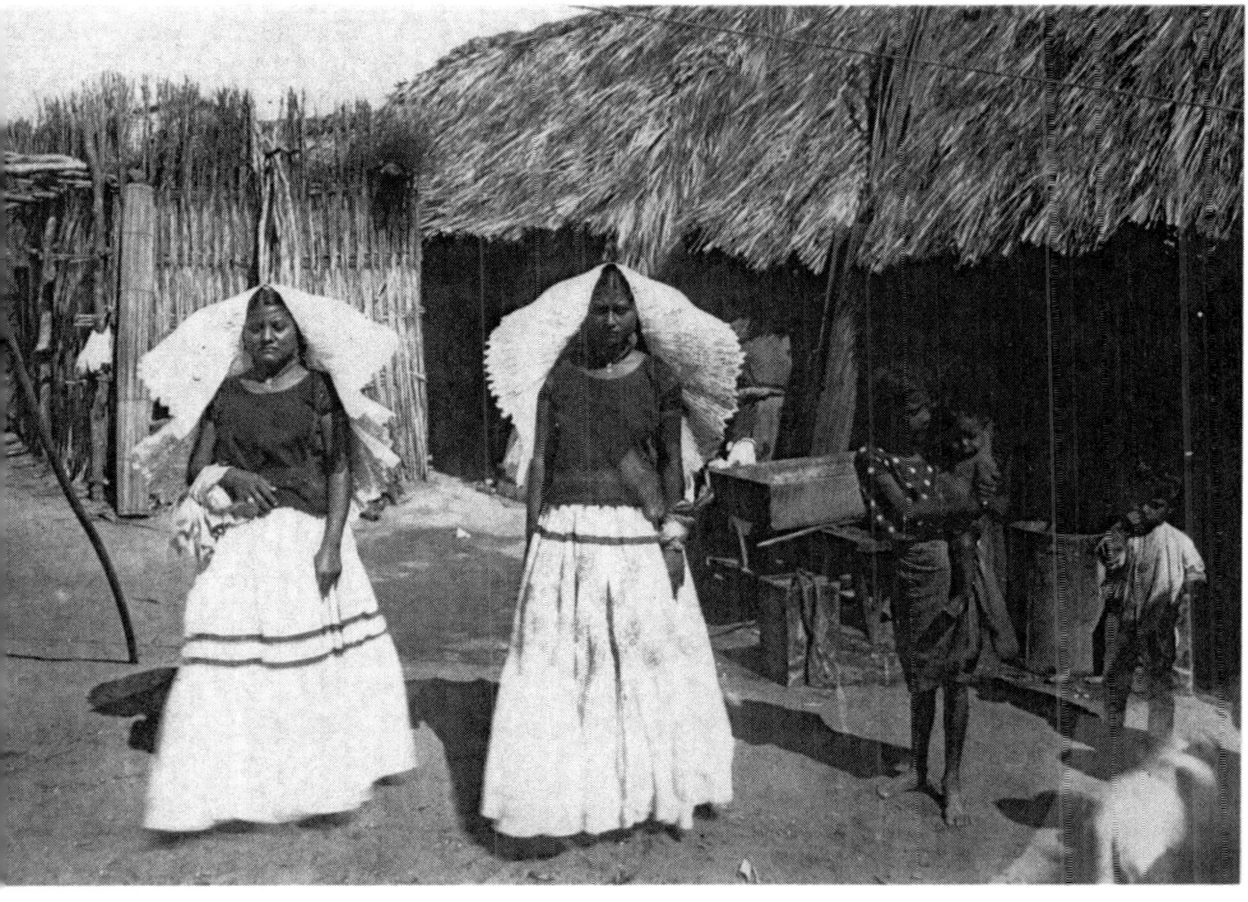

age seven. While there actually was not an epidemic in our village, the conditions in that rural region of Mexico were conducive to disease. The waters were unclean, there was no sewage system, animals roamed where they pleased, and the design of the homes, with open courtyards and unscreened windows and doors, did little to safeguard us from infectious illnesses.

Maria, after moving her shrine, replete with all the Catholic altar trappings, into my room, began each morning of my illness with the gathering of dried and fresh medicinals at the markets. She knew by training and intuition the exact amount of each medicine to use, and how to blend them into the proper dosages. Her work was never experimental; it was a strict application of principles and knowledge learned over a lifetime. For the first ten days of my illness, I was unconscious, and during this time I was administered donkey's milk and medicines made from plants that Maria purchased from the vendors, who also sold such things as dried lizards, herbs, small fish, insects, snakes, and the ground bones, horns, and hooves of livestock, many of which were—and still are—used for other cures. The eggs of a hen that had flown into my room and nested on my bed one feverish day were fed to me in the final stages of recovery. Seeing that I drew great strength from the eggs, Maria declared that the hen had been sent by God. Although death came four times to our Mexican home (to my sister Anna, at age eight; my mother; and two brothers, thirteen-year-old Alfred and infant Albert), I recovered from the raging fevers and delirium.

Quickness of mind and body are shared characteristics, or gifts, of curanderos and avisadores, for both these professions demand split-second decisions and rapid follow-through. Both are greatly humanitarian, for their work is universally for peaceful purposes; for protection, or simply samaritan. Rewards are incidental, if not unthinkable, for avisadores and curanderos. Avisadores are secretive—an openness about their work would endanger the security of the villagers—while curanderos are highly visible, even specious, in their work. Contacts in my youth with both were, as I have told, fleeting, intense, and memorable.

It might seem, after leaving San Luis in good health, that I would not care ever to return. Obviously that was not the case. My love for Mexico, its people, and their lifestyles was not diminished; my longings to know more only swelled. I knew that my stay in San Antonio would be temporary, that it surely would not be a stepping stone to points north or east; at age ten I felt bound to return to Mexico.

The cultural and geographical switch from San Luis to San Antonio, from Mexico to the United States, was not shocking. Indeed, San Antonio was more Mexican than Texan in those days. My obsessions with Mexican lore, customs, and, I liked to think, magic were well fed in Texas. After all, my first face-to-face contact with an avisador was in San Antonio.

Shortly after we moved to San Antonio, I decided to become a photographer. But in 1910, paid photographer apprenticeships just didn't exist. After a brief period at Schuler's Sign Shop, I accepted work at two photography studios, Archer's Art Shop and Rayburn's Studio, at no pay. Archer and Rayburn taught me all the basics from which I developed my own style. Afternoons spent in Archer's and Rayburn's studios and darkrooms encouraged my ever-growing determination to become a professional photographer. I say "afternoons" because those were the only times I could work at photography. For half a decade I studied with these two only after a full day of other work. I drove a two-horse ice wagon, loaded with fifty- and one-hundred-pound blocks, twelve hours a day for fifty dollars a month. Hard work, but I loved the horses and the idea of providing people with a needed commodity. After a couple of years of that, I drove the two-mule team of a road-building contractor's dirt scraper, for the not-too-generous pay of a dollar a day, plus meals. My brow sweated and my muscles hardened, and the experience with work animals proved invaluable. Whenever I could make the time, I'd run off to hang around the cavalry troopers stationed in the city, for their lives surely seemed the most exciting.

Until I was 17, my notions of photography were strictly reportorial. I wanted to be a photojournalist, a correspondent, and I have free-lanced this work periodically all my life. Free-lancing was a natural for me, wanting to find my own stories. The death of Juan Vargas, in 1910 at the age of 114, gave me a deeper focus. Thinking of all the things this old man had seen that could never be recaptured, I began to feel that my photography should direct itself to historical and transient subjects—vanishing lifestyles, primitive cultures, old faces, and odd, unconventional professions. Before my camera I wanted huts, vendors, natural majesties, clothing, tools, children, old people, the ways of the border. I was to find all of these and more in the Big Bend.

The skills that I acquired—photography, sketching, riding, plus a love of work, complemented all the objects of my curiosity. There also was a bit of restlessness, which I still feel today. And when the bugle sounded, as it literally did, I was ready, with rolled sleeves and film.

Cavalry Mounts and Pack Mules

Great Britain and France entered World War I in July, 1914. In a year of fighting, 250,000 horses were purchased at San Antonio by the English and the French. Thousands were bought each week to meet the needs of the French cavalry and field artillery. From San Antonio, the animals were shipped by rail to a Gulf of Mexico port and loaded on cattle boats for the voyage to France.

Early in 1915, I took an interest in those large purchases of horses and soon went to work for one of the horse dealers at one dollar per day. In several jobs that I had worked at since 1910, I had learned much about handling horses and mules and therefore was an asset to these operations. In fact, I almost signed up to make those ocean trips to France with the horses. The pay was good: fifty dollars per month for the entire voyage, plus meals, a bunk in the ship, and no work on the return trip. But I lost interest on hearing of German U-boat attacks on the horse ships. So instead of signing on I went to work at the army's remount unit at Fort Sam Houston, where men with knowledge of horses were needed.

In 1915, there were few motor vehicles in the United States Army. Although the Quartermaster Corps was testing motor transport units, all the combat and technical branches were horse and mule powered. Cavalry and artillery branches had the most horses, as wagon trains and pack trains required many animals. Even in the infantry, all officers above the rank of lieutenant were mounted, as were the Medical Corps's doctors. Wagons and buckboards were used for official transportation and all ambulances were horse drawn. Throughout the army, it seemed there were more horses than men.

The Remount Service supplied the horses and mules to all units. Prior to 1915 there were four remount units in various sections of the United States; Fort Sam Houston was one of them. But soon the Mexican Revolution had worked up to the United States-Mexico border, and troubles increased as bandits and revolutionaries in search of horses raided American ranches and villages. Border troubles worsened and hundreds of American soldiers were stationed between the regular army posts along the nearly two thousand miles of boundary.

New remount units had to be organized to meet the needs of the new cavalry troops, and pack-mule and wagon trains were in demand to supply them, some as far as one hundred miles from their base. Pack and wagon trains were the only means of delivering the supplies, so our mission was crucial. To augment the remount unit at Fort Sam Houston a new one was organized at Leon Springs, sixteen miles north of San Antonio, and I volunteered for transfer there. It soon became one of the largest units in the country. Within a year, a second Leon Springs company was formed to handle its large work load.

Train loads of horses and mules—whistling, wheezing, whinnying—arrived every few days from various parts of the country, sent from army purchasers throughout the United States. Every remount man was waiting at the railroad spur when a shipment came in, for the animals had to be unloaded immediately. They were first put into a large quarantine corral, where they were fed and watered and examined by a staff of veterinarians. Once the horses got medical clearance, they were divided into two herds: the light ones for the cavalry and the draft types for medical or artillery service. Mules, after quarantine, were separated for wagon or pack-train work.

Each horse and mule, in turn, was led out of its assigned corral to a smaller one. A leather halter was secured and a serial number was burned onto the animal's left front hoof. Then either a "C" for cavalry or an "A" for artillery was branded on the right shoulder. "US" was grilled into the left shoulder. A service record, much like that of a soldier's, now became a part of the animal's life. Mules were marked similarly, but also were branded with a "P" for pack train, or with a "W" for wagon train. Both cavalry horses and pack-train mules were branded on the right hoof with the identification number to be used in troop or pack train, one to sixty for cavalry mounts, one to fifty for pack mules.

"IC," inspected and condemned, was the last brand for a military animal. It was reserved for aged or disabled horses and mules, which usually were sold at public auction. These animals often were used for many years of civilian work after discharge. The retired animal's service record was filed in Washington, the same as a discharged soldier's.

From four large pastures at the Leon Springs remount the horses

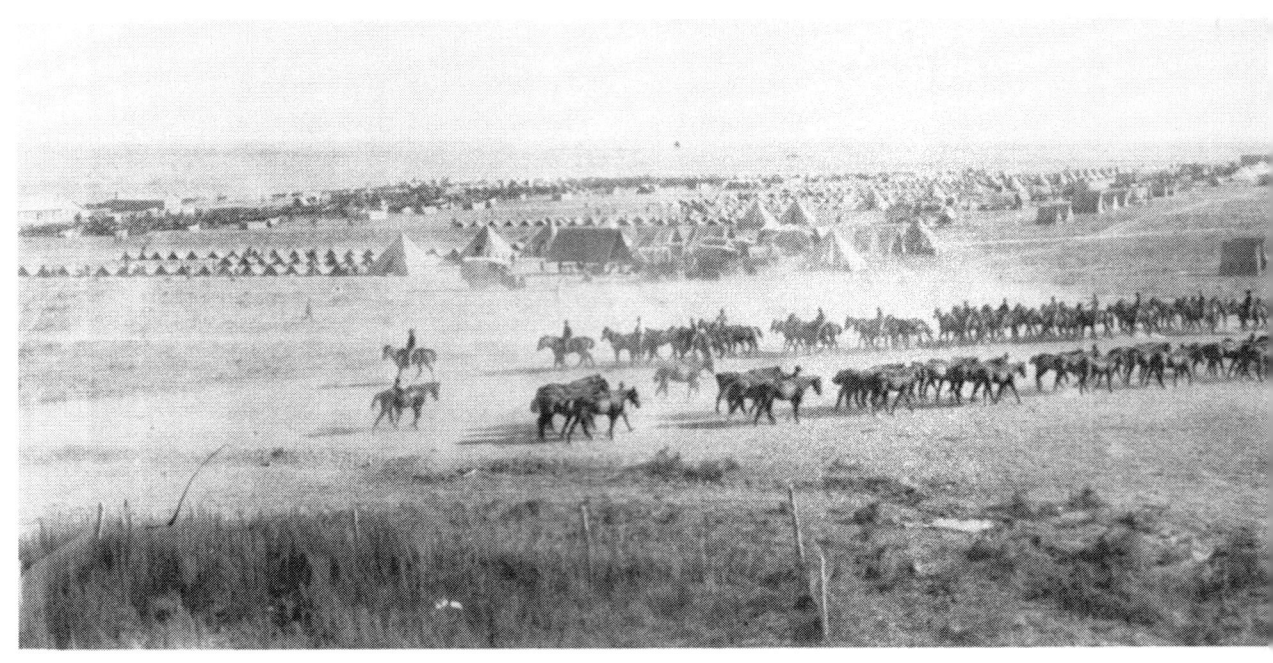

After a hot, lengthy march, such as this one from Fort Bliss to Camp Marfa (above), it was necessary to cool the horses by walking them before they could be tied on the picket line. Below, Troop M of the Eighth's camp at Ruidosa, Texas.

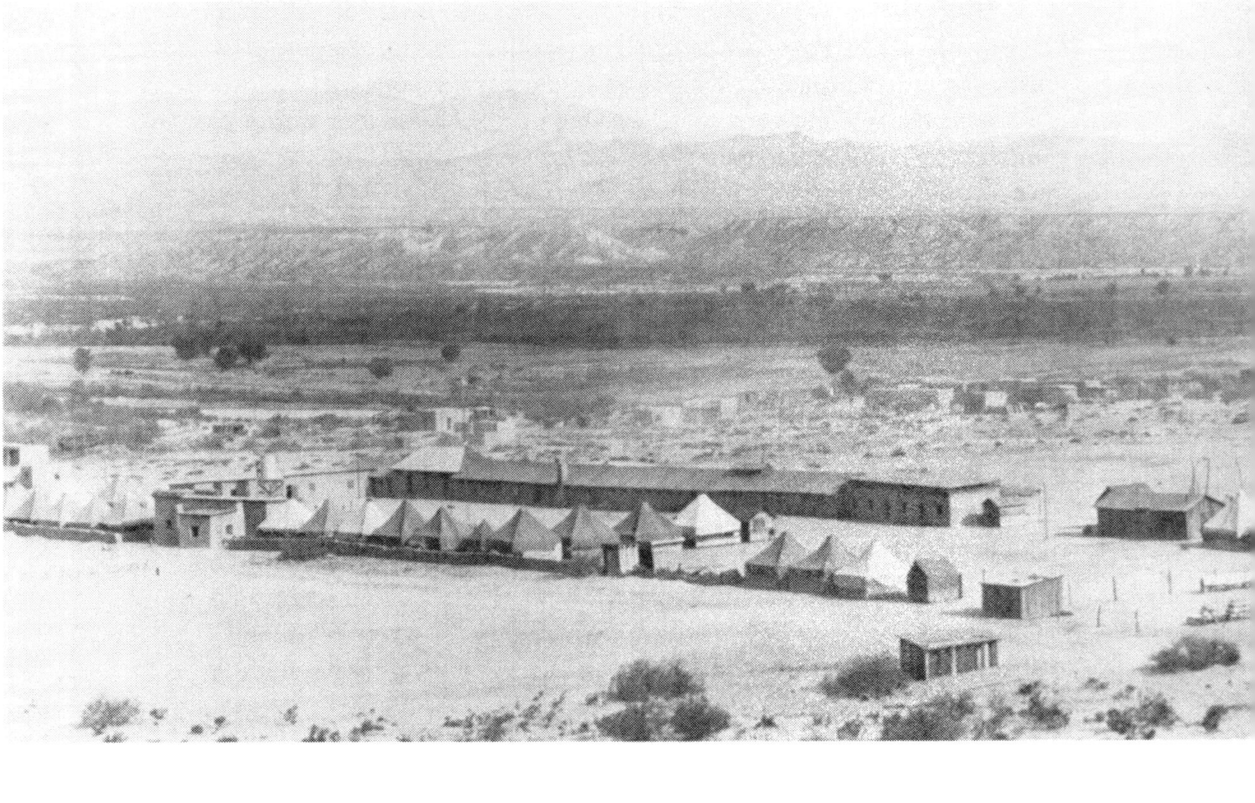

and mules were called into service in large numbers: 1,000 horses required for a cavalry regiment, 124 mules and 6 horses for a wagon train, 140 horses for an artillery regiment, and 64 mules and 1 horse for a pack train. One thousand of the best horses, reserved for officers, were kept in a small pasture. Wild horses—and some were incurably wild and ornery—were sold readily to rodeo men, always looking to promote their shows with outlaw animals.

The remount service required horse trainers and bronc riders, horseshoers and veterinarian helpers, as well as teamsters. Although I qualified specifically as a teamster—to drive a six-mule team requiring six pairs of reins, hauling oats and hay to the pastures—my duties were varied. Unloading new arrivals, dispatching requisition shipments, and unloading train loads of feed also were part of my seven-day-a-week routine that began before daylight each morning and for which I was paid fifty dollars per month. Meals and quarters (an army cot in a large bunkhouse) were furnished.

The wagon I drove was a creation the likes of which I'd never seen. It was called a buffalo wagon because it was designed for hauling feed to Yellowstone National Park's buffalo. Top-heavy, slope-sided, and without a conventional bed, the vehicle was a trick to drive but

Displaying the skill of "pickup" at a cavalry Fourth of July field meet. Here a battle situation is recreated in which a trooper is rescued by another when his horse is wounded.

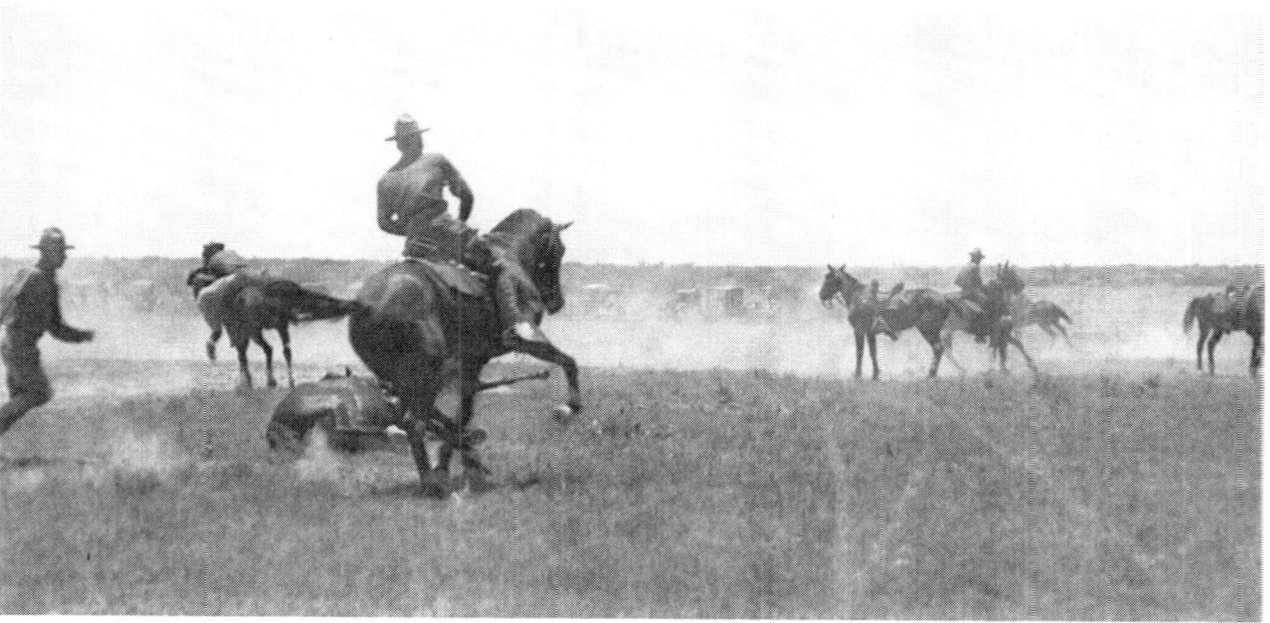

ideal for remount work. At least three times the load of a regular army escort wagon could be carried in each buffalo wagon.

After the wagon was loaded with baled hay, the teamster sat on the front bale, at least nine feet above the ground. He had to use a rope to operate the brake lever. When the wagon was empty, the teamster had to stand to drive the mules—a precarious position made more risky by rutted or hilly roads. My pasture, the farthest of all from headquarters, was for artillery horses. Six large hayricks in the pasture had to be filled every morning. The daily ration for each animal was twelve pounds of oats, fourteen pounds of hay, and five to fifteen gallons of water. We also had to be on the lookout for sick and injured animals, keep salt blocks in the pasture, and fill water troughs.

Each teamster was allowed to select six mules from the large wagon-train mule pasture for his team. It's hard to believe, but I found three sets of twins of matching size for my six mules, each one adapted to the different positions—leaders, swingers, and wheelers. The two wheelers of a six-mule team were hitched to the wagon, one on each side of the wagon tongue. The swingers were hitched in front of the wheelers, but without a tongue between them. They were hitched instead to a doubletree attached to the end of the wagon tongue. The two leaders were hitched to a doubletree connected to the end of the tongue with a chain. Each pair of mules pulled a share of the load, but the wheelers pulled the most.

This drawing I made of the "off" (right) side of a four-mule army wagon team details the intricate harness. Front mules were called "leaders" and rear mules were known as "wheelers."

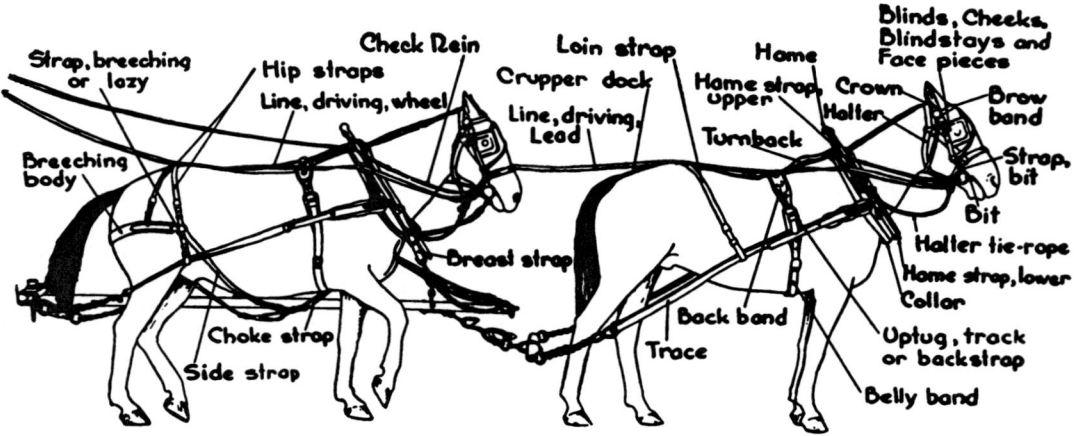

—Nomenclature of harness, ambulance or escort wagon.

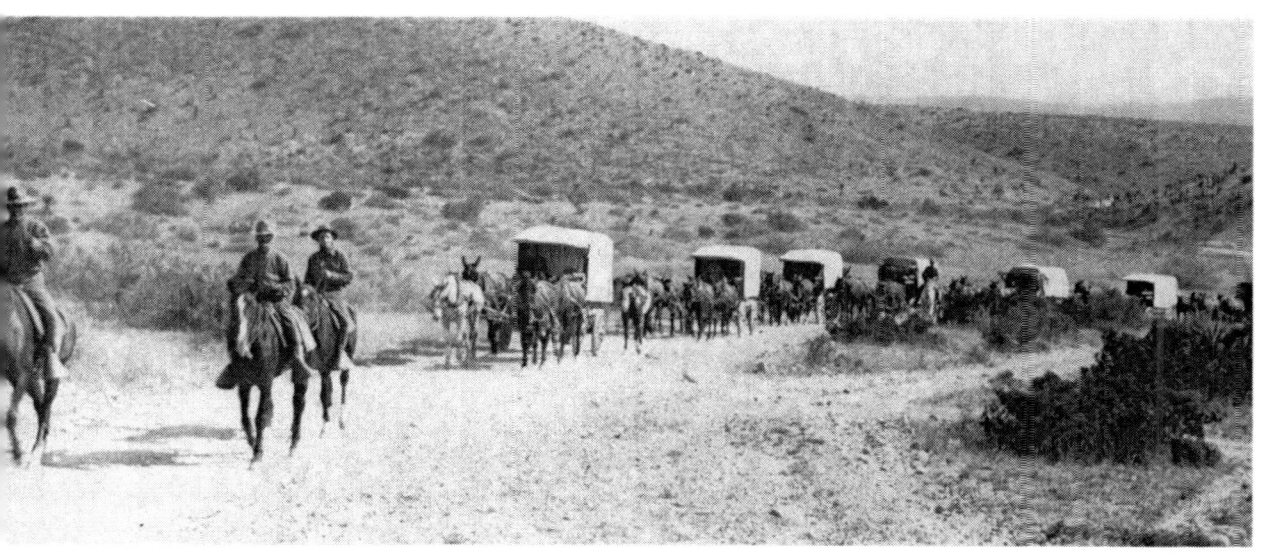

Above, a Medical Corps unit of the Fifth Cavalry on an overland march from Fort Clark to Camp Marfa, 1919. Doctors and enlisted personnel rode horses or traveled in mule-drawn ambulances. Below, trooper, horse, and equipment in the Eighth Cavalry at Marfa. The trooper's saber was on the opposite side of the saddle, his sidearm at his right.

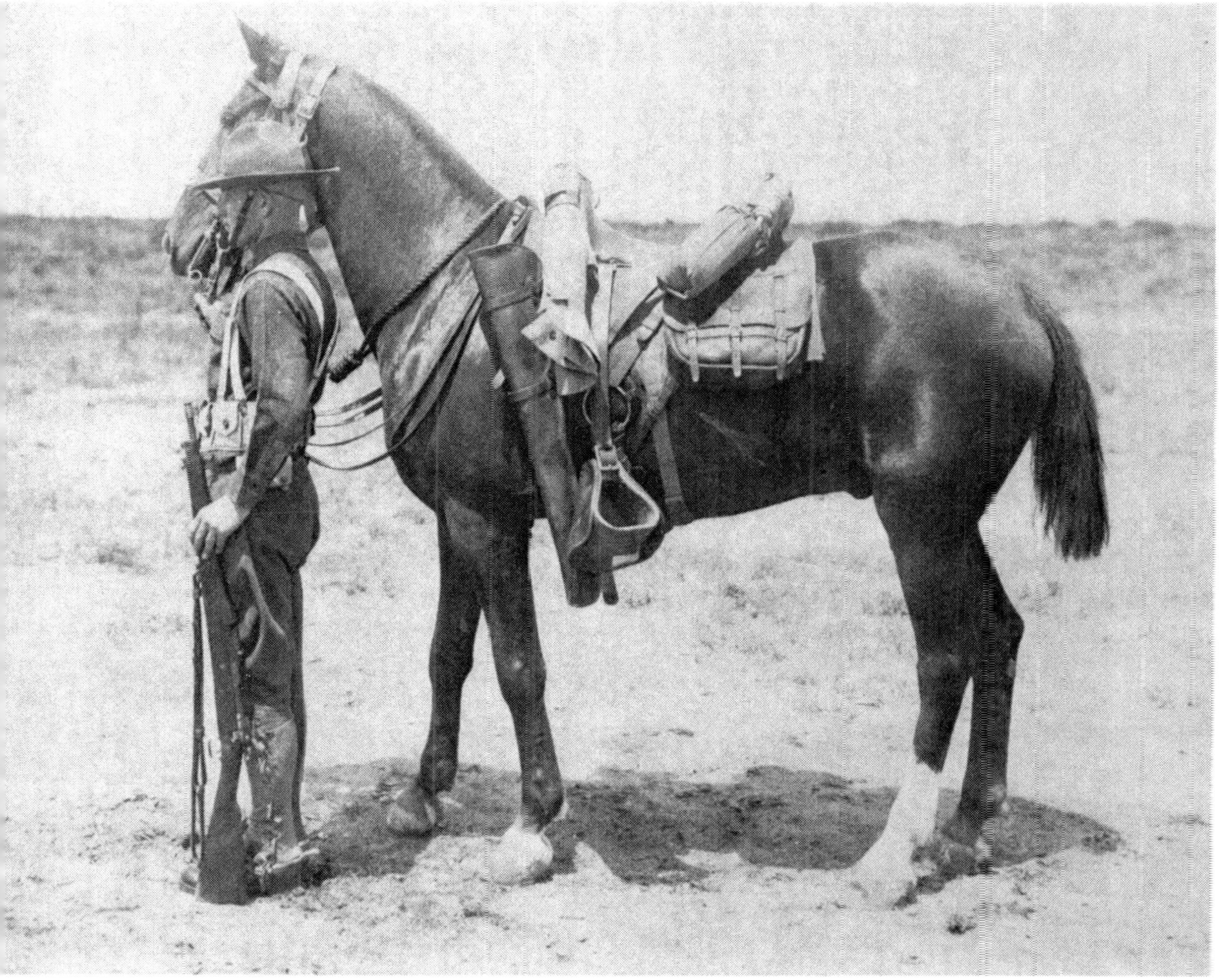

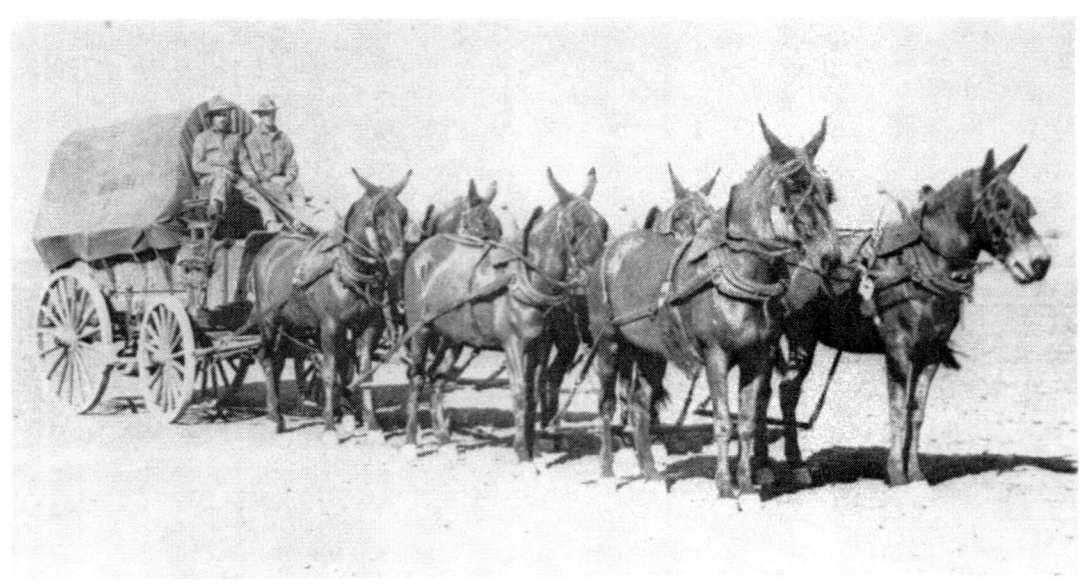

Above, one of the few six-mule teams used by the quartermaster at Marfa. Below, dummy mules used at Marfa Quartermaster Supply Base to instruct neophyte teamsters in harness and wagon rigging. When final exams were passed (one question called for naming the forty-five parts of a wagon's running gear), a teamster degree was awarded.

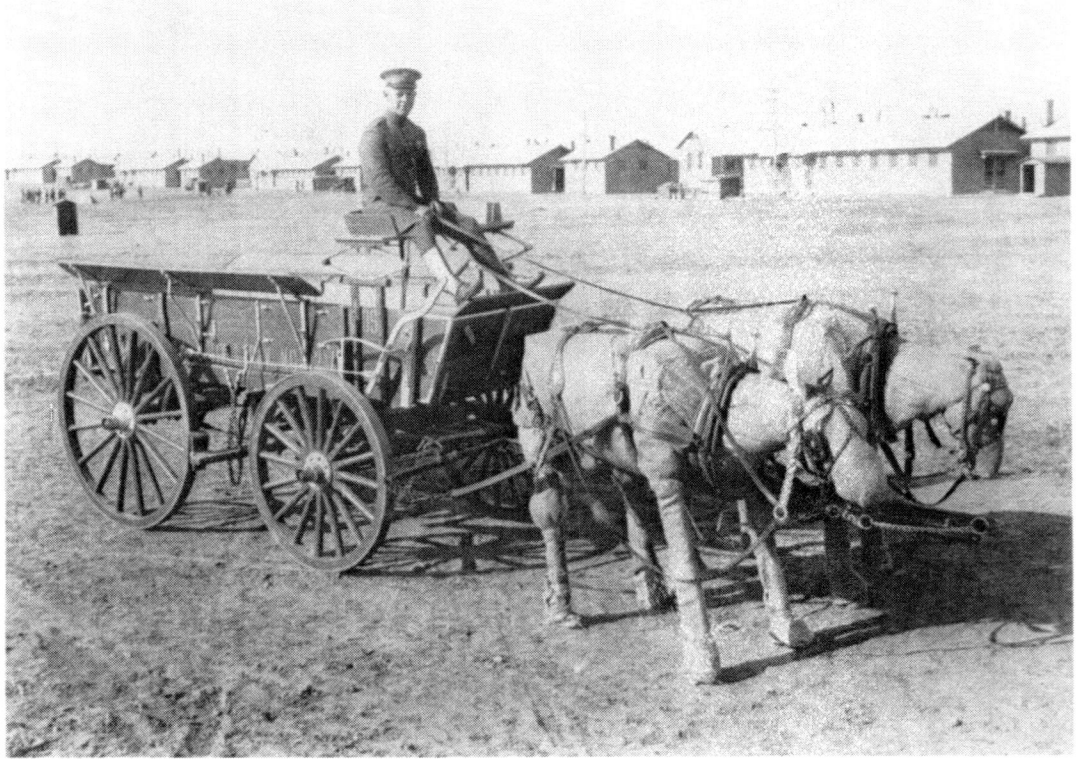

The six mules were controlled with three pairs of reins of varying lengths. In each hand the wheelers' rein was held between the little and ring fingers; the swingers' rein between the ring and middle fingers; the leaders' between the third and index fingers. The excess rein fell into my half-closed hand so that I needed only press the leaders' rein with my thumb to create a pull sufficient to guide the team.

Mules and horses responded readily to kind treatment, and most of the teamsters I knew were affectionate and patient with their teams. Even with gentle and cooperative mules, hitching them was tricky. Breeching harness for each wheeler, necessary for helping brake the wagon, weighed ninety pounds and consisted of thirty-eight different parts. The harness for a leader and a swinger was not as complex but, even so, it weighed about seventy-two pounds.

The breeching, consisting of a network of straps attached to the basic harness and the breast yoke and fitting around the wheeler's haunches, enabled the animal to use his full weight to hold the wagon back on a downward slope. Despite the complexity of the harness, reins, and other equipment, driving a well-trained team was easy. Army regulations required that all reins be held at all times but, with good mules, this was not necessary.

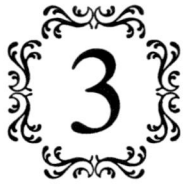

Mule Trains on the Border

In January, the Leon Springs remount began to organize new pack-mule trains. Finding enough qualified packers for the new trains was a problem, but several of the teamsters, myself included, had learned on mules that were being trained. A group of us volunteered to transfer to a new pack train. I knew what was in store: the same pay, and hard conditions, since packers slept on the ground in the open with only a saddle blanket for bedding.

With regrets I left the remount but eagerly headed for the bandit-plagued border, never without camera and note pad. Our train enjoyed fame of a sort, being the reorganized quartermaster Pack Train 29, which had been in the Philippines years earlier.

Bound for the Indio Ranch, about twelve miles below Eagle Pass, Texas, we went out the Laredo road to Dilley and thence west through Carrizo Springs. It was a 4½-day trip from Leon Springs, as we were taking a load of oats for a troop of the Second Cavalry stationed at the ranch.

We guessed that our Indio Ranch assignment was temporary, that we soon would go on to a rougher area where pack trains were needed to do the work they were suited for. Sure enough, on May 10, our train was ordered to Del Rio, 68 miles from Indio Ranch. At Del Rio we loaded the train with 98 sacks of oats for delivery to the quartermaster at Marfa, Texas, 275 miles farther west. Averaging better than 35 miles per day, we reached Marfa on May 19, 1916.

What grand preparation that rugged trip was for rookie teamsters! After loading and unloading the fifty mules each day for nine days, we considered ourselves veterans. And what a place Camp Marfa was! It consisted only of a single large tent and lots of land, but it was bustling with the National Guards of Texas, New Mexico, and Arizona. These units had been called into federal service on May 9, following the May 5 raid by Mexican bandits on Glenn Springs, and the entire U. S.-Mexico boundary was being patrolled. Part of the Sixth U. S. Cavalry also was in the Big Bend, helping patrol the border. The rest of the Sixth was in Mexico with General John J. Pershing, chasing Pancho Villa following his raid on Columbus, New Mexico, the previous March 12. The Sixth Cavalry was a favorite of General Pershing and, in 1917, he took the entire regiment with him to France. In June, all National Guard units in the country were called up for border service, and many of them came to the Big Bend.

Camp Marfa's quartermaster depot was a large and busy place. We got a cheering welcome when we arrived with supplies, the first it had seen for days. The nearest outpost was fifty-four miles from Camp Marfa, and others were more like one hundred miles away. In the Big Bend district, there were twelve outposts all together, and their soldiers and animals had to be supplied by pack or wagon train. Many outposts could be reached only by pack trains, so rough was the country. The troop at Lajitas, on the Rio Grande, is a good example.

It took the train 3 days to get to Lajitas from Marfa. So much was needed by the troops and their horses that it required three trains to supply them, each making a round trip every 6 days carrying 9,600 pounds of food for the men and hay and oats for the horses.

Besides being the most difficult outpost to supply, Lajitas was one of the most strategic, for it guarded the western approach from Mexico to the quicksilver mines at Terlingua. Another cavalry troop at Castolon, sixteen miles below Terlingua, guarded the eastern approach. Without these two troops, the mine stores, as well as the mines themselves and several ranches in the area, would have been subject to continuous bandit raids.

In early 1916 Castolon was supplied by pack trains from Alpine, where cargoes were received by rail. Later that year, a road was built from Alpine to Terlingua and Castolon, easing the supply problem somewhat, although wagon training was neither easy nor altogether economical. The typical wagon train consisted of 28 wagons managed by nearly 40 men. It carried something like 65,000 pounds—7 times a pack train's capacity. Just as one mule in a pack train carried cooking utensils and food for the train's 14 men, one wagon of the wagon train carried cargo for the troops. And trains of both kinds had to carry feed for their own animals.

A pack train was a complex organism, winding its way through treacherous terrain, providing nourishment at its many stops. Of the sixty-four mules in a train, fifty were carrying cargo and fourteen

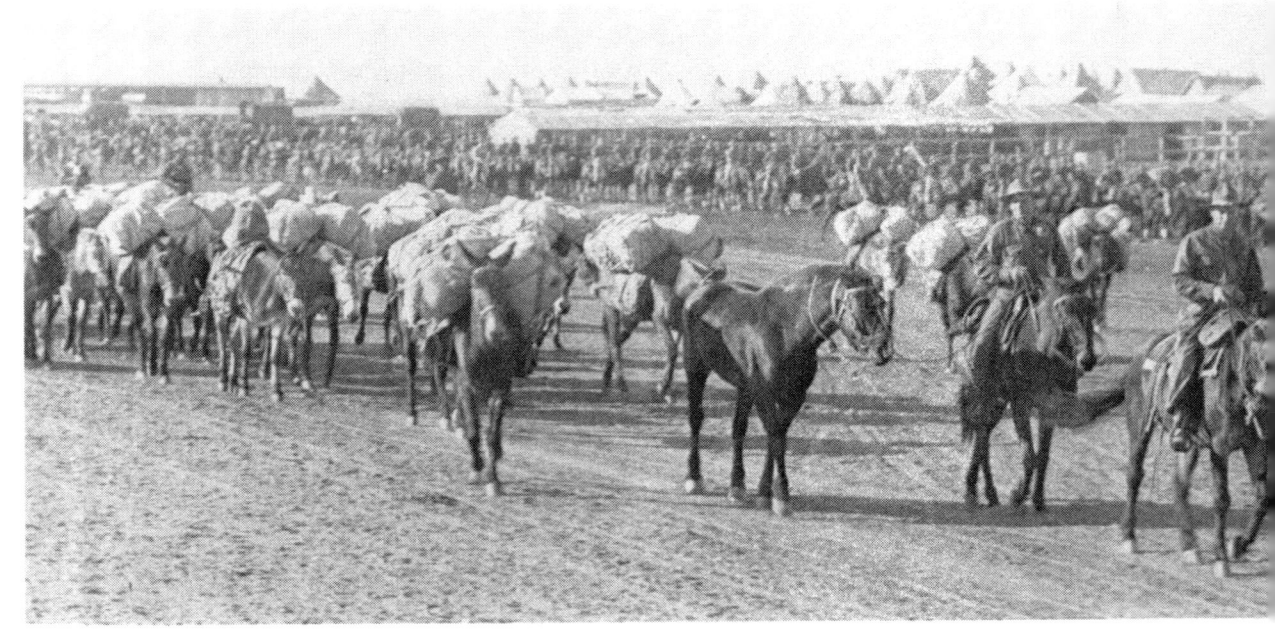

Above, pack trains lined up in preparation for travel to outposts. Below, an army wagon train unloading cargo at Dublan, Chihuahua. This train was part of the Pershing expedition and had brought the supplies 125 miles from Columbus, New Mexico.

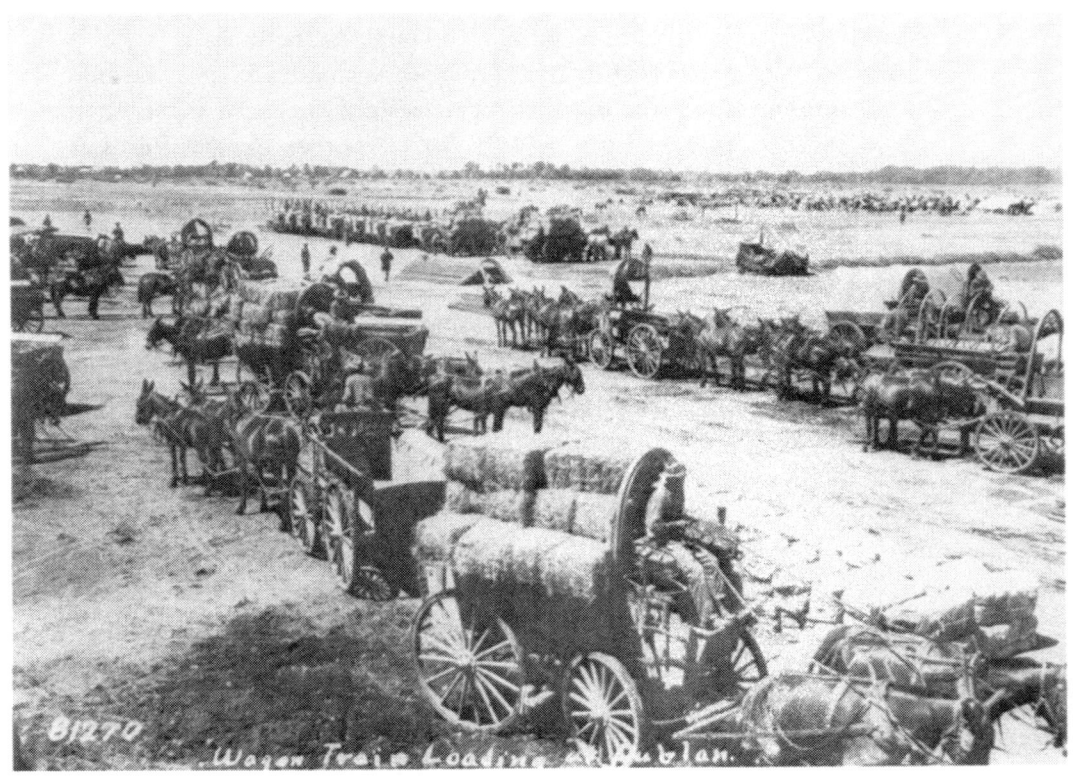

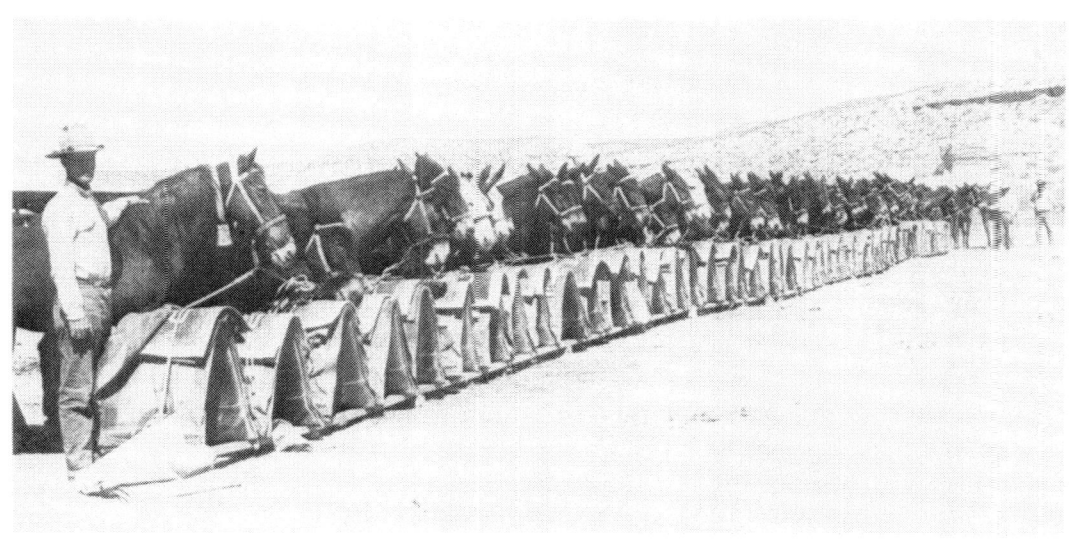

Above, the packmaster of Army Pack Train 1 standing with the bell mare by the line-up of fifty pack mules, fourteen saddle mules, and fifty pack saddles. Below, scene at Lajitas, where mules and men of a pack train could bathe in the Rio Grande between the Texas shore and an island in the river.

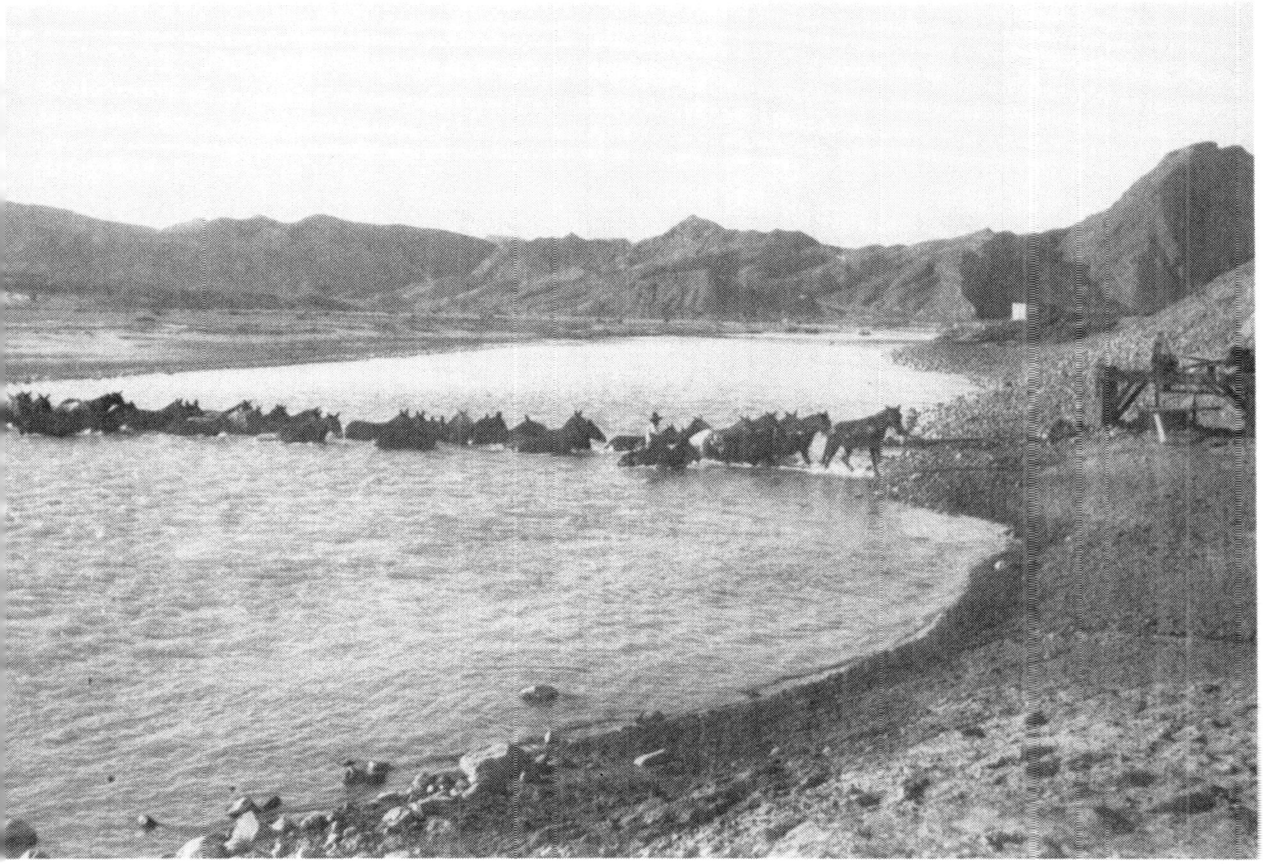

were the mounts of ten packers, the packmaster, a *cargador* (saddler), and the blacksmith. The cook led the bell mare, and the mules followed, heeding an uncanny instinct that drew them to a female horse. The bell mare was the pivot and the leader for the mules, and it was rare for the mules to wander from her. In camp she was the only animal staked. The mules, turned loose to graze, would never stray. When time came to picket the mules for the night, the bell mare was led around first, to one end of the picket line. The mules would all line up, awaiting their turn to be tied.

Each mule's number—the one branded on the right hoof at the remount station—was stamped on the headband of its leather halter for ease in identification. The number also appeared on the pack-saddle a mule wore, for the gear was individually fitted.

The 10 packers were divided into 5 2-man teams, each with 10 mules in its charge. Grooming, watering, feeding, tying: those were

Drawings I made to illustrate the diamond hitch to fellow teamsters.

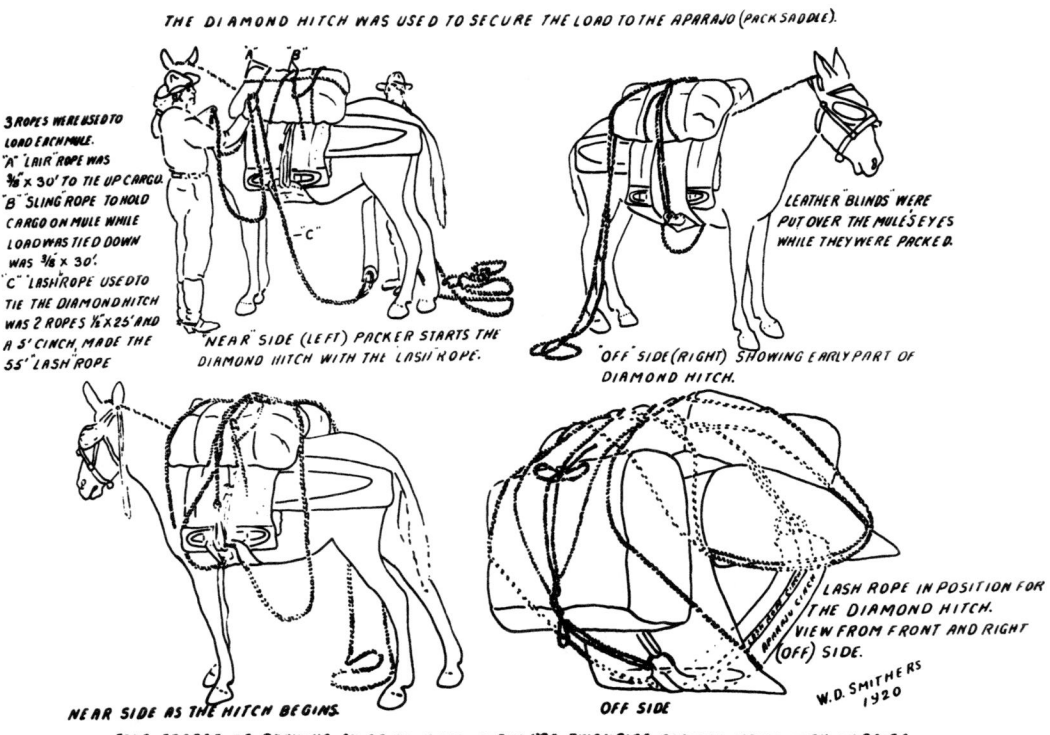

THE DIAMOND HITCH WAS USED TO SECURE THE LOAD TO THE APARAJO (PACK SADDLE).

3 ROPES WERE USED TO LOAD EACH MULE.
"A" LAIR ROPE WAS ⅜ x 30' TO TIE UP CARGO.
"B" SLING ROPE TO HOLD CARGO ON MULE WHILE LOAD WAS TIED DOWN WAS ⅜ x 30'.
"C" LASH ROPE USED TO TIE THE DIAMOND HITCH WAS 2 ROPES ½ x 25' AND A 5' CINCH, MADE THE 55' LASH ROPE

"NEAR" SIDE (LEFT) PACKER STARTS THE DIAMOND HITCH WITH THE LASH ROPE.

LEATHER BLINDS WERE PUT OVER THE MULE'S EYES WHILE THEY WERE PACKED.

"OFF" SIDE (RIGHT) SHOWING EARLY PART OF DIAMOND HITCH.

NEAR SIDE AS THE HITCH BEGINS.

OFF SIDE

LASH ROPE IN POSITION FOR THE DIAMOND HITCH. VIEW FROM FRONT AND RIGHT (OFF) SIDE.

W. D. SMITHERS 1920

FOUR STAGES OF PACKING AN ARMY MULE IN THE PRE-TWENTIES. PACKERS HAD TO WORK IN PAIRS.

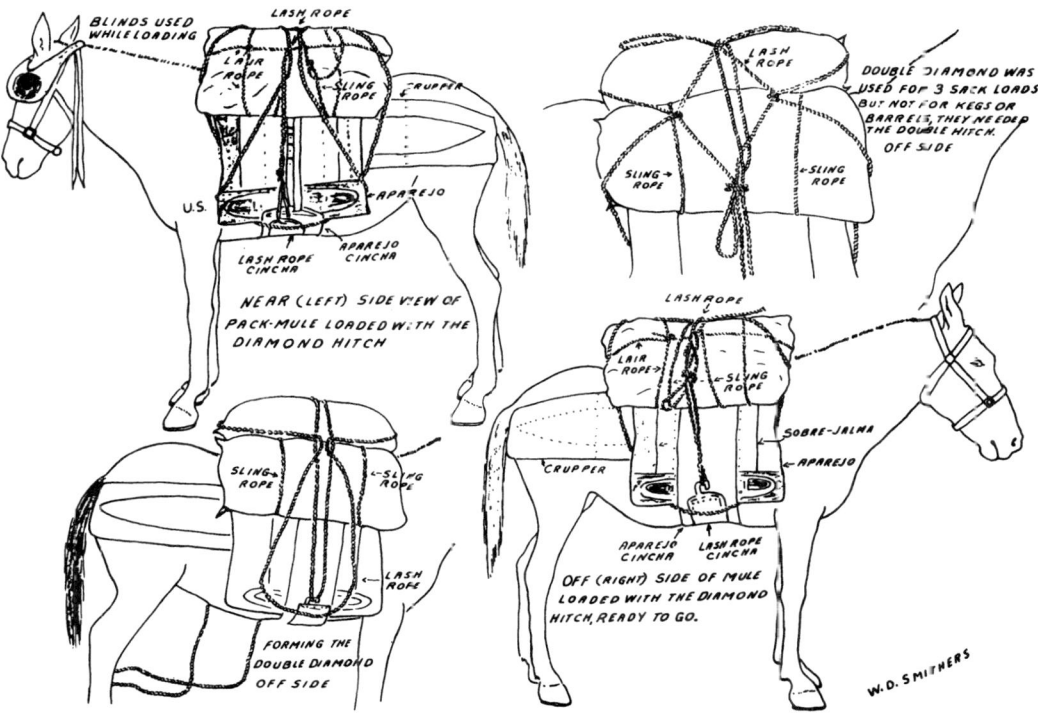

BLINDS USED WHILE LOADING
LASH ROPE
LAIR ROPE
SLING ROPE
CRUPPER
U.S.
APAREJO
APAREJO CINCHA
LASH ROPE CINCHA

NEAR (LEFT) SIDE VIEW OF PACK-MULE LOADED WITH THE DIAMOND HITCH

LASH ROPE
DOUBLE DIAMOND WAS USED FOR 3 SACK LOADS BUT NOT FOR KEGS OR BARRELS, THEY NEEDED THE DOUBLE HITCH. OFF SIDE
SLING ROPE
SLING ROPE

SLING ROPE
SLING ROPE
LASH ROPE

FORMING THE DOUBLE DIAMOND OFF SIDE

LASH ROPE
LAIR ROPE
SLING ROPE
SOBRE-JALMA
CRUPPER
APAREJO
APAREJO CINCHA
LASH ROPE CINCHA

OFF (RIGHT) SIDE OF MULE LOADED WITH THE DIAMOND HITCH, READY TO GO.

W. D. SMITHERS

our responsibilities to the mules. But the real work was in loading them with 250 pounds of cargo. The 80-pound packsaddle went on first, secured with an extra-strong cinch. Then each packer lashed a 125-pound cargo bundle to his side of the mule, using a 30-foot sling rope. Great strength and skill were required to hoist the heavy bundles onto the mule's back, balance them, and tie them on with a diamond-hitched 50-foot lash. The slinging and lashing, hoisting and tugging were done in rapid movements by expert packers who developed a keen sense of load balance and position. I made many sketches of the lash-and-sling process, which novice packers later used to learn packing techniques.

On the pack train, we began our day three hours before daylight. We slept on the ground, wrapped in army blankets that served during the day as padding beneath the packsaddles. There was no space for bed rolls, tents, or other comforts; all we had was what we could carry in our saddlebags.

Most of the day was spent in forward, linear movement, stopping only once for water. Because packers could not carry canteens and only one water stop was made during ten hours of travel, our drink-

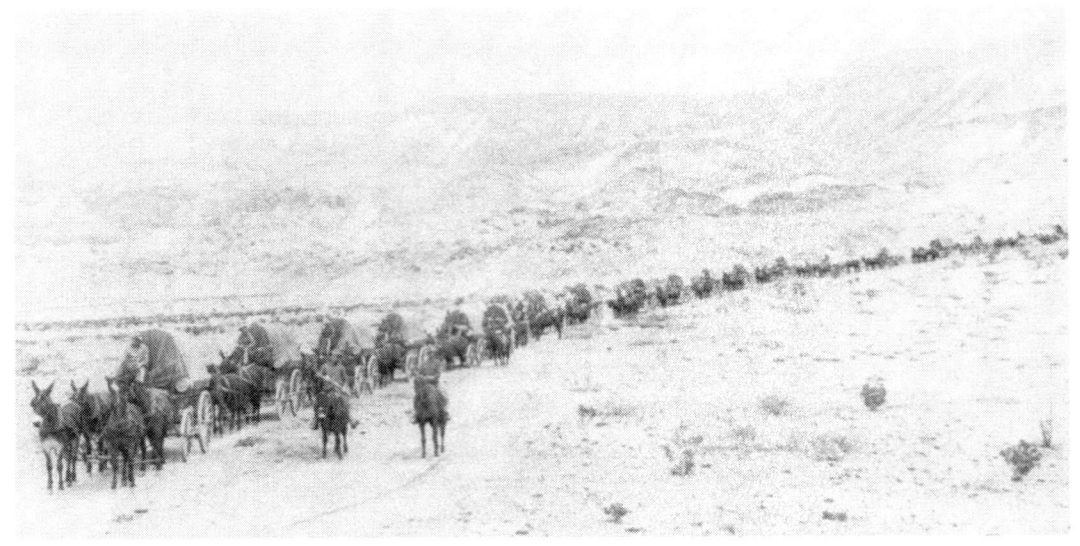

Above, twenty-two wagons in formation come off the Candelaria Rim. Below, a wagon train winding down the rim, the longest and steepest rise in the Big Bend—more than seventeen hundred feet.

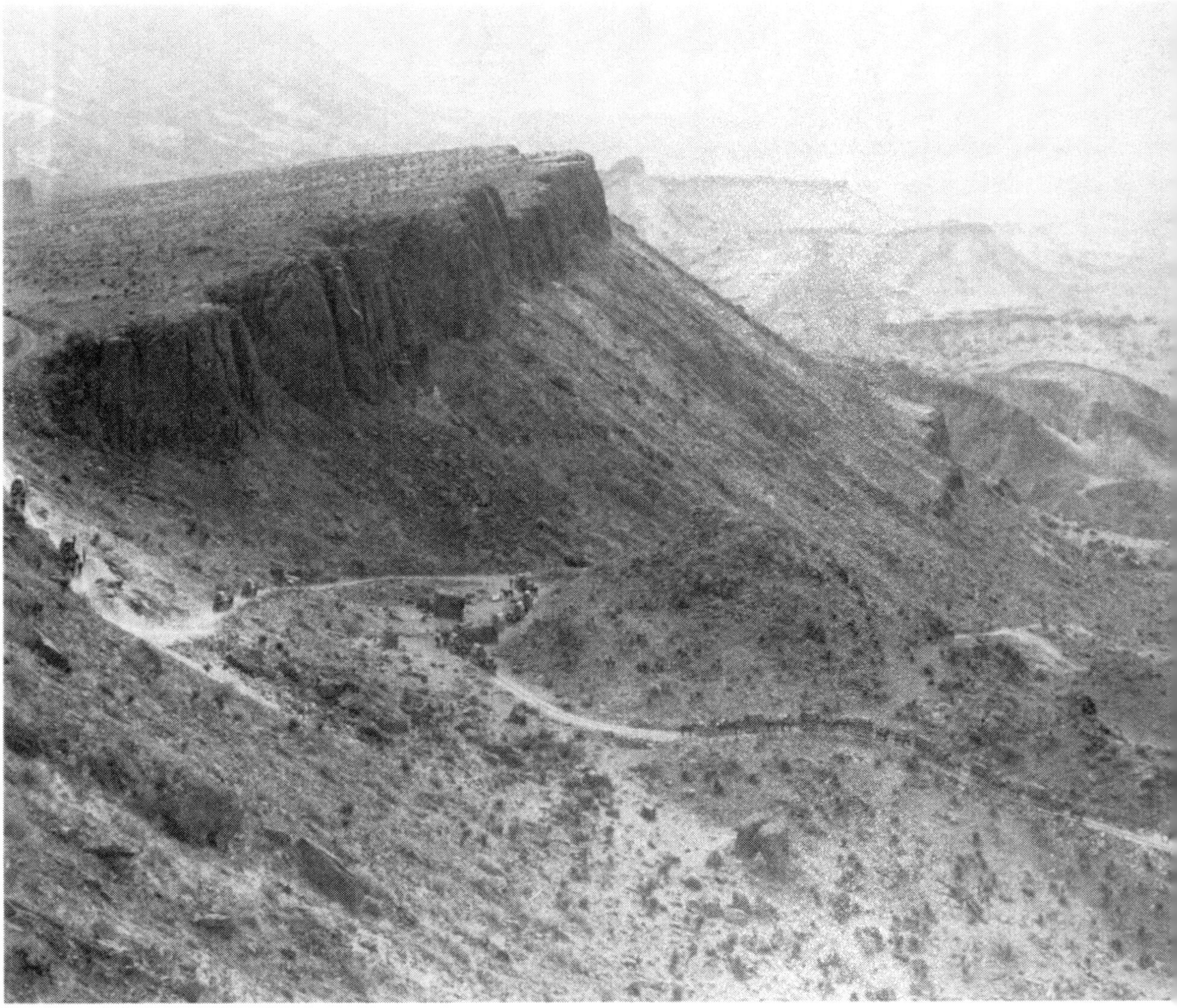

ing habits were altered considerably. But the day began and ended
with monumental meals (although we fed the mules before ourselves)
and even this seemingly casual process was refined and disciplined.

As the train approached its overnight camp, the cook dashed
ahead to select a cooking and camping site. By the time we caught up
with him, the fires were burning, and the meal was in preparation as
soon as the blacksmith and the *cargador* brought the cook's mule and
unpacked it. The coffee pot went on the fire first; the packers wanted their black brew before the meal, as well as during and after. One
of the 50 pack mules was allotted to the cook, with 2 strong wooden
boxes, each about 24 x 24 inches, placed on the packsaddle. At the
start of our trips to Lajitas, the 2 boxes had to be carefully packed
with food sufficient for 168 large meals. In addition to foodstuffs,
utensils—dutch ovens, coffee pot, skillets, sauce pans, plates, and
knives, forks, and spoons—had to be included.

The pack-train cook, unlike the wagon-train cook, who had an
army range, was disadvantaged: he was stoveless. Still, our cook
could prepare a fourteen-man meal quicker, and one that was tastier,
than some could fix for four. By the time we had unpacked and fed
the mules at the campsite, coffee was poured, potatoes were boiling,
onions frying, and corn, beef, peas, and beans stewing. And half a
dozen batches of baking-powder bread would be rising. For breakfast, there was oatmeal with evaporated milk, beans with lots of
bacon, fried potatoes, and prunes, jam, and molasses. And coffee.
While the meals at Marfa were better—with eggs, fresh beef, and lots
of dairy products—we never hungered while on the road. And at Lajitas, we were lucky that the local Mexicans sold us young goats, catfish, and fresh vegetables.

On the march, the packmaster headed the procession, followed by
the cook leading the bell mare. The fifty pack mules were spaced out
with two packers dividing them by tens. The blacksmith and the
cargador brought up the rear except when they would ride forward
to see if any of the mules had lost a shoe. When this happened, the
animal was reshod in camp that night.

It was the packmaster's responsibility to ride along at various
points of the train, checking mules for lameness, packsaddle sores, or
illness. Loads had to be checked as well and, if a loose tie was discovered, he would have the responsible packers readjust the hitch.
When a load needed reworking, both packers galloped out of the
train and rode ahead of the mule and dismounted. As the train
passed, one packer would dash in and grab the mule that needed re-
loading—no easy task. The second packer was ready with blinders,

always kept ready on the packer's right shoulder, which he put around the mule's eyes. Without the blinders, the mule would continue to follow the train. Once the cargo had been readjusted and the diamond hitch retied, they galloped ahead to catch up with the train.

Pack Train 6 had a problem at one time that caused a bit of embarrassment and a small cash outlay: a goat-hating mule. Our train was in the large valley, part of Pinto Canyon, when this particular mule made his second attack on a large herd of Mexican goats. The first night's camp during that trip had been at Cleveland's Ranch Tanks, two large earthen impoundments for watering cattle, whose owners had allowed the wagon and pack trains free use of the water and campsite. As we rode out of camp the next morning, the herder and his goats were at least one hundred yards away. But suddenly number seven mule broke out of his place in the train and raced toward the goats, his two packers and the packmaster in pursuit. The mule seized a goat in his teeth, raised it off the ground, and tossed it aside, then went after another. As he went for a third victim, the two packers grabbed the mule's halter and subdued him. Packer Steve Harris just about somersaulted the mule as he braked him. The rest of the train kept moving the whole time. Once a pack train started on its day's journey, it took a dire emergency to halt it except when it made its one water stop, and then the packmaster had to give the word. While I was with the pack train, no special halt ever was called.

After the goat incident, it took the packmaster a while to catch up with the train, as he had to make matters right with the goat herder. The selling price for adult goats was two dollars, while kids and young goats brought from fifty cents to one dollar. Packmaster George Hickle settled the four-dollar debt from his own pocket, as too much red tape would have been involved in an army settlement.

On the Marfa-Lajitas trip, two overnight camps were necessary each way. Thirty-five miles out of Marfa, we camped at the small village of Plata, then forty miles beyond, near a spring in Fresno Canyon, through which Fresno Creek runs. The last thirty-mile stretch from Fresno Canyon to Lajitas was always a slow, rough trip. At Lajitas, we camped below a large hill where a troop of the Sixth Cavalry had pitched its tents.

The next morning we would return to the Fresno camp, then on to Plata and finally to Marfa to conclude our 6-day, 210-mile trip. The morning after our return to Marfa, we would begin a new trek to Lajitas.

Arrival at Marfa, like that at Lajitas, was followed by loads of work. At Marfa, the quartermaster had the next trip's cargo of hay or

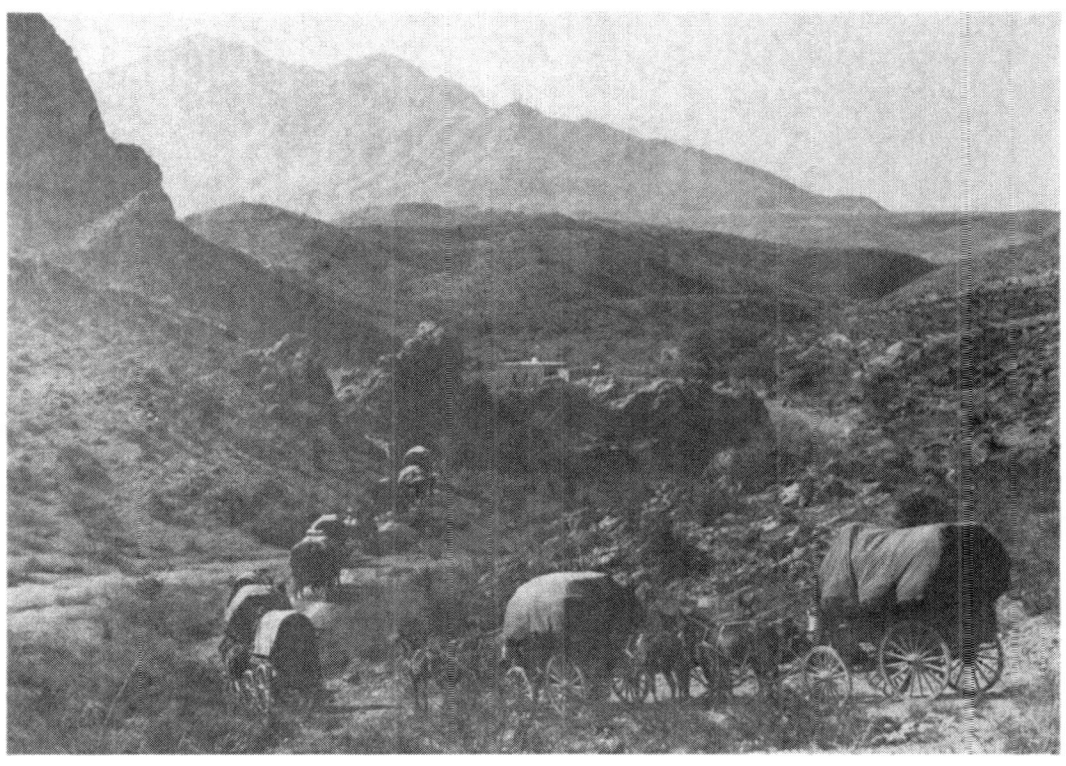

Above, twelve wagons loaded with hay and oats for the cavalry at Ruidosa.
Mule packs often needed readjusting and retying (below).

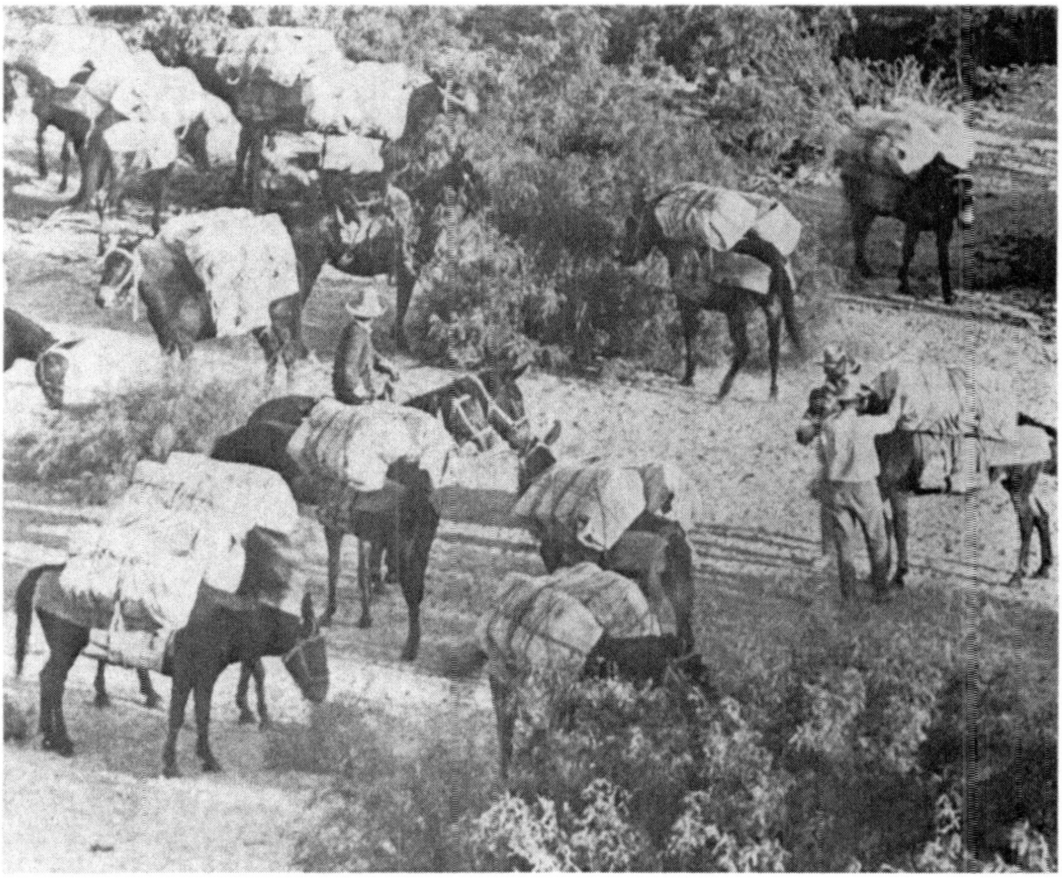

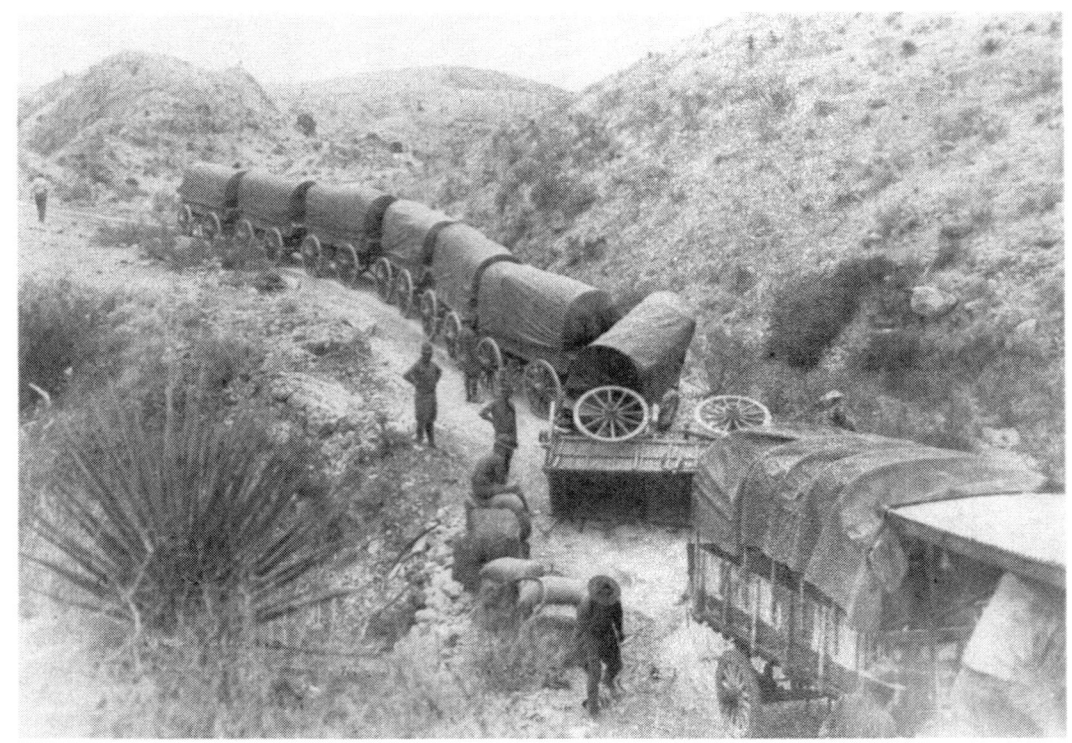

The tractor trains (above) sometimes had mishaps resulting from inability of wagons to keep up with the tractor's quick turns and jerks. Heavier trailers eventually were built, greatly increasing loads and decreasing time and manpower required to deliver them. Below, the tractor train in one of the rougher parts of Pinto Canyon.

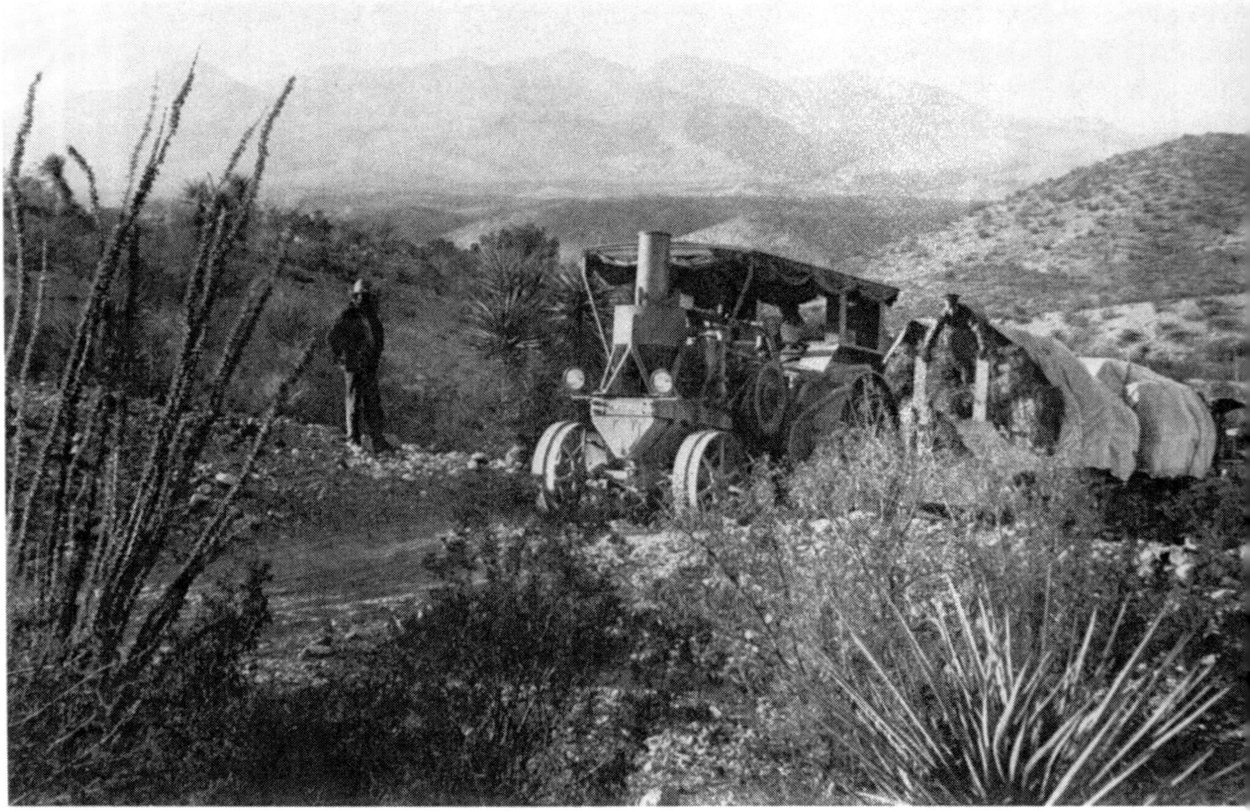

oats ready for us to bundle. We wrapped the cargo in heavy twelve-foot-square pieces of canvas, then tied each with a thirty-foot lair rope. At Lajitas, we of course had to unwrap these bundles for the troops.

Arrival days at Marfa and Lajitas were our longest, averaging about sixteen hours. But we never complained about the hours, for everyone truly liked the work. Good thing, too, since our weeks totaled something like ninety-two hours. We actually were "on duty" twenty-four hours a day, since we slept near the mules' picket line. When commotions arose—and they did when mountain lions or snakes frightened the mules—we had to bounce up to quiet them.

Although there were some drifters in pack trains, we were a stable lot for the most part. For me, the packer life offered opportunity for countless fascinating observations, some of which I found time to photograph. A photographer couldn't ask for better subjects than the packer and cavalry life, or the natural beauties of the Big Bend.

Once I made a trip with a pack train from Columbus, New Mexico, to Dublan, Chihuahua, where the Pershing expedition was head-quartered. Leaving the pack train at Dublan, we returned to Columbus with one of the quartermaster truck trains and got back to Marfa by rail. Those Nash and Jeffey Quad trucks, with four-wheel drive and four-wheel steering, were a curiosity.

World War I called many of us away from Marfa, and I was sent as an enlisted cavalryman to Fort Sam Houston for induction. So I left the Big Bend, hoping to be assigned to the Eighth Cavalry, stationed again on the wondrous curve of the Rio Grande.

A Desperate Land

Until mid-1919, I was in soldier's uniform, but the farthest I was sent from the Mexican border during that period was San Antonio. Having enlisted in the cavalry, I spent only a few weeks at Fort Sam Houston. Then, for the rest of my two years of army service, I was assigned to Otay Mesa, on the California-Mexico border, where I transferred to the aviation section of the Army Signal Corps, forerunner of the U. S. Air Force. I was discharged on April 7, 1919, at Fort Sam Houston.

To get back to a pack train, I went to the transportation office at Fort Sam Houston, where experienced packers were in great demand. Packer pay had gone up—to seventy-five dollars per month plus rations—and I got a coach seat on the next train to Marfa.

Camp Marfa had changed little since 1916. When I arrived, I was assigned immediately to Pack Train 6, to leave the next morning for Ruidosa. Finding the train encamped at the railroad stock pens, I spent the evening taking in the familiar scene: mules resting contentedly in pens, cargo and packsaddles laid out for the early-morning start, packers bedding down for the night. It was good to be back.

I decided on three rules for my pack-train routine, hoping they would assist my research. One was to make detailed mental notes of things I saw; two, jot down as much material as possible; and, three, take photographs whenever I could. Regretfully, I found it difficult to scribble notes or snap the shutter as often as I would have liked, but the memory of many of my observations are as clear today as they were the day I made them.

My packmaster was George Hickle, who had been in mule pack trains more than twenty-one years since signing on in 1898, during the Spanish-American War. He was one of the best men that any of us packers had worked under, and he was more knowledgeable about mules and packs than anyone I knew. Pack Train 6 had a fine crew.

For the first few days I was a little awkward, but soon my hands toughened and I fell into the routines of roping, lifting, and loading. The two years in the aviation section had pampered me but in little time I was back in top shape—essential for a packer. The major change that greeted me in 1919 was the construction of a few good roads to several of the outposts. Tractor-drawn wagon trains now could supply areas previously reached only by pack train. One such road ran from Alpine to Terlingua, only twenty-two miles from Lajitas. In 1916, Lajitas had been a hard three-day pack-train journey from Marfa but tractor-drawn wagons now made the trip to Terlingua, where a pack train was stationed, ready to relay the load to Lajitas. The pack train would return to Terlingua the next day, load up, and head to Castolon, sixteen miles down the Rio Grande. How it had changed! Three years previously, five pack trains had been in motion every six days between Marfa and Alpine and Castolon. Now such trips were occasioned only when a tractor broke down.

The road from Marfa to Candelaria was about the same as it had been in 1916. Nothing could be done that would improve that terrible trip over the Candelaria Rim. Even fifty years later, with modern road-building equipment, the rim could not be bridged.

Pack Train 6 had come to the Big Bend in May, 1917, from Fort Bliss with the Eighth U. S. Cavalry. While I was away, Mexican bandits had made many raids on Big Bend ranches. The most treacherous attacks were on the Nuñez ranch, near Ruidosa, the Brite ranch, near the Candelaria Rim, and the Nevill ranch, up the Rio Grande from Candelaria. Ranch people often were the victims of grisly murders, some of which were avenged by the Eighth Cavalry with its pursuit of the outlaws beyond the Rio Grande. The cavalry's invasions of Mexico, which often recovered much stolen loot, were not sanctioned by Washington, but the commander, Colonel George T. Langhorne, had an ace up his sleeve: the 1884 treaty between the United States and Mexico, allowing both countries to cross the international boundary in pursuit of raiders.

In the Big Bend, cavalrymen made constant patrols along and near the Rio Grande. There were several detachments of half a dozen Texas Rangers each, stationed at various points, also patrolling on horseback. The purpose of both Rangers and cavalry patrols was to catch illegal Mexican aliens. There were many Mexicans living in all parts of the Big Bend, many in the villages near the outposts, and others scattered along the river. They were legal residents, and should

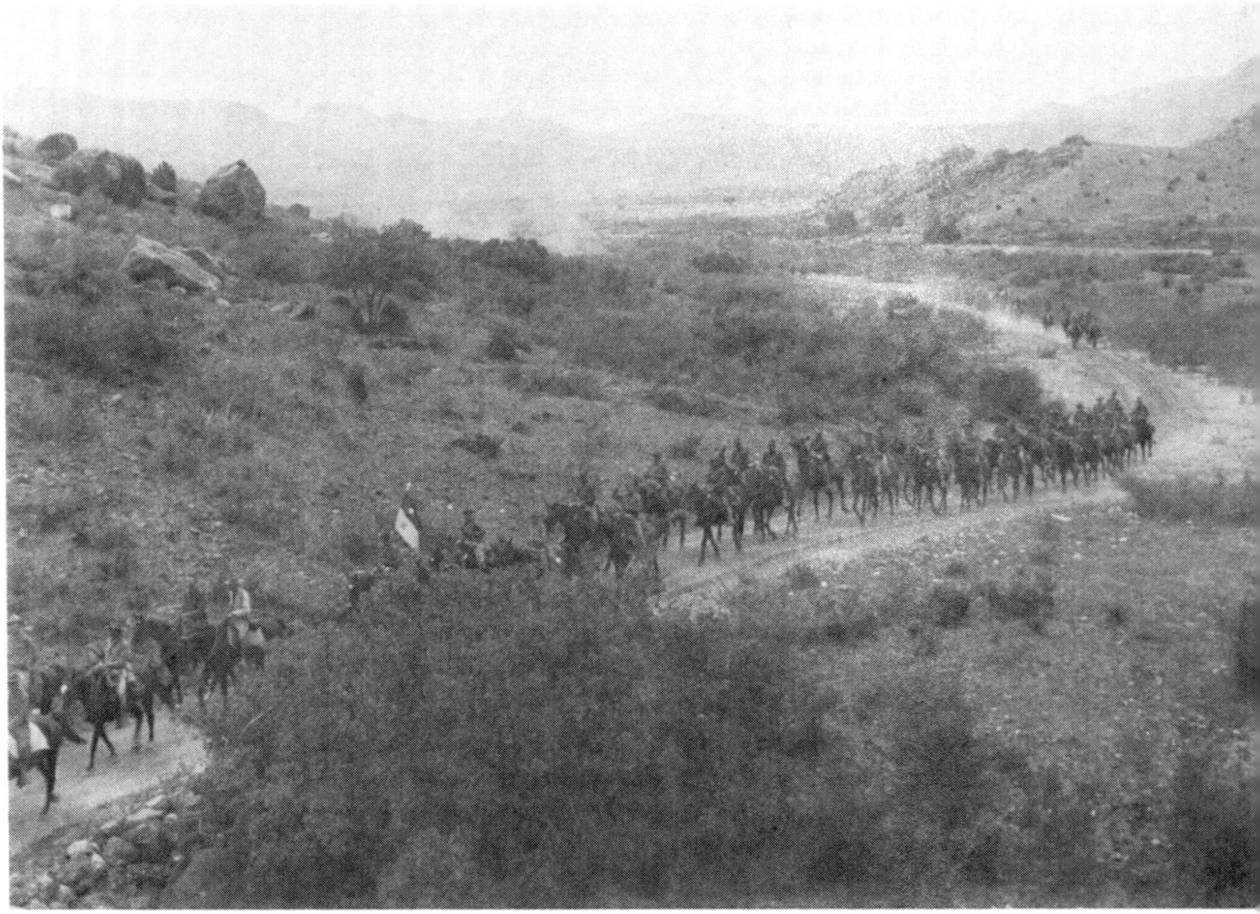

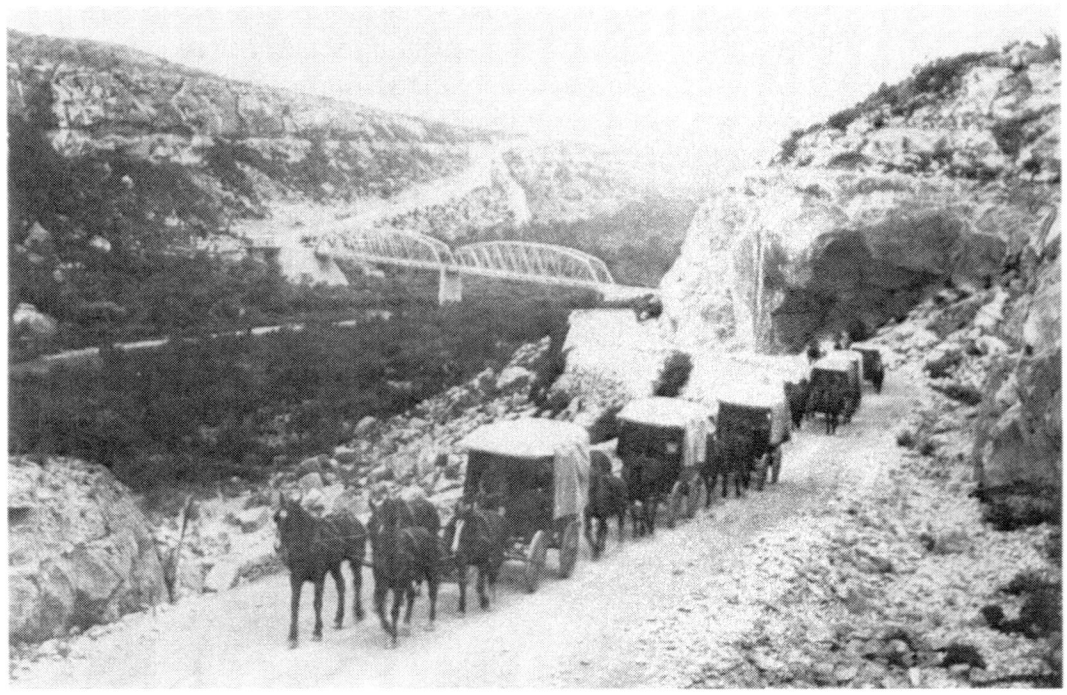

Troop H of the Eighth (above) marches from Marfa to Alpine. Below, ambulances of the First Cavalry Regiment cross the Pecos. The bridge later was washed away and replaced with a higher one.

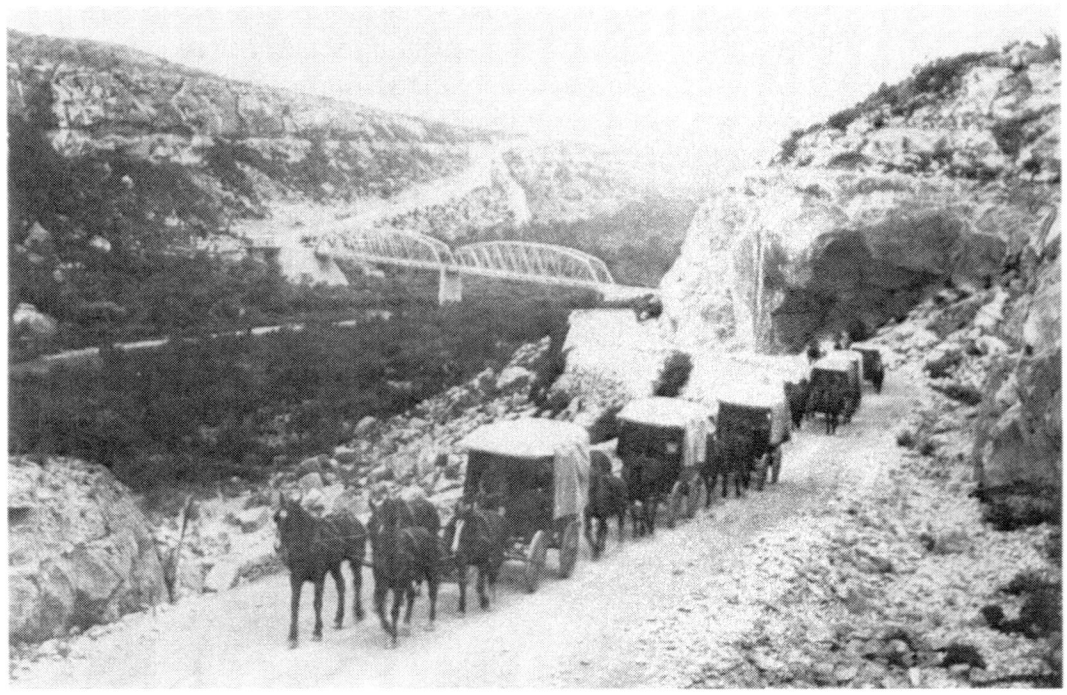

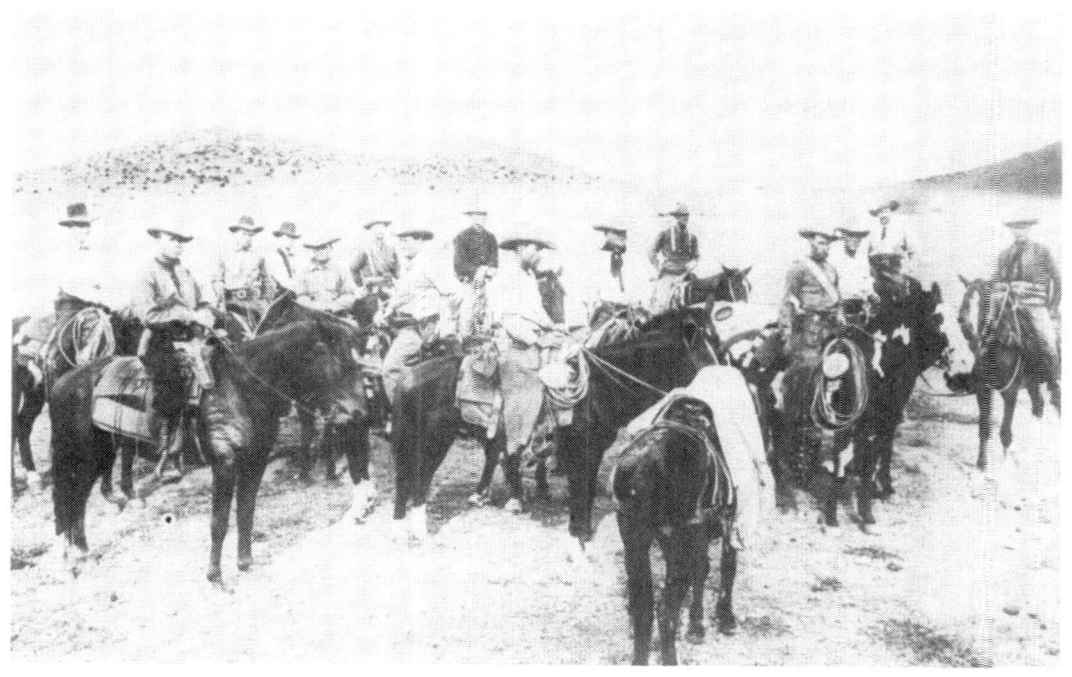

Above, Company B of the Texas Rangers; S. F. (Buffalo Bill) Sherman at extreme right. Below, Troop A of the Sixth Cavalry at Glenn Springs two weeks after the bandit raids of May 5, 1916. The rest of the Sixth was with the Pershing expedition.

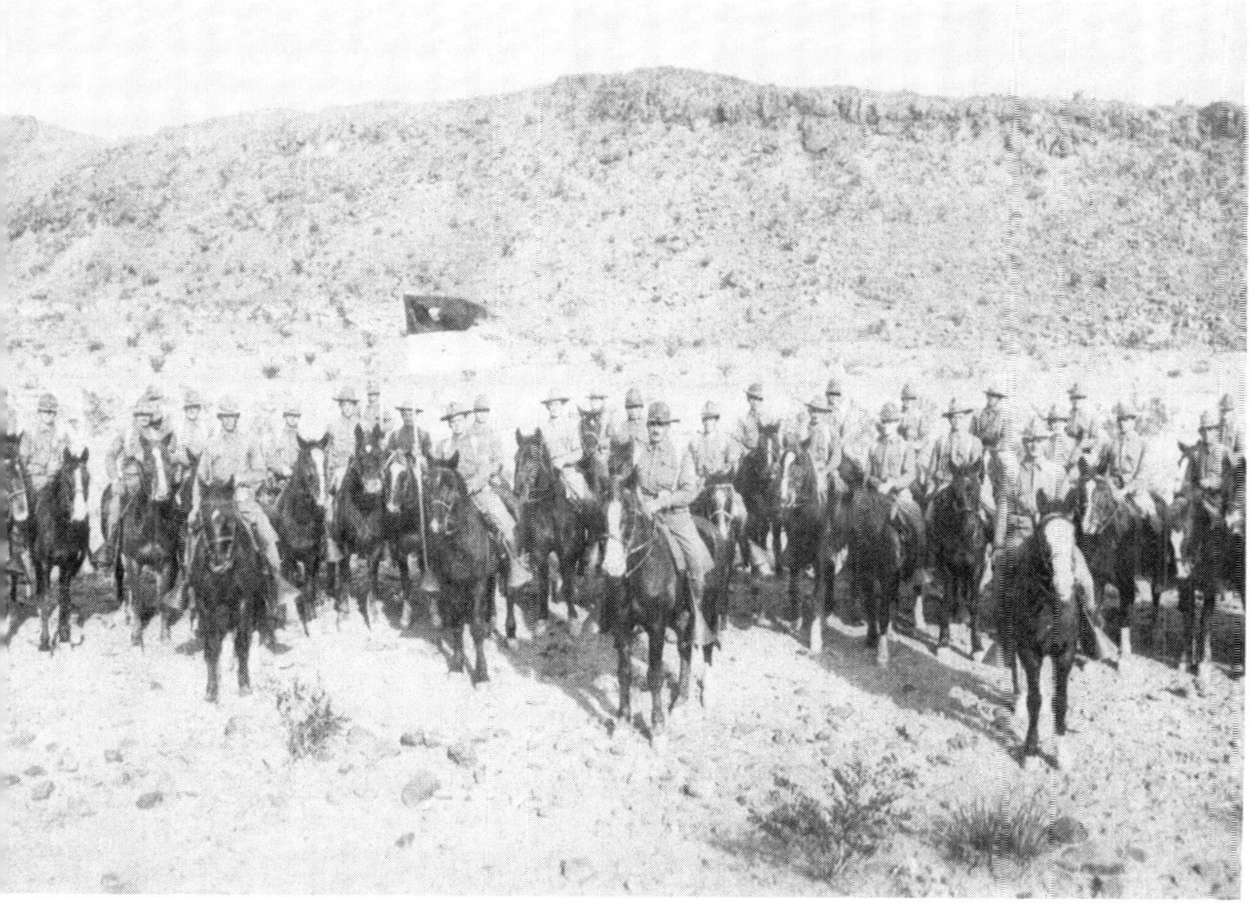

34

not have feared the cavalry or the Rangers, but they often did. It was these Texas Mexicans who sent avisos about the patrols, enabling bandits to dodge pursuit. The Rangers and cavalrymen knew that messages were being sent, but they did not know how—"grapevine telephone" was their name for the Mexicans' silent, effective communication system.

In 1919, the bandit raids were far from over, and my fellow packers who had witnessed the results of the raids and helped supply the pursuers related many stories to me. It was clear that the bandits were going to be very much a part of my life in the Big Bend. Certainly not all Texas Mexicans assisted the raiders, for many had been robbed of their goats, pigs, and cattle.

The cavalry got its first break in its continuing war with the bandits on June 20, 1919. The Border Air Patrol was started, and four DeHaviland planes were assigned to Marfa. Two planes, on a morn-

Texas Rangers came to Lajitas in 1917 to track down the bandits who raided the Brite ranch.

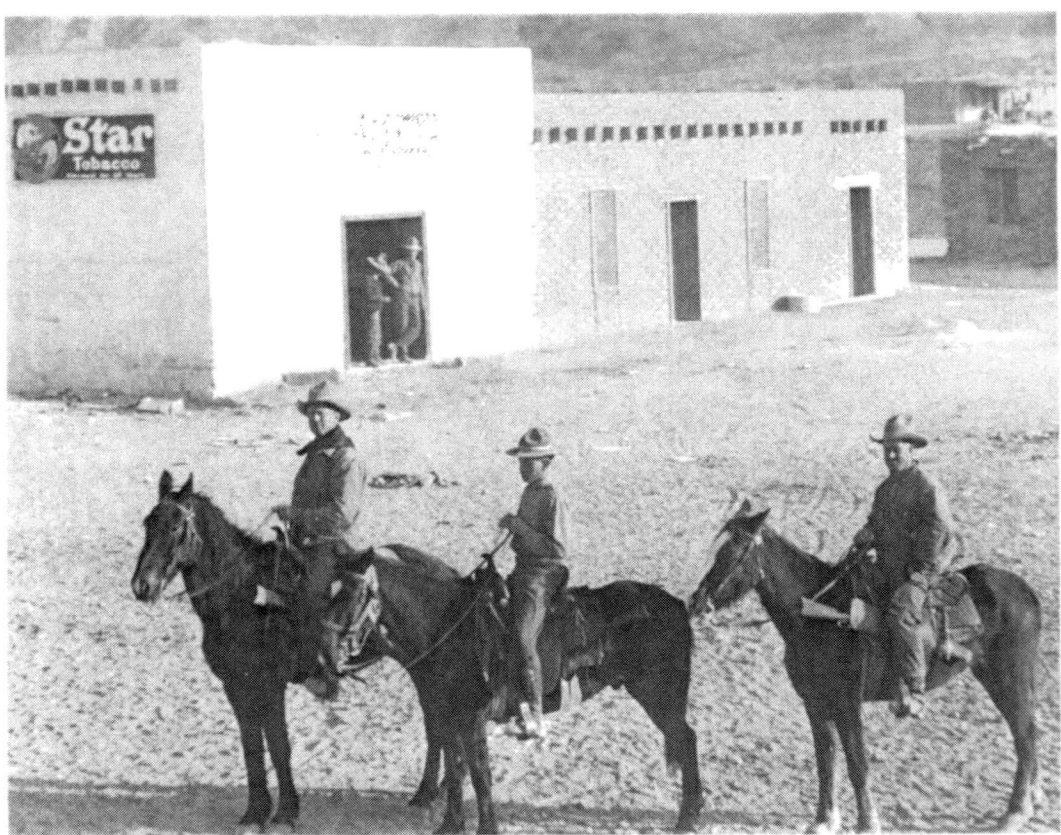

ing patrol, flew the entire Rio Grande perimeter of the Big Bend. Two others would make the same flight in the afternoon. The presence of the planes instantly reduced the number of raids, but some small bands continued to cross the river at night. The cavalry patrolled both day and night, complementing the observers in the air. Those flyers had a pretty effective way of publicizing their presence and mission in the Big Bend. The DeHaviland planes could land in very small spaces, and they would do so near settlements, to be seen by as many people as possible, some of whom had never before seen a flying machine. The soldiers encouraged them to take good, long looks—especially at the machine guns. The flyers gave demonstrations, too. Flying low, they would fire at oil drums, using tracer bullets to emphasize the effectiveness of the cavalry's new bandit-deterring machinery. We knew that detailed avisos describing the cavalry's capacities soon would be flashed to the bandits. Those demonstrations were almost as good as having the bandits there as spectators, for they were informed by avisos of *balas calientes*, the fiery bullets.

The raiders came from all along the Mexican border, from Boquillas to El Paso, but they represented only themselves, not the Mexican people or their government. In their looting, they were indiscriminate; both Texans and Mexicans were their victims. Many of the border bandits emerged from bands of various revolutionaries that had roamed northern Mexico for several years. Others were military deserters. The spoils they most desired were saddle horses and commissary goods. Some of the families they came in contact with condoned their activities by allowing their homes to be used as hideouts, but many refused to harbor the bandits, having been misled or even robbed previously.

The sections of the Big Bend that had the most violent bandit activity were up the Rio Grande from Ruidosa to Candelaria, then farther up, a few miles beyond the village of Porvenir. These three villages were on the Texas side and each had a cavalry outpost. Across the Rio Grande from Porvenir was Pilares—a regular outlaw haven. It was at Pilares that the Eighth Cavalry destroyed some of the bandits' houses—and a few bandits—that had raided the Brite and Nevill ranches.

Even more bandits made their headquarters in the village of San Antonio de Bravo, directly across from Candelaria, Texas. One of its most noted desperadoes was Chico Cano—feared, hated, and hunted for six bloody years. On May 23, 1915, Mounted Customs Officer Joe Sitters and Eugene Hulen, a cattle inspector, were ambushed and killed by Chico Cano and his gang of bandits southeast of Porvenir.

Sitters and Hulen, Rangers Sug Cummings and one Tollinger, and Customs Officer Craig Head were on the trail of Chico Cano and his band of bandits when they found themselves surrounded. The other three managed to escape. Cano was a leader of sorts of San Antonio, wielding a powerful influence over the village into the twenties. San Antonio's prominence as a bandit center increased and it was surely where the raids were planned, although the bandits rarely returned there directly following a raid; they would head for Pilares instead.

The San Antonio-Candelaria area made national headlines later, in 1919, when two U. S. aviators were held by Mexican bandits for fifteen thousand dollars ransom.

It was Sunday morning, August 10, 1919, when Lieutenants H. G. Peterson and Paul H. Davis, Border Air Patrol flyers, were soaring over the Rio Grande on a routine patrol. Their regular route was from Santa Elena Canyon, in Brewster County, up the Rio Grande to the corners of Presidio and Culberson counties, where they would meet the patrol from the El Paso base, and thence back to the starting point. On that Sunday, though, Peterson and Davis flew up the Rio Conchos—official reports said they had taken the wrong river by mistake—and were about eighty miles into Mexico when their motor died. After maneuvering to a safe landing, they dismounted their machine guns and hid them in bushes, then walked toward a Mexican home they had seen from the air.

They found hospitality in the home, and the Mexican man furnished burros and headed toward the border with them. After six miles, there suddenly appeared a band of forty bandits, led by the menacing Jesus Renteria, known as Gacho, for the steel hook he had in place of his left hand. He had lost his hand while working for a railroad in the United States and, after receiving a settlement for the accident, had returned to Mexico. Before coming to the San Antonio de Bravo area, Gacho had been in one of Villa's armies, but thought he could do better with his own band—possibly even replace Chico Cano as bandit king.

In English, Gacho told the two flyers that they were to be held for fifteen thousand dollars. If they refused to write the ransom note, they would be killed. Lieutenant Peterson wrote the note at a Mexican's home in the town of Coyame and scribbled another note requesting that telegrams describing what was happening be sent to the Big Bend commander, Colonel Langhorne; Major General Joseph Dickman, commander of the Southern Department; the secretary of war; the commander of the Border Air Patrol (Major J. A. Walton); and to the fathers of both flyers.

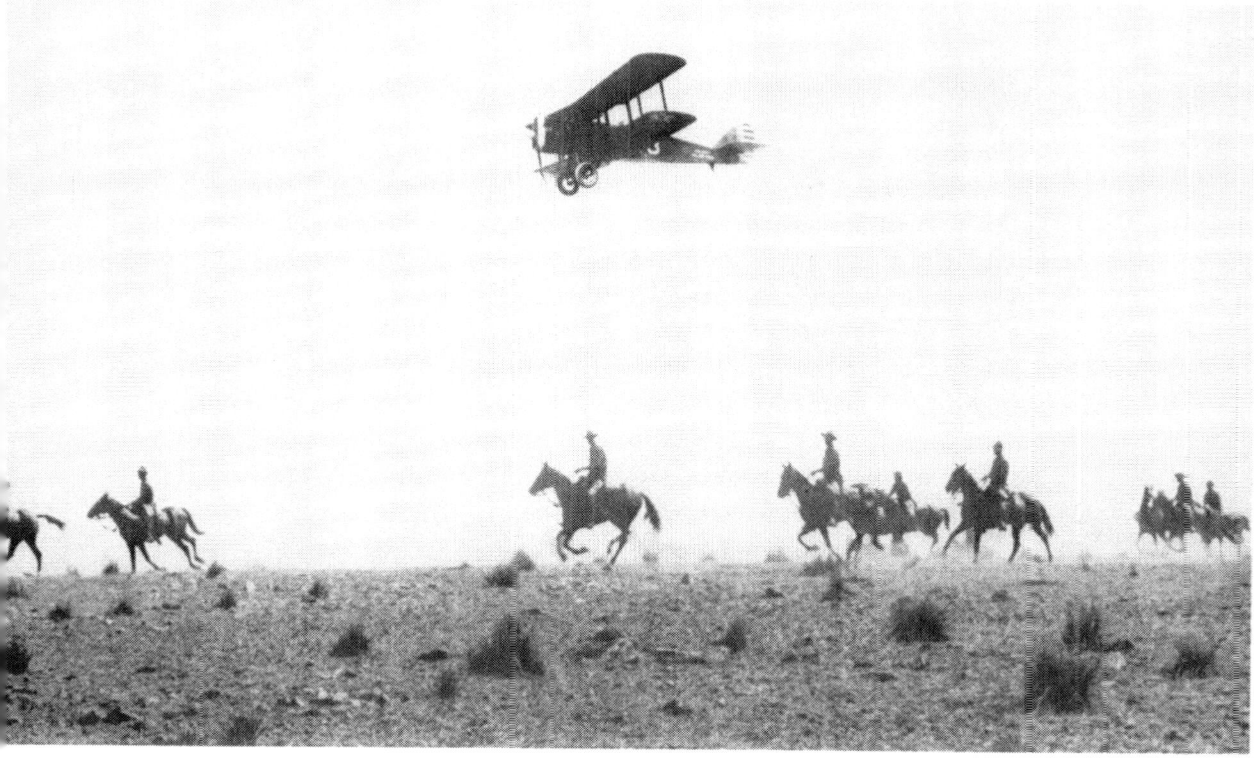

A DeHaviland plane (above) prepares to drop a message to galloping troopers. Below, Border Air Patrol plane at Marfa, 1919.

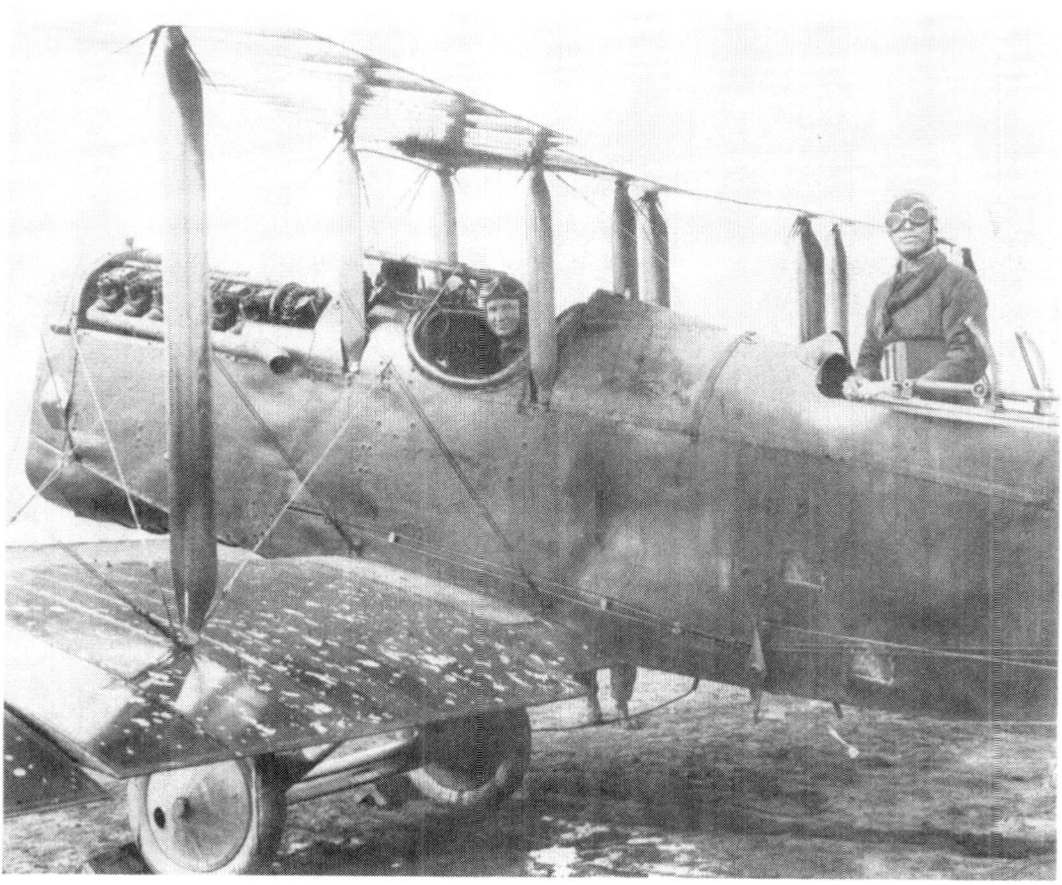

Soon the most extensive air and ground search ever seen in the Southwest began for Peterson and Davis. Planes from Sanderson and El Paso bases joined the search, and four Martin bombers flew out from Kelly Field. Permission to fly over Mexico in the search was refused by President Carranza, which impaired the quest, since even the high-flying Martins were insufficient for the job.

Everyone felt that the plane was surely down in Mexico, but there were no hard facts. Troop K, at Candelaria, had a government scout, Miles Scannel, whose job included getting information from informers, but in this instance his sources could not provide much. The avisos were even more secretive than usual, apparently using a different code. Meanwhile, our pack train was kept on the Marfa-Candelaria run, two days each way. The cargo we hauled to Candelaria increased beyond what was needed for one troop, and it was rumored that many more men would arrive soon. Something big was going to take place at Candelaria.

The ransom note arrived a week after it was written. On Sunday, August 17, a Mexican boy, holding a piece of paper, crossed the Rio

Two cavalrymen clown it up in bandit gear.

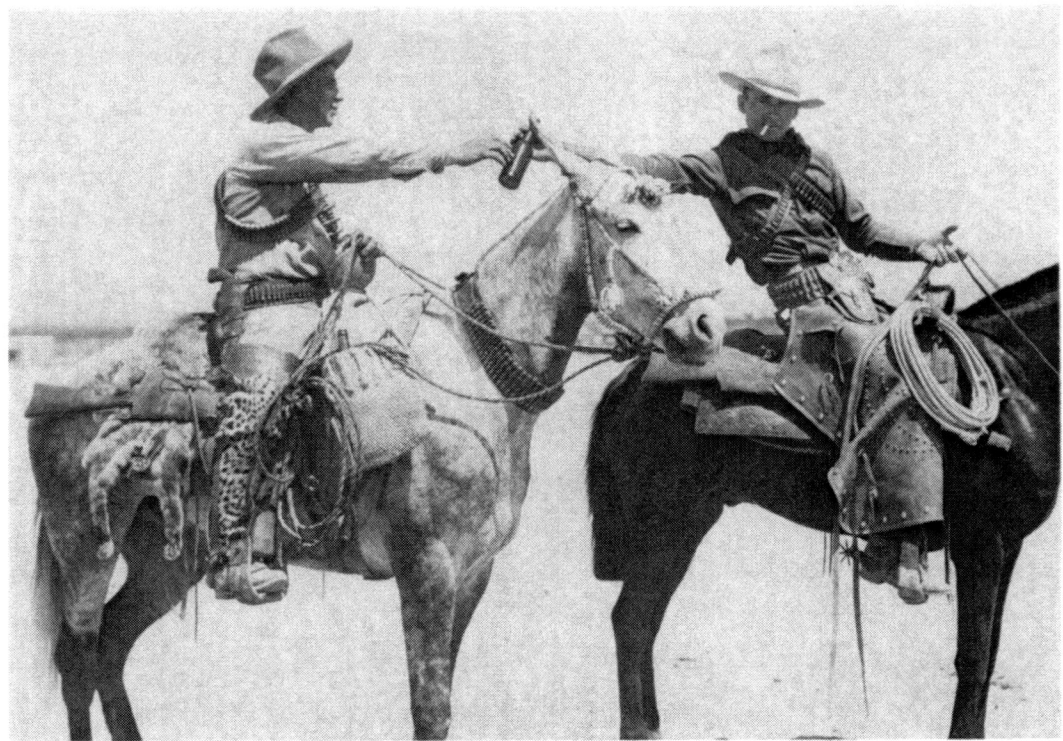

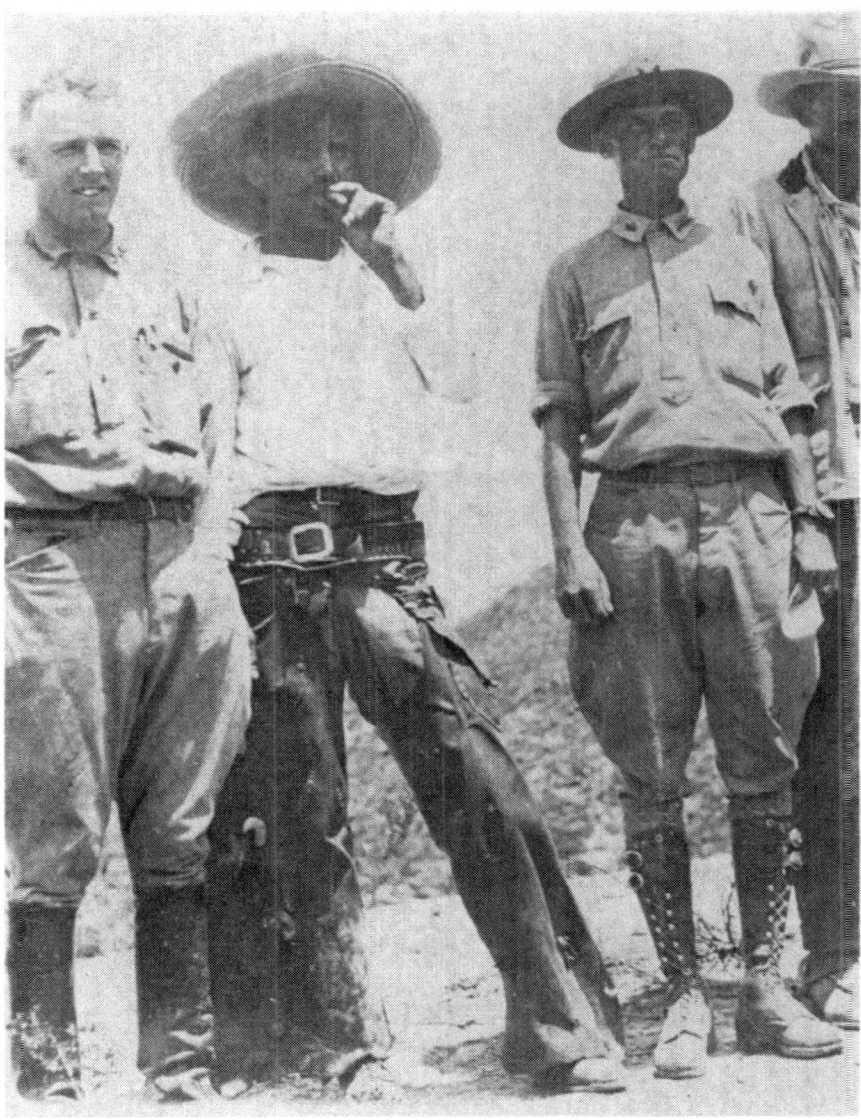

Left to right: Major Roy J. Considine, Chico Cano, Captain Leonard F. Matlack.

Grande on a burro and delivered it to Captain Leonard F. Matlack, commander of Troop K of the Eighth Cavalry.

Upon receipt of the note, Matlack phoned his commander, Langhorne, at Camp Marfa and read the message over the Signal Corps telephone line. It was assumed that action on the demands would not begin until the next morning. But as fate would have it, the ranch families of Marfa, Valentine, Fort Davis, and Alpine had gathered

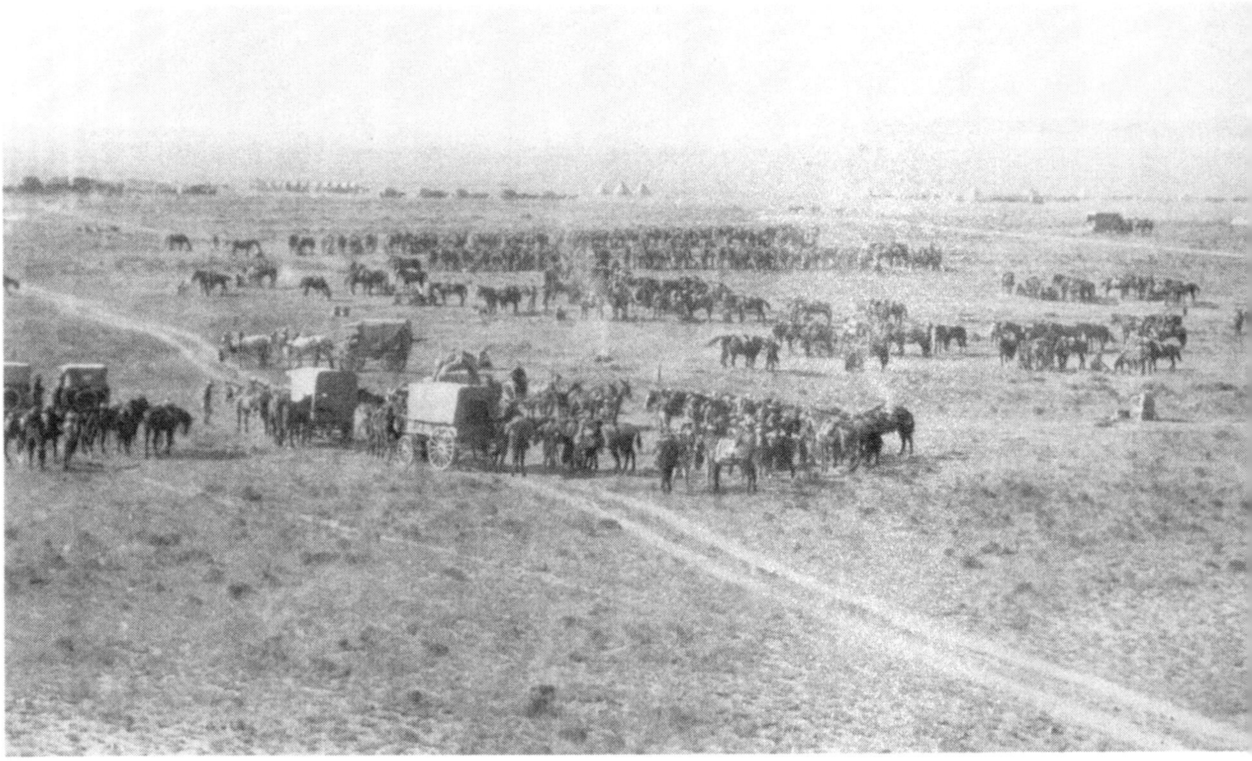

Above, a cavalry company sets up camp at Marfa. Below, one of three telephone operators on twenty-four-hour duty at Marfa. All cavalry outposts in the Big Bend were connected to Marfa headquarters by Signal Corps lines.

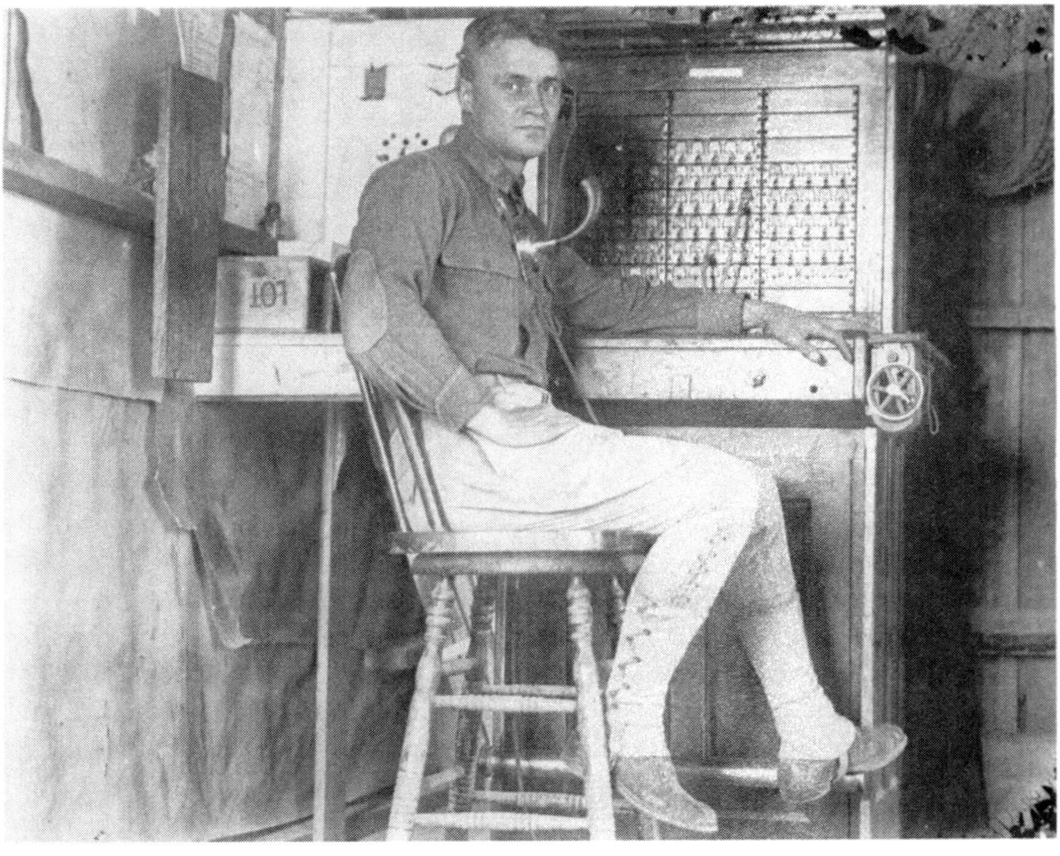

that Sunday for the annual Bloys Camp Meeting, and word of the fifteen-thousand-dollar demand soon spread to them. By afternoon, five local ranchers had located their banker, H. M. Fennell, at the camp meeting and instructed him to go for the fifteen thousand dollars and send it to Langhorne for delivery to Gacho.

Langhorne called Captain Matlack to tell him that the ranchers had raised the money and it was being delivered by Major C. C. Smith and Fennell. Langhorne also sent a letter urging Matlack to secure the release of the two aviators. That letter to Matlack was fateful for many.

Matlack tried all that Sunday and Monday morning to negotiate with Gacho by messenger—a long and tedious ordeal—but Gacho rejected all offers. Finally, Matlack sent Gacho word that if he did not accept one of the arrangements, or if any harm came to the two flyers, he would hold every Mexican in the San Antonio area responsible. The captain also threatened Gacho with personal revenge. It worked: Gacho replied with acceptance of one of the Matlack proposals.

It was arranged that when Gacho signaled with a light from the slope of the mountain behind San Antonio (about 3 miles from the river), Matlack would cross over, travel the old San Antonio trail, and meet a bandit with one of the aviators. Matlack would pay $7,500 and take the aviator back to the Texas side, then return with the other $7,500 for the second flyer. The exchange was set for midnight, Monday, August 18. Nerves were tight, and all attention was on Matlack, who certainly had the most incredible kind of courage to ride 2 brushy miles at midnight toward the hideout of at least 30 desperate men with $7,500 in his pocket.

Matlack mounted his horse and, after a considerable wait, decided that he must have missed Gacho's light signal. He crossed the shallowest part of the river and started into the Mexican midnight. Sure enough, a mile down the winding road, he met one of the bandits and one of the aviators. Through the darkness he asked for identification. "It is Lieutenant Peterson, United States Aviation."

He gave the bandit the $7,500 and told Peterson to mount the horse behind him, and they recrossed the river. After delivering Peterson to headquarters, Matlack took the second $7,500 and returned to the rendezvous for the other aviator, but no one was there.

Then he heard two horses coming through a cornfield to the left of the trail. As they approached, he heard one of the riders say to the other, "*¿Mato los dos gringos?*" The other answered, "*Seguro.*"

42

("Kill both Americans?" "Sure.") As they rode past, Matlack heard them say that they would get him when he passed through the thick brush near the river.

After they passed out of hearing, Matlack moved ahead about one hundred yards and saw the burning cigarette of a rider coming down the trail. The rider waved the lighted cigarette in a circle—a signal to alert the two riders that Matlack was approaching. Matlack carried on as if unaware of their plans, while Lieutenant Davis walked toward him, ahead of the mounted bandit. When they met, Matlack told Davis to jump up behind him, then whispered to Davis to take the pistol out of his right holster.

On the first trip, the bandit had seen Matlack take the money from the bosom of his shirt, but this time he got a surprise. When the captain's hand came out of his shirt, it held not the money but his six-shooter.

Captain Matlack was near the bandit as his gun appeared like a flash. The bandit, too terrified to make a move, could only sit in his

Candelaria, 1919. In the background is the river crossing where Matlack and Davis crossed into Texas.

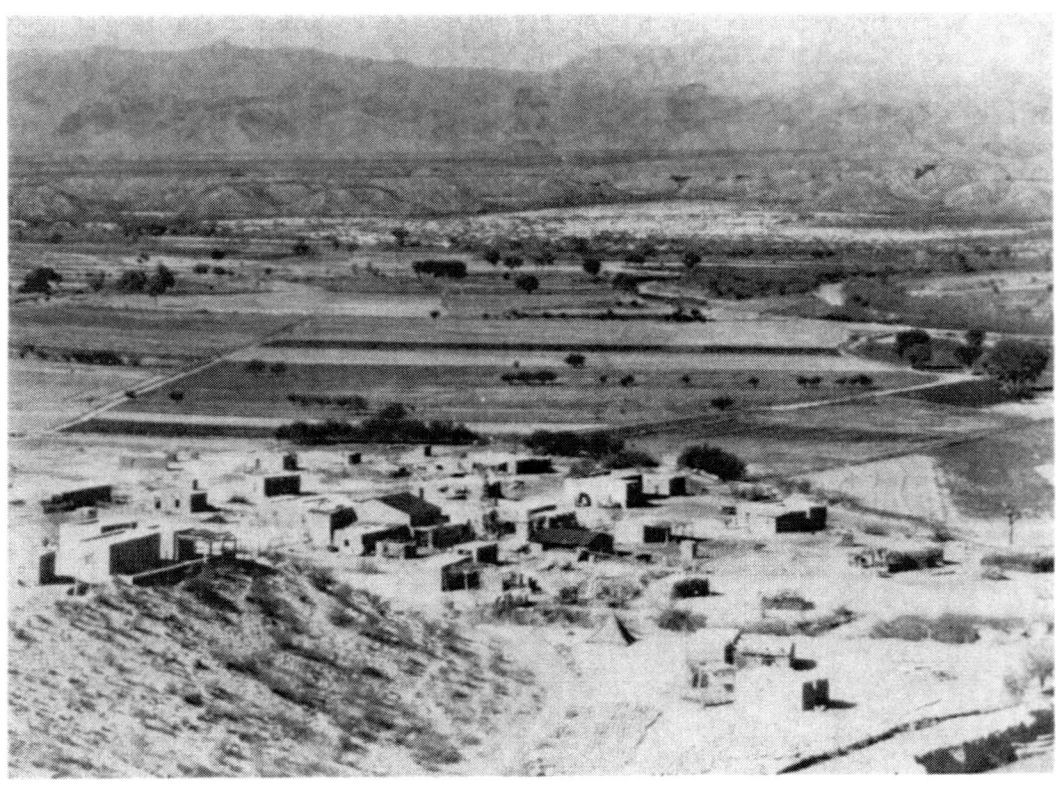

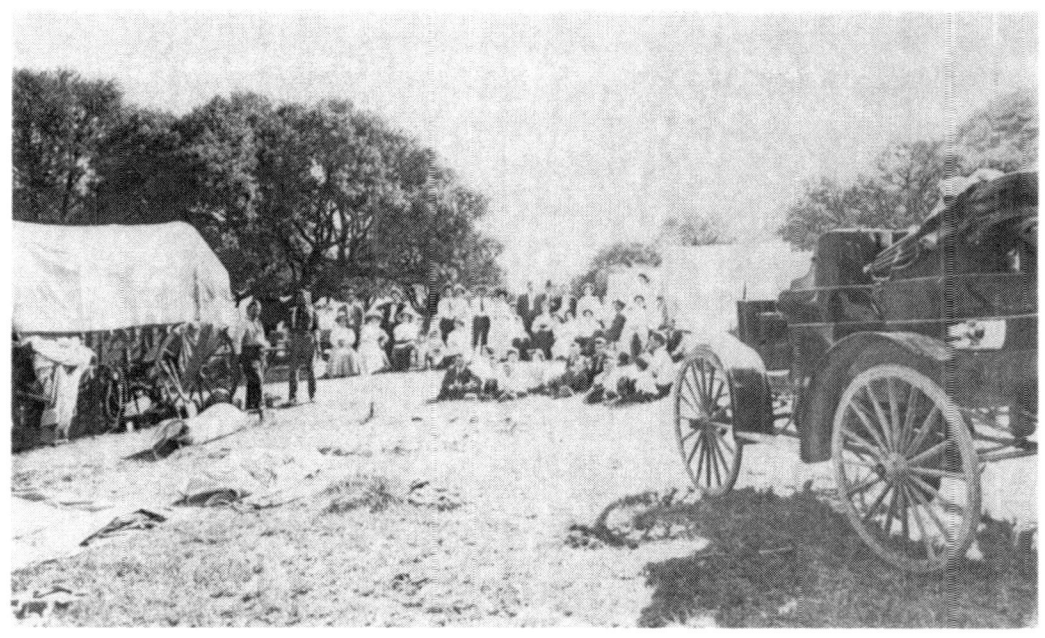

It was at a camp meeting like this one (above) that the ransom money for Lieutenants Peterson and Davis was raised. Photo, by Nick Merfelder, was taken about 1912. Below, Captain Matlack leading Troop K at Candelaria

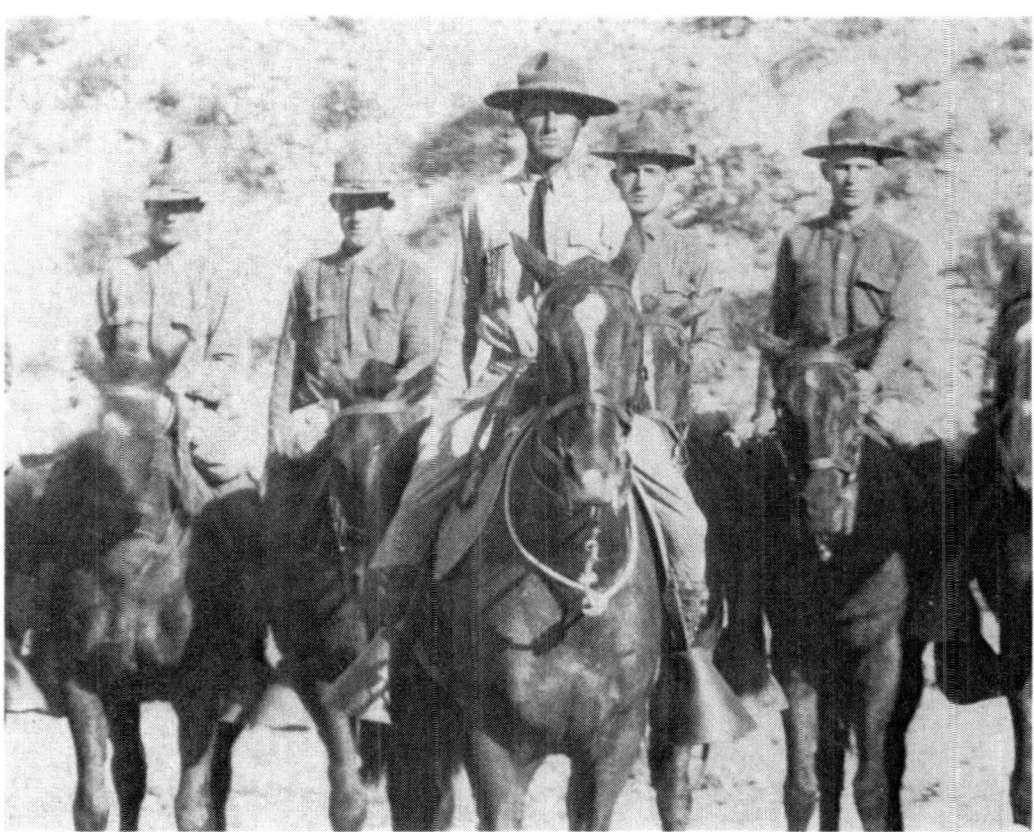

saddle and stare as Matlack ordered him to go back, and added, "Tell Gacho to go to hell. He's had his last American dollar."

Matlack spurred his horse and dashed for the Rio Grande, to cross at a different ford from the one where the two riders he had overheard were waiting to kill him and Davis.

Davis was delivered safely to the troop headquarters and Matlack returned the $7,500 to the banker. Matlack said nothing about his mission except that it would all be in a report he hoped to make within a few days. The captain first had to go back into Mexico, this time at the head of his troop.

Between 5:30 and 6: o'clock the morning of August 19, Troops K and C of the Eighth Cavalry, under Matlack's command, crossed the Rio Grande into Mexico. Two other troops crossed at Ruidosa, about twelve miles downstream from Candelaria—Troops A and E of the Fifth Cavalry, under Major James P. Yancey, who also was in command of the expedition. A third contingent embarked from Indio, twenty miles below Ruidosa and thirty-two miles from Candelaria. The Indio force consisted of Troop C of the Fifth Cavalry and the machine-gun troop of the Eighth. All the troops at Indio were commanded by Major C. C. Smith.

With those troops were Pack Trains 11, 13, and 26. Our Pack Train 6 was ready to go with the two troops at Candelaria, but someone confused the orders. The packmaster had been told to have the train loaded with oats, be in the wheat field near the lower San Antonio crossing at five o'clock, and wait there for further orders—which never were issued.

Matlack's Troop K, from Candelaria, was to flush out any of Gacho's bandits that had not scattered in the 5 hours since the $7,500 was paid. Troops that crossed at Ruidosa and Indio were to cut off the bandits' escape routes to the towns of Coyame and Carrizo, where all the troops were to meet. None of Gacho's bandits was found. Those who had not evacuated found good hideouts until the troops left. Four armed outlaws were captured by a Troop K patrol, but Matlack and his scout, Miles Scannel, knew they were not part of Gacho's gang.

Later, Major Yancey gave custody of the four prisoners to the civilian scouts, as Matlack had said that all four were wanted in Texas for various crimes. The four prisoners were taken into a canyon and shot, although no one learned which of the scouts did the killing. The prisoners were last seen by the soldiers in the custody of John Kerr, cavalry scout; A. G. Beard, Marfa town marshal; Presidio County Deputy Sheriff Mark Langford; and Pablo Chaves, a Mexican employed as a United States government scout. Beard and Kerr also had been Texas Rangers in 1917 and 1918. Those names were not learned until the 1920 court martial of Major Yancey.

The region penetrated by the expedition provided the greatest opportunities for avisadores to demonstrate their skills. There is a long range of high mountains, the Sierra Grande, between Candelaria, Texas, opposite San Antonio de Bravo, Chihuahua, and El Carrizo and T and O Tanks, where most of the events of the expedition oc-

Leading politicos of Ojinaga, Chihuahua, 1919 (left), and federal soldiers.

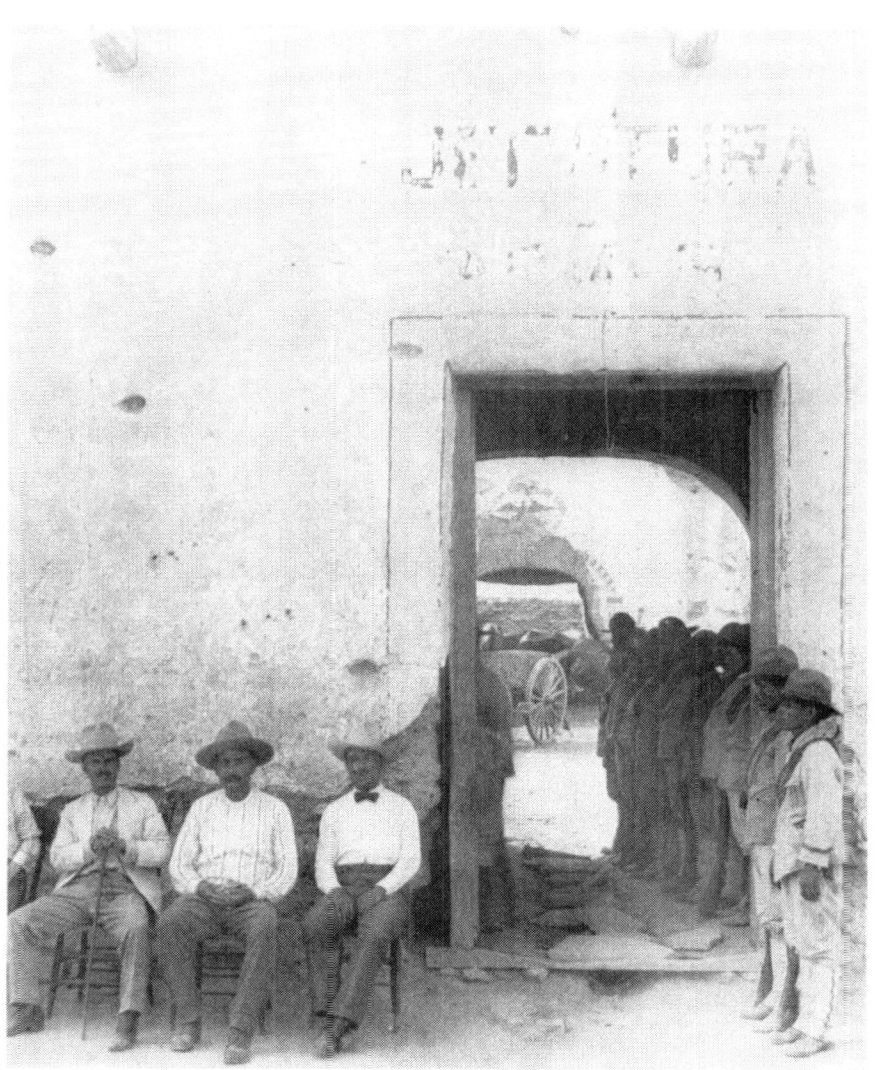

curred. It seemed impossible that messages could be sent from beyond those high, rough mountains, but they were. Ten years later, after learning that they were sent by mirror flashes, I concluded that the transmission must have been in relays, but I hadn't identified this procedure in 1919.

During the expedition, avisos were not as secretive as those concerning the two aviators. Friendly Candelaria Mexicans willingly told of avisador-related happenings several times during the five-day expedition. The accuracy of the communications was validated. The avisos were brief, omitting specifics of names and places, but they told the essentials of the troop movement.

There was one event of the expedition that avisos failed to detail. On that Tuesday, the first day of the U. S. Cavalry expedition into Mexico, one of the planes made big news. Lieutenants Frank S.

Jim Watts, civilian scout for Troop M of the Eighth Cavalry.

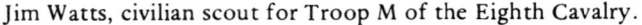

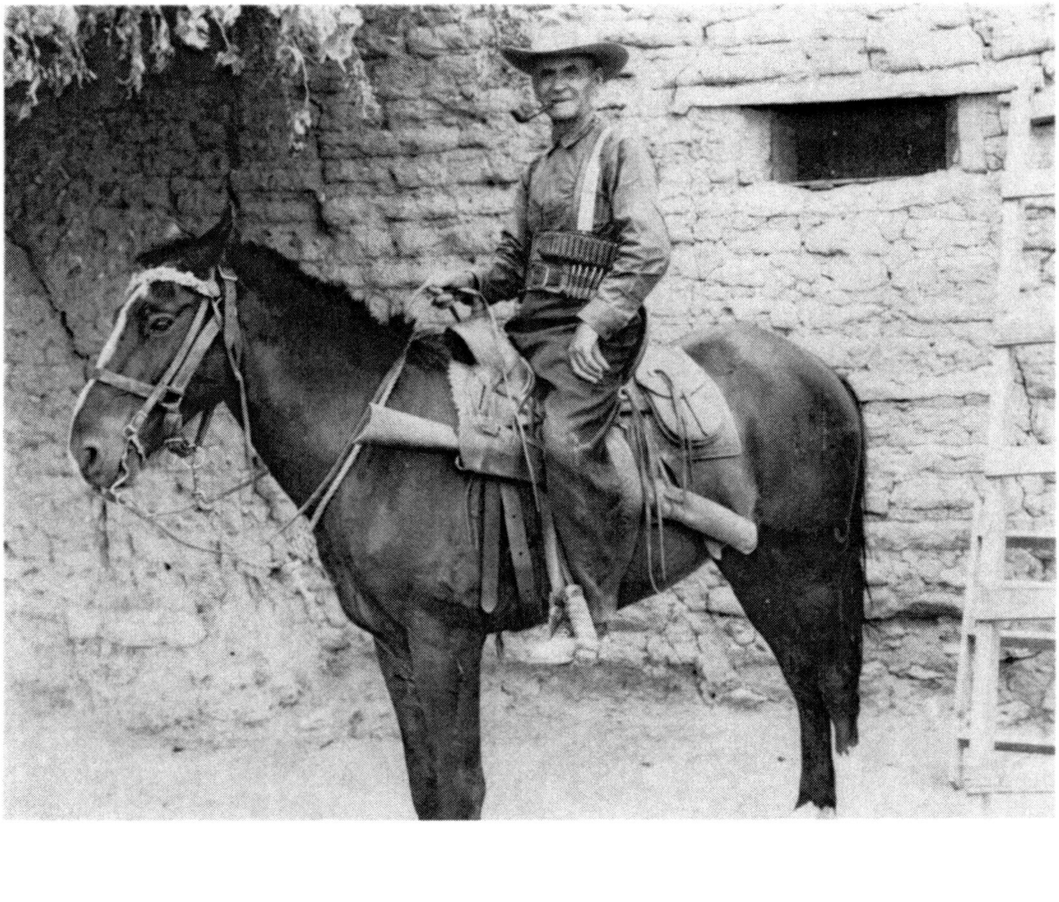

Estill, pilot, and Russell H. Cooper, observer and gunner, were far ahead of the cavalry, searching for bandits that may have taken refuge in the rugged mountains. They were flying over the rough area near Quatralvo, about fifteen miles south of San Antonio.

Three mounted riders were spotted going up a slope strewn with large boulders. Lieutenant Estill swooped in to see if they were armed bandits. They were. A rifle shot from below ripped one wing of the plane, and Lieutenant Cooper retaliated with a burst of machine-gun fire. Estill circled and came back over, lower than before, and both flyers saw a riderless horse, another horse lying on the ground, and a man scrambling over the large boulders, and another man lying prone. The third man and horse apparently had escaped.

Again they flew low over the spot and both flyers saw the man lying face down. At the end of one of his outstretched arms was a gleaming steel hook. Gacho! It was hard for Estill and Cooper to believe what they saw and they made several more dips to make sure about the hook.

There was no landing place nearby, so they flew directly to Presidio, Texas, opposite Ojinaga, Chihuahua. Because Presidio had the largest landing field of any of the border towns in the Big Bend, it had been made the base of operations for this expedition. Presidio erupted in excitement, and no time was lost in spreading the news. Colonel Langhorne, informed by the Signal Corps telephone, dispatched radiograms to the Southern Department and to Washington.

The airplanes had no radios, but the Signal Corps radio stations at Fort Bliss, Camp Marfa, Dryden Aviation Field, and Forts Clark and Sam Houston spread the news about Gacho. The only communication between the Border Air Patrol planes and the cavalry was by means of notes dropped in message bags. The bags were twenty-four-inch strips of yellow cloth, pocketed at one end to hold the note and weighted with lead. As the message fell, the bright yellow cloth announced its own arrival.

The news about Gacho thus was dropped to the cavalry units, but the news was premature: Gacho and his horse had disappeared. Only one dead horse remained at the scene. The first assumption was that one or both of the bandits who had fled had returned after the plane left and removed their dead leader, but the sharp eyes of the troop commander and his scout found conflicting evidence.

Cavalry scouts, all veteran cavalry officers, and some of the older enlisted troopers possessed exceptional tracking abilities. They could study the ground and find clues the average person would never notice. Facts that might seem insignificant to others enabled those experts to ferret out the most mysterious elements of a given situation. In this case, traces of disturbed soil showed that a man had lain at Gacho's "death place," but there was no sign of blood, as there was near the dead horse. This fact raised speculation that Gacho was not dead. Matlack, his scout, and a Mexican informer encouraged further investigation.

The various troops of Yancey's command made rendezvous as planned. On Saturday morning, August 23, the united force left its overnight camp at El Toro and headed southwest toward Coyame. That's when they came across the dim trail of two of Gacho's bandits. The trail came from the direction of Navarrete Canyon, the only pass through the mountains from Ruidosa, Texas, and a popular bandit route. It led past Rancho Paredero, where Yancey halted his troop to talk with the owner, Preciando Cerando.

Cerando told Yancey he had seen two men leading a wounded horse pass by the previous day, en route to Coyame. Their names, he said, were Bernino Olivas and Dolores Navarrete. Olivas lived about a mile from Coyame, and it probably was at his house that Lieutenant Peterson had written the ransom notes.

At nine o'clock that Saturday evening, Matlack split off from the main force with ten men and a scout, headed for Coyame to get the two men. In a narrow arroyo some distance away, they came upon a Mexican cavalry patrol positioned across the trail. There was no way to get through without a clash, and Colonel Langhorne's orders were to avoid such incidents. Matlack and his men returned to the main force about four hours after they had left it.

Yancey now received War Department orders to withdraw, prompted in part by fear of a clash between the American troops and Mexican cavalry but mainly by a letter the department had received in Washington. The letter, from J. J. Kilpatrick of Candelaria, related the killing of the four prisoners.

Beginning the withdrawal immediately, the troops rode all day Sunday through driving rain and hail storms, typical of the Big Bend in August, to reach the Ruidosa crossing at midnight.

During the entire episode, avisos about Gacho were notably absent, and no one knew whether Gacho was dead or alive. Yet this message-sending technique surely played an important part for the bandits during the six days the cavalry was in Mexico. Olivas and Navarrete, thus informed of troop movements, also timed their getaway and fixed their route by avisos. This timely information, plus the bandits' knowledge of the country, gave them a day's start before Yancey's cavalry found their trail.

Had the troops been able to make all their moves after sundown, the bandits could not have followed their progress, since avisos cannot be sent without sunlight. Had Matlack not been blocked on the road to Coyame by the Mexican patrol, therefore, his night maneuver might have succeeded.

For official reasons, Matlack had been summoned from the Mexico expedition the previous Tuesday, by a drop from a Border Air Patrol plane. The following day, the message informed him, Lieutenant E. Eubank would land his plane near the troop to fly the captain to Camp Marfa: Major General Joseph Dickman, commander of the Southern Department, was coming to inquire as to why all the fifteen thousand dollars had not been paid to the bandits. The general had received a telegram from the same J. J. Kilpatrick who had writ-

Colonel George T. Langhorne, second from left. To his right is Major General W. A. Holbrook, commander of the Southern Department at Fort Sam Houston, later to become chief of cavalry in Washington. Marfa, 1917.

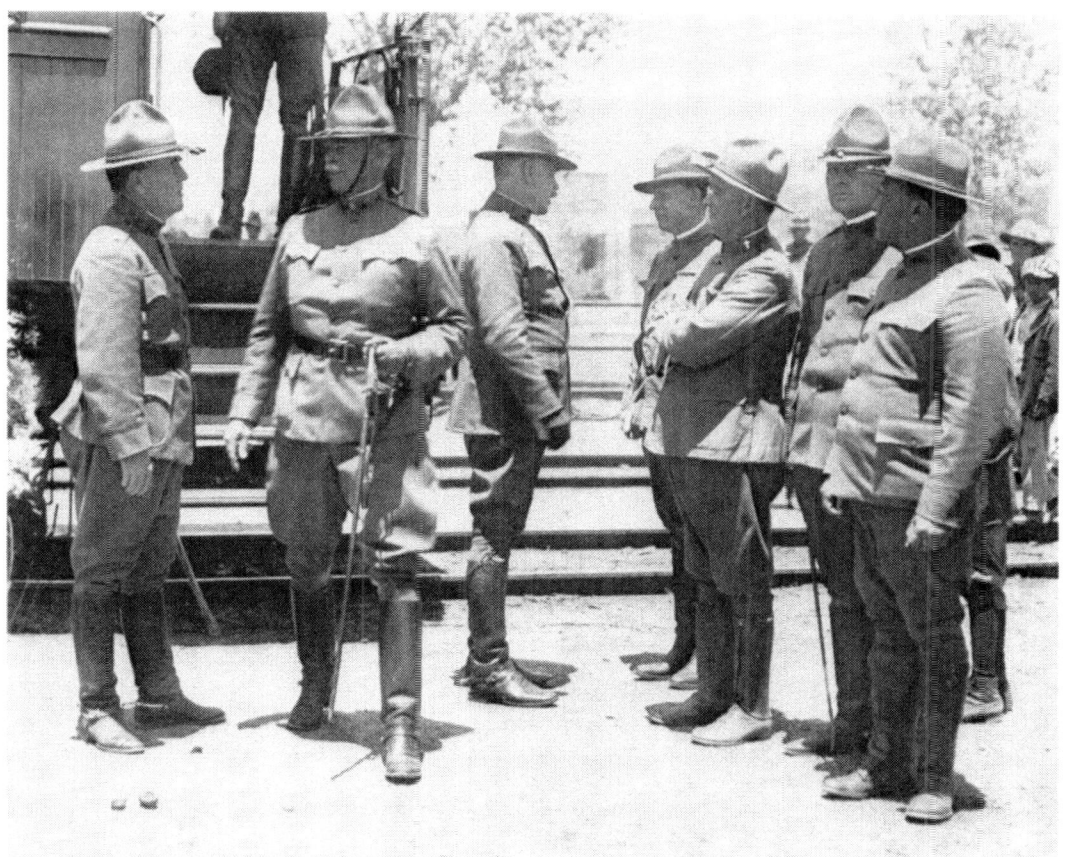

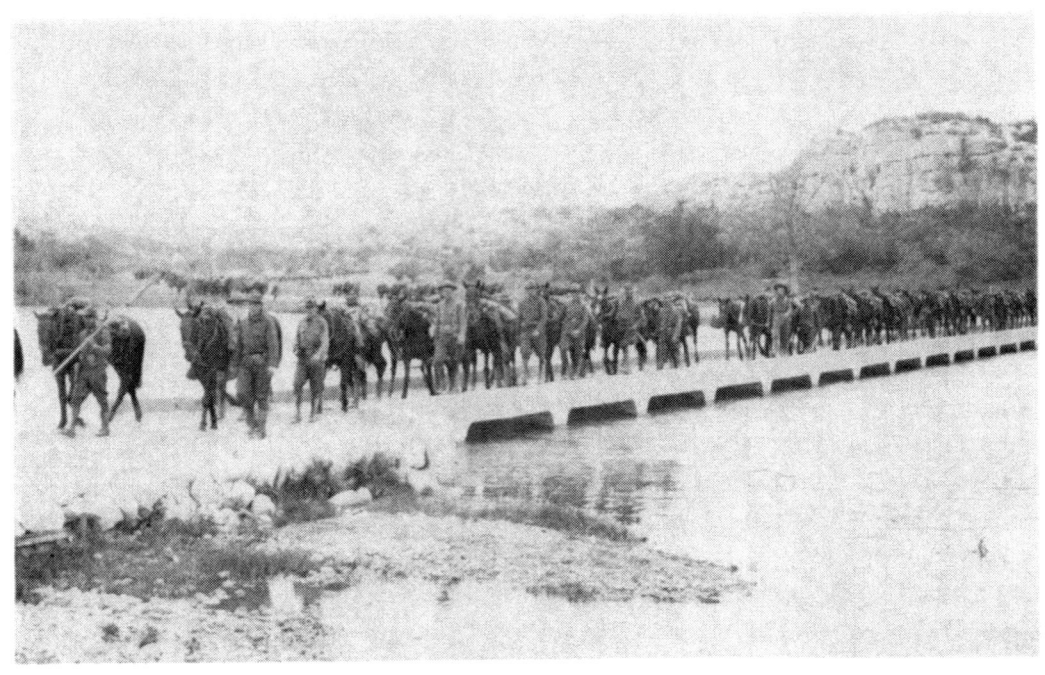

It was a cold morning, with snow, as the troops of the First Cavalry (above) crossed the Devil's River in 1922. Below, the mess sergeant (left) oversees his cooks in this typical cavalry outpost kitchen.

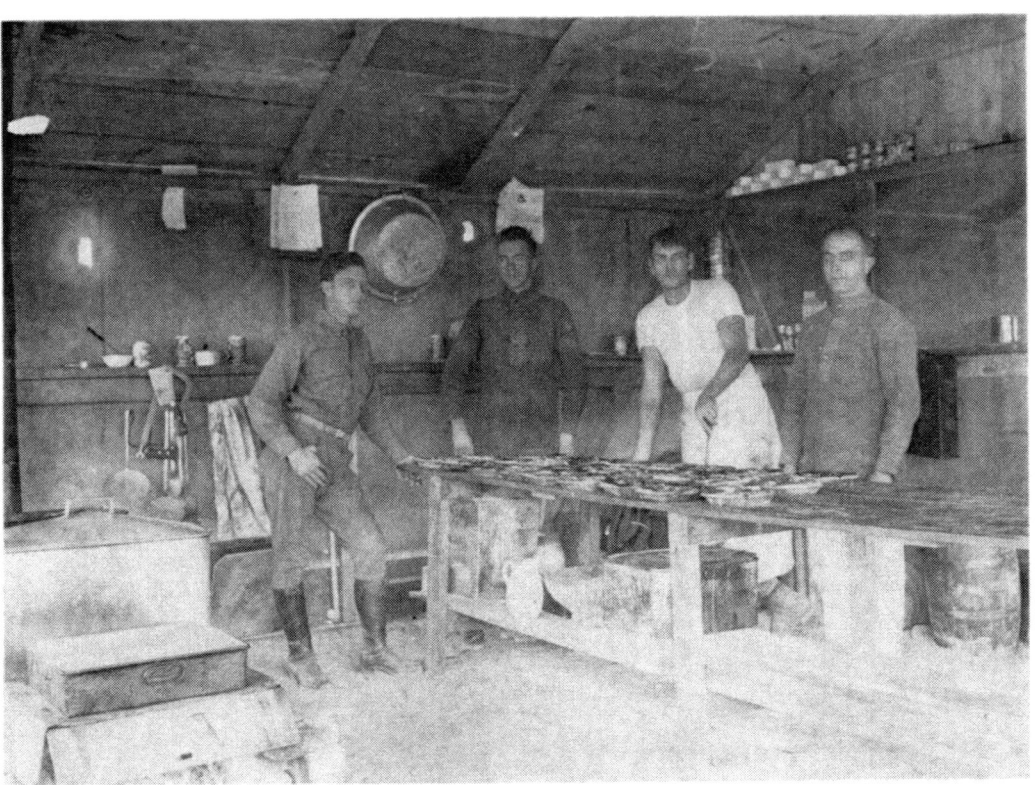

ten the War Department concerning the killing of the prisoners. There were some matters relating to the ransoming of the two flyers that the general wanted to clear up.

In Langhorne's presence, Matlack related to General Dickman details of the rescue and the march into Mexico—a report that normally would have waited until the troops returned. After hearing the account, the general complimented Matlack for the courage he had displayed by going alone into Mexico twice to rescue the two pilots.

Previously, Dickman had made a statement to reporters about the ransom, saying, "If we do not keep our promise, we would furnish excuses for treachery in the future. . . . " After hearing Matlack's account, he retracted the implication and told newsmen, "The report has put an entirely different light on the matter. He [Matlack] was in danger of being cut off with Lieutenant Davis at the time he made the dash to the river as he heard them planning an ambush. Captain Matlack did a very brave thing to go alone nearly two miles into Mexico. . . . It is appreciated."

Thus Dickman ended speculation and rumor that Matlack would be court martialed for failure to pay all the fifteen thousand dollars to the bandits.

Matlack went back to the expedition in Mexico.

When the troops returned to Texas, everything seemed normal, with cavalry and air patrols continuing, as well as pack-train trips from Marfa to Ruidosa and Candelaria. Still, the bandit situation was critical and rumors of a government investigation were soaring.

It seemed likely to all of us that the Fifth Cavalry would relieve the Eighth, as Major Yancey and two troops of his Fifth were a mainstay of the cavalry expedition into Mexico. By September, the Eighth had been in charge of the Big Bend District twenty-six months longer than any other regiment, and the wild, bandit-infested area had exhausted the troops. In October, the transition came, as the Eighth returned to Fort Bliss and the Fifth moved into the Big Bend. Some of the troops came up to Marfa from Mexico but most came overland—nearly a six-hundred-mile trip—from Fort Brown.

By early September, 1919, Matlack, still commander of Troop K, Eighth Cavalry, felt he had heard enough reliable reports of Gacho's being alive to justify an investigation. Juan Delgado (an alias) was selected to locate and talk with Gacho if he was alive; if not, he was to confirm that he had been killed by Lieutenant Cooper's machine gun.

Juan was one of the most trusted and efficient informers in the Big Bend, above suspicion. He had relatives and close friends living on both sides of the river, and he was always welcomed in homes on both sides of the Rio Grande. It is believed that he was born in Candelaria, Texas—an American citizen—and, considered a Mexican national, he was able to go to Mexico as he pleased.

Juan and others like him were not considered traitors to Mexico or to the Mexican people, just as the bandits on whom he gave information did not represent in any way their government or people.

Juan Delgado located Gacho in El Pueblito, but it took time to lead the bandit chief into a conversation about Cooper's shooting. Gacho and Juan saw and spoke to each other in the cantina for three days, but Juan was careful not to arouse Gacho's suspicions.

Gacho liked tequila and it seemed to make him talkative. On the fourth day Gacho and two of his compadres were drinking at a table in the cantina. Juan was near their table, also having a small glass of tequila, but he was a silent listener and did not intrude on Gacho's conversation.

After a couple of hours, one of Gacho's friends said that he had to leave, and Juan quickly asked if he could join the others for a drink. Juan ordered a litre of tequila. Several hours later, with about half the bottle consumed, all three were talkative, but not about banditry—until Juan casually mentioned Gacho's recent shooting at the airplane.

Gacho spoke up and said that it was not he who had fired at the plane, but one of his companions.

Lieutenant Cooper's gunburst had hit Gacho's horse, but no bullets had hit Gacho. As his horse went down, Gacho related, he deliberately leaped off and fell to the ground as if he were dead. One of his companions came to his aid while the plane was circling for another pass. Gacho told his companion that he was not wounded but would play dead, and his companion fled afoot. (That checked with the flyers' report that they had seen a man running among the rocks; also the story of a horse standing near Gacho.)

In the cantina, Gacho shuddered as he told of his close brush with death. He said the plane had passed over seven times—a variation of the flyers' report. When the plane was gone, Gacho had remained in his prone position until the sound of the engine could no longer be heard, then left with his companion on the one horse.

Gacho talked without prodding from Juan and probably would have told more had Juan pumped him. It was a congenial, confidential talk among friends, but Juan was aware that it revealed exactly what Matlack and many others wanted to know. It was of no real military value, except that it proved Gacho still alive. Juan also learned from Gacho that his future plans did not include any more involvements with Americans, and he lived up to that resolution; thereafter he stayed at least thirty miles south of the Rio Grande.

What has been told about Gacho's talk in the cantina was obtained from Matlack's reports to Colonel Langhorne, and the captain's testimony at the U. S. Senate hearings in El Paso on January 5, 1920. The information that Juan brought back did not, of course, convince everyone that Gacho was still alive. Records of the Border Air Patrol still related that he had been killed by Cooper, though there was no proof. The army's records listed him as being alive, but they had no documentation of that either.

The complete story of the Matlack case was not told until it came out in the Senate hearings, which were instigated by New Mexico Senator Albert Fall and J. J. Kilpatrick, the owner of the large store and trading post at Candelaria. They were intent on seeing Matlack court martialed for disobeying orders to pay the bandits the full $15,000. Matlack was the star witness at the El Paso hearings, and all the residents and officers who had been involved in any raids, battles, or other disturbances were summoned to testify. Their testimony gives an accurate picture of the general border situation. Senator Fall questioned Matlack about his having withheld the second $7,500. Had he not realized that the U. S. Government had committed itself to paying the full ransom? Matlack said he had known only that the money was from Texas ranchers and therefore had considered it his duty to return as much of it as possible. The letter from Langhorne to Matlack confirmed Matlack's story.

My dear Captain Matlack:

Major C. C. Smith, Eighth Cavalry, and Mr. Fennel, vice president of the Marfa National Bank, bearer of this letter, take to you fifteen thousand dollars ransom money demanded for the return of the aviators, Lieutenants Peterson and Davis. This money has been advanced through the Marfa National Bank by the prominent ranchmen and citizens of this and surrounding counties, subscribed yesterday afternoon within five minutes after the news of the demands of the bandits was announced at a camp meeting.

> Yours very truly,
> George T. Langhorne
> Colonel, Cavalry

The letter saved Matlack from court martial. Fall and Kirkpatrick had assumed that an official order from Washington had been issued to Matlack to pay the full ransom, but such an order was never sent.

In the mid-1930s, Matlack retired with a glowing record of army

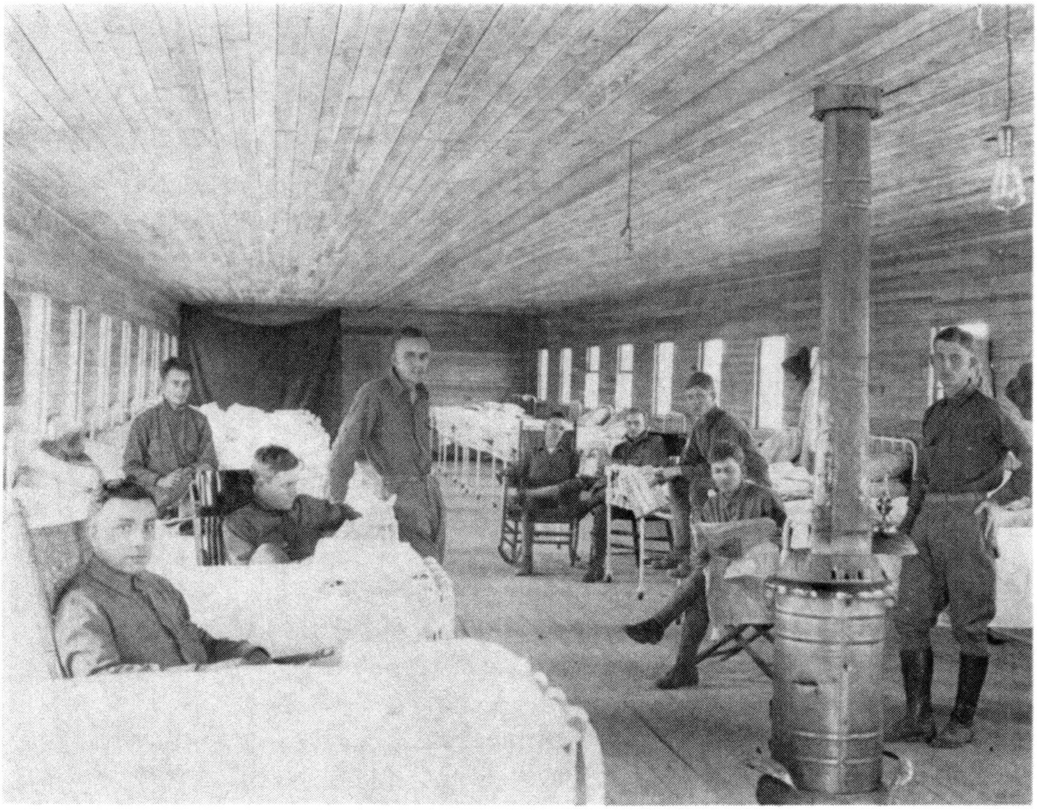

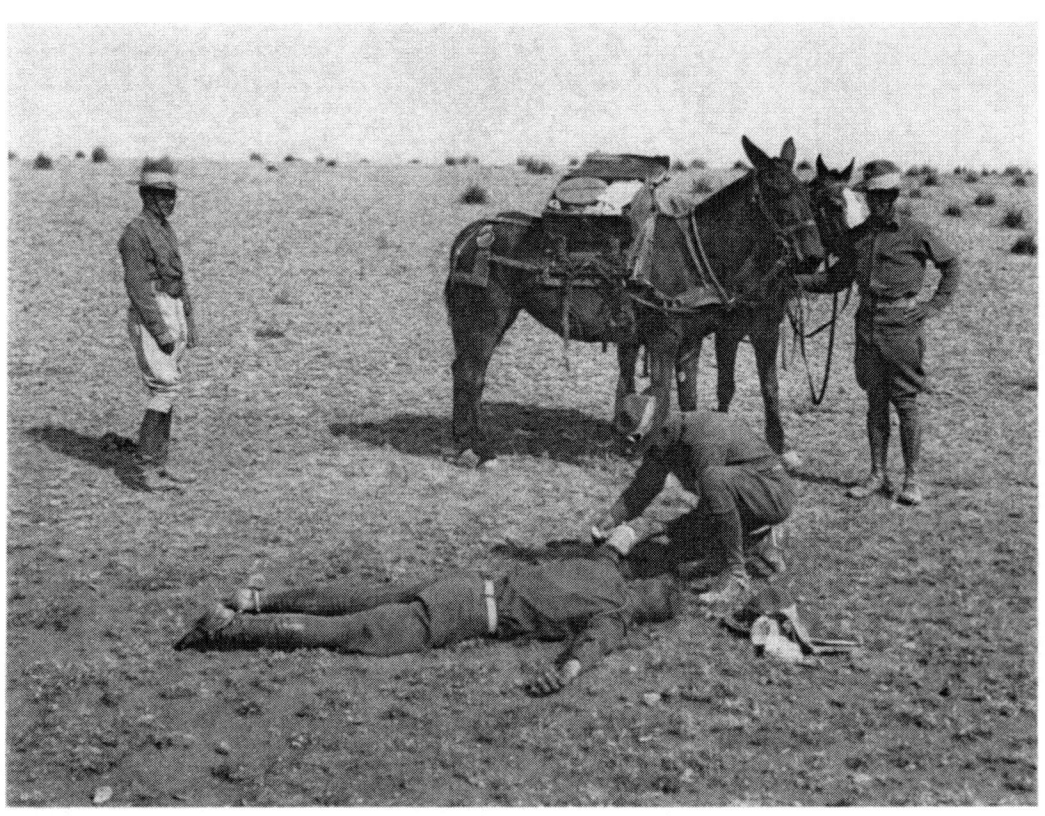

Above, the convalescent ward of Camp Marfa hospital, 1919. Below, one of the Medical Corps's "hospitals on four legs."

service. During World War II, he worked as a guard in a defense plant, then returned to his farm in Kentucky. Having survived nearly forty years of dangerous cavalry campaigning, he died of injuries received in a fall from an apple tree.

Kilpatrick was determined to have Major Yancey court martialed also, and the case against him was tighter than that against Matlack. Two errors on Yancey's part sparked Kilpatrick's zeal: he had turned over the four Mexican prisoners to the scouts who had executed them, and he had authored an expedition report that did not agree with the War Department's.

As told earlier, Kilpatrick had been informed of everything that happened during the expedition into Mexico by receiving timely avisos. Kilpatrick and his three collaborators, his son D. D., H. R. O'Neill, and C. C. Hurst, had urged Yancey to allow them to accompany the expedition as scouts, since they knew all the Mexicans in the area and could serve as interpreters. Permitting them to go along—wholly unnecessary, since the expedition had its own scouts and interpreters—was Yancey's most serious mistake.

Major Yancey's report of the expedition was turned in to Langhorne's office in Marfa, then dispatched to General Dickman. It soon came to light that Yancey's version of the fate of the four prisoners differed from Kilpatrick's. Both were filed with the War Department.

Dickman tried to persuade Yancey to change his report so that it would agree with Kilpatrick's, but he refused, and was charged under three articles of war. He was found guilty on two of eight specifications, but an even more interesting outcome was the disclosure of what lay behind Kilpatrick's aggression toward both Matlack and Yancey. Kilpatrick finally acknowledged that he had never been on good terms with the armed forces at Candelaria and that he had been influenced further by an adverse report on the expedition circulated by one of his family members. What was being admitted, finally, was the festering feud between the Kilpatricks and the army.

Court martialed, Yancey was found guilty and reduced to the rank of captain. Pardoned by President Woodrow Wilson, he retired in 1922 with his old rank of major.

The bandit raids became history by the end of 1920. With troops of the Fifth Cavalry still at all the outposts along the Rio Grande, the Eighth had moved into Mexico to make a show of force that discouraged further bandit activity along the border. The Eighth's avenging of the Brite, Nūnez, and Nevill ranch raids had left one hundred outlaws dead. Too, there were other developments that would divert the bandits' attention.

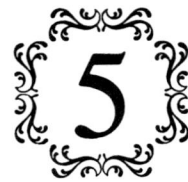

The Rum Runners

The Volstead Act—the Prohibition Law—which came to be on October 18, 1919, did a lot to end the border bandit troubles, but it created new woes for customs officials, Texas Rangers, *fiscales*, and several new law enforcement agencies. "Enforcement," though, is not actually the word, for in the Big Bend, as in other parts of the United States, the Prohibition Law was constantly violated until its repeal in 1933.

The only good that I could see in the law was that it provided an alternative to banditry. Hundreds of the bandits became liquor smugglers—a more dangerous life, perhaps, but more profitable, too. The smugglers would purchase liquor from other Mexicans who brought it to the border in pack trains from interior Mexican cities. The smugglers then would handle the risky business of crossing the river with the intoxicants to rendezvous with American liquor runners, who arranged to distribute the stuff in various thirsty cities.

The smuggling business was messy, and it was punishable by a prison term and a stiff fine. Smugglers were always armed and most preferred a shoot-out with American officers to capture. The toll of dead and wounded after thirteen years of Prohibition was staggering on both sides.

Smuggling rose rapidly as a profitable enterprise; within a month of the proscription law, smugglers, runners, and law officers had their hands full. Becoming a smuggler required only enough cash to buy an initial load of liquor. Each investment was virtually assured of doubling itself by the time the merchandise was sold to runners on the Texas side. After a few crossings, a smuggler could be well established in the business.

Such successes bolstered the courage of some of the smugglers, who not only tripped the loads across the river, but also transported them overland toward Marfa. The price was higher outside the intensely guarded border country, but the smugglers earned the pay; the overland routes were rough, and chances of their getting caught much greater on the longer runs. Most of these hauls were delivered to big-time bootleggers, who retailed the liquor to individuals or wholesaled it to runners supplying Eastern and Northern cities.

The smuggling operation was complex, employing about a dozen mules and burros in each pack train. A Texas Mexican guide was used by smugglers making deliveries beyond the immediate border area. Three smugglers usually traveled with a train, taking hidden trails over rough country in preference to well-traveled roads on which the chances of detection were greater. They traveled at night, hiding out in canyons during the day.

One of the most significant factors in successful liquor smuggling was the immense unpopularity of the Prohibition Law, which blinded many ranchers to the smugglers' trailing through their property. When officers questioned the ranchers about smuggling, they could be counted on to reveal nothing.

The smugglers had the further advantage over the officers of a communication system: avisos. The messages, sent from just over the border in Texas not long before sundown, instructed the smugglers to begin fording the Rio Grande, or to hold off until officers left the area. If urgent directions had to be sent at night, fire signals were devised by covering the flame with a blanket, like smoke signals, a fair substitute for the sun-dependent avisos. Even when there was no sign of danger, avisos were sent to the smugglers to assure them that their friends were on the lookout.

The river crossing was the most crucial point of the smuggling journey, for once the smugglers were across and into the rugged Texas country, officers stood little chance of catching them. Smugglers always made their crossings at fords, where the Rio Grande was shallow and the river bed accessible, free of quicksand and bog holes. Usually, the home of a Mexican family was built on top of a small hill or on the slope of a higher one at those fords—strategic lookouts for the smugglers.

One night in late 1923, I made camp three miles below Castolon, near the Rio Grande. I was awakened by two smugglers and their many pack burros as they passed within twenty feet of my bed roll, unaware of my presence. I pretended to be asleep when they finally noticed me. "*Es el fotografo*," I heard them whisper, and they proceeded in silence with their forbidden cargo. Avisadores must have

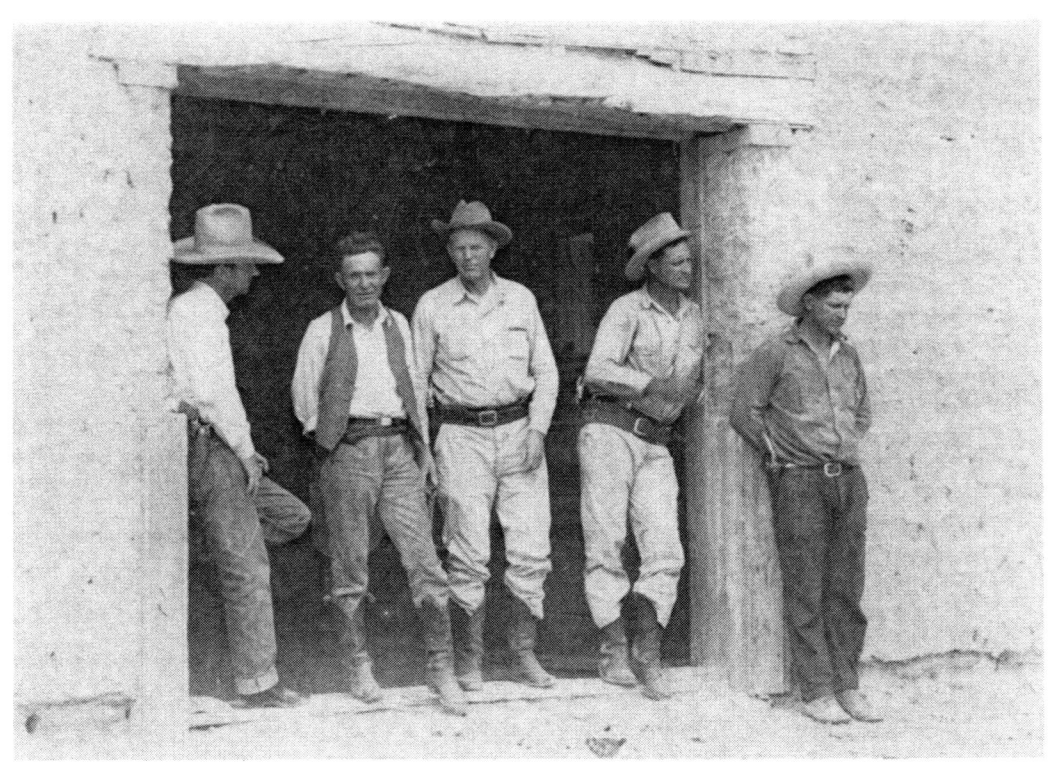

The law in the lower Big Bend, 1919 (above). Left to right: Pete Crawford, Texas game warden; Ray Miller, justice of the peace; Bob Pool and Arch Miller, Texas Rangers; Steve Bennett, constable. Below, the gear of a Mexican *fiscal*: mule, saddle, rifle, and bandolier. The *fiscales*, federal officers, were in charge of enforcing all federal and some local laws along the Mexican border areas.

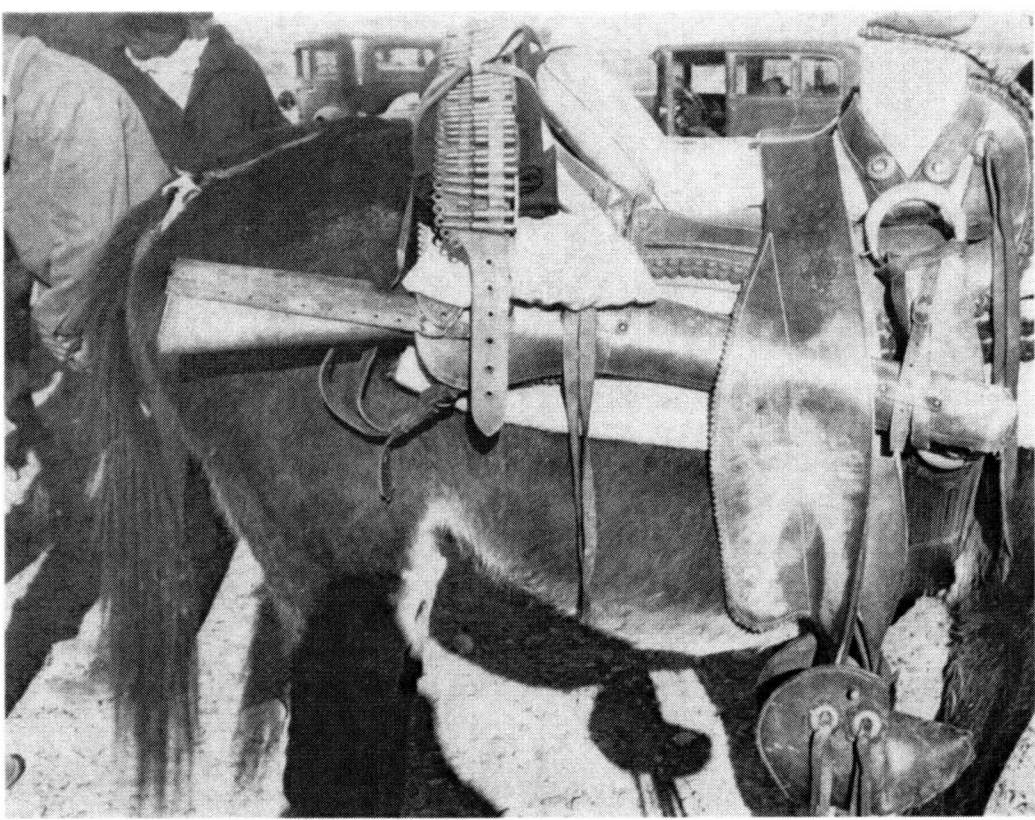

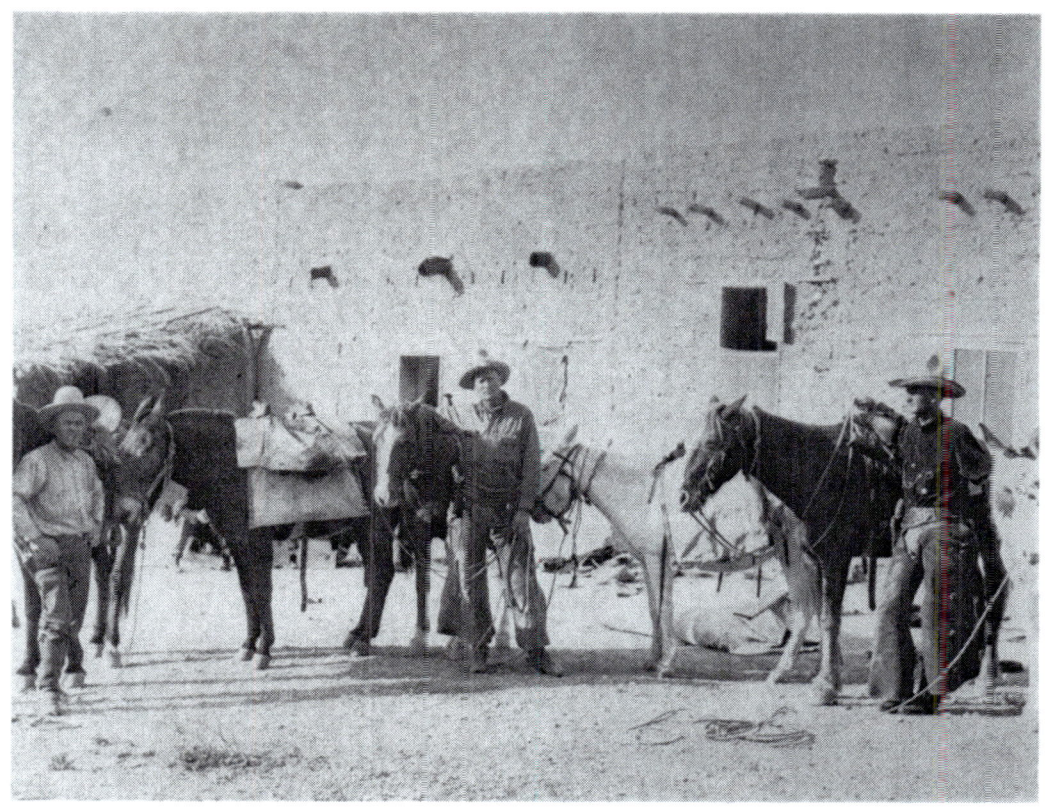

Texas Rangers in Boquillas (above) were a smuggler's nightmare. Arch Miller, who had the distinction of being the only one-armed Ranger, stands between Bob Summerall and John Hollis. Below, the Border Patrol acting on secret information seized this well loaded Model T in Pinto Canyon.

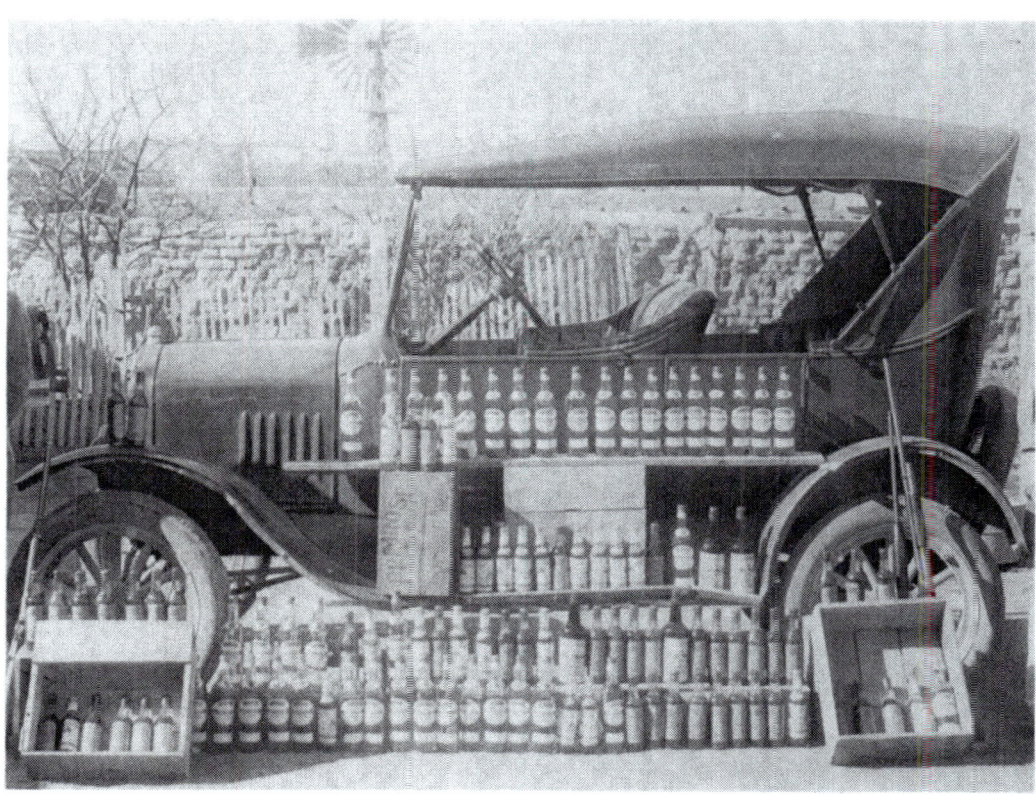

told the smugglers that I was in the area, which they knew to be no cause for alarm.

Although smugglers stood less chance of being caught than runners in autos, the runners continued working, lured by the profits of the trade. The towns and cities involved in smuggling connections were many: Valentine, Marfa, Alpine, Marathon, and Sanderson served as initial delivery points for the contraband. From such points runners would venture to West Texas oil towns, then farther east to Fort Worth and Dallas. San Antonio, Texas, and points north were supplied by smugglers from the Laredo area, a more lucrative run than the Big Bend connection.

Retail and wholesale demand for liquor was growing every day, and the distributors in Marfa were hard put to meet it. More smugglers were needed to bring the liquors from Mexico and before long a new idea was conceived.

The bootleggers approached regular army pack and wagon trains about running booze. The deal was tempting, as the trains were making weekly trips from Marfa to Ruidosa and Candelaria. Soon every packer and teamster was approached by a bootlegger, whose terms were generous. But, to my knowledge, no one in Pack Train 6 accepted such an offer, as transporting liquor in an army train carried severe penalties. Besides, under the watchful eye of Packmaster Hickle, not one bottle could have been stashed in the train undetected.

I never learned how the trains got involved in smuggling, but it happened. It was fairly common to see a train being searched by customs officers. I remember one wagon train in particular which, having shared our overnight camp at Cleveland's Tanks, left about half an hour earlier than usual. The teamsters, experts all, were Mexican. Later that day, the train was caught with about twenty or thirty of its wagons loaded with Mexican liquors. Creed Taylor, U. S. Customs chief in the Big Bend, and three of his officers were in charge of the search, and they soon had unloaded scores of boxes and sacks of bottles. As we passed the seized train, we learned that twenty of the teamsters would be taken to El Paso to be tried in federal court.

Our train left early the next day for Ruidosa and, on returning to Marfa four days later, we learned nothing new about the arrest. A week later, though, we caught up with the train, its twenty arrested teamsters now free. They explained that they had been acquitted on technical army evidence that teamsters do not load or unload their own cargo. All loading and unloading was done at various outposts; therefore, the teamsters had not actually loaded the liquor but merely transported it, perhaps unwittingly. (Pack trains, of course, were different: the packer loaded and unloaded his own bundles.)

Three weeks later another episode illustrated the extent to which informers were being used, much as narcotics agents use them today. Pack Train 9, rumored to be carrying liquor every now and then, was a mixed train. The packmaster, blacksmith, *cargador*, and four of the packers were enlisted men, but the six other packers and the cook were civilians. (When their enlistments were up, packers could continue in trains at seventy-five dollars a month.) When our train arrived in camp one day, Pack Train 9 was being searched by customs officers. Nothing was found except the cargo covers and regular equipment. Several mysteries remain about how the customs officers were tipped off, and why the train's packmaster—a former army sergeant—disappeared.

During Prohibition sotol was the only popular alcoholic drink that was both hard to police and really too cheap for a smuggler to handle. Sotol is made from the fermented juices of *Dasylirium leiophyllum* and many families made it for themselves. Burro-powered grinders

Some Texas Rangers, like Pete Crawford, seen here roping his mount, were former cowboys.

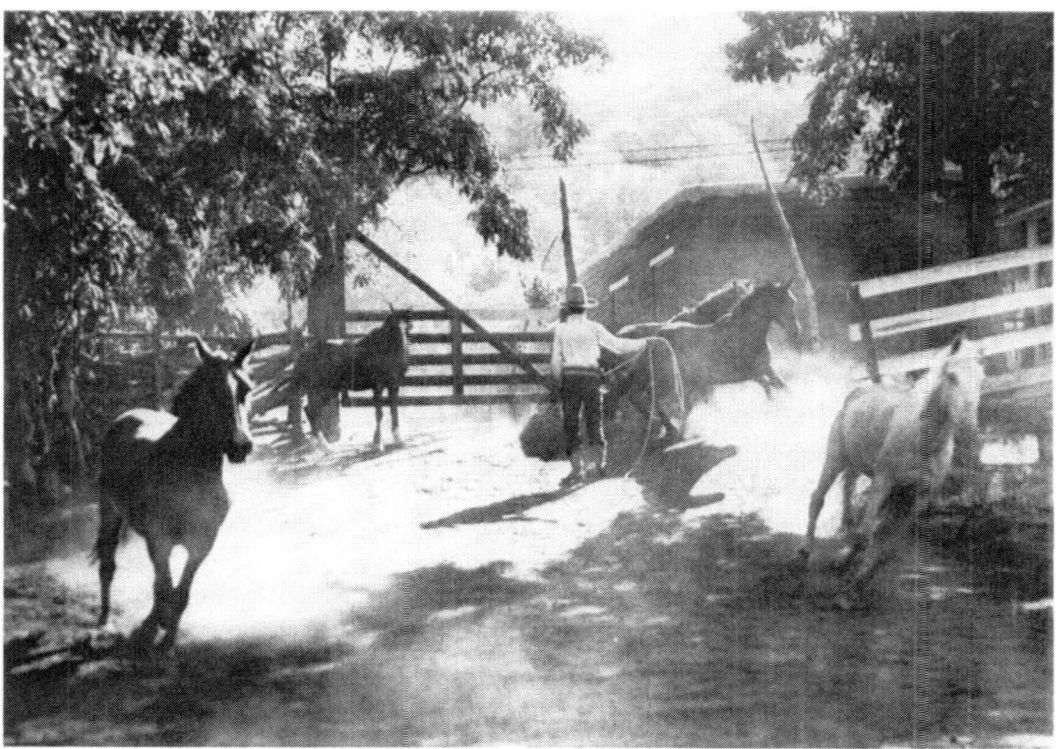

extracted the water-clear juices, which were delivered in goat-skin bags to distilleries.

Texans in the area found the strong drink to their liking and a steady flow of sotol kegs and bottles crossed the Rio Grande during the thirteen-year moratorium on legal liquor trade.

As 1920 wore on, things quieted on the border, and the need for trains lessened. I had saved a bit of money—something over six hundred dollars—and wanted to return to San Antonio, Texas, to open a photo shop. I told Packmaster Hickle of my plans, agreeing to stay on through August to give him time to find a replacement.

That last month was a momentous one for, in addition to the sentiments I felt at leaving, Pack Train 6 was almost lost.

The morning of August 30, 1920, the train left Ruidosa on its return trip to Marfa in a pouring rain that had caught us at noon the day before and drenched us all night. By the time we had reached Cleveland's Tanks at three o'clock, we had been washed with twenty-seven hours of rain. And there was no sign of a dry sky that night.

While packers unsaddled the mules, the packmaster, *cargador*, blacksmith, and cook set about erecting shelter in which to prepare the evening meal. Our camp site was at the southeast side of the largest of the two earthen tanks, where the dirt embankment was highest. From the top of this embankment, canvas cargo covers were stretched out and tied to large rocks, to make a sort of half tent. It served well enough to protect the cook's fire, a boiling coffee pot, and our buoyed, dryer spirits. After dinner, thoughts focused on the logistics of sleeping. Saddle blankets were like wet sponges; no clothes were dry. Two more half tents were constructed to turn the rain.

Then, the flood. The high earthen embankment suddenly broke, releasing thousands of gallons of water that gushed directly onto the kitchen area, then through the sleeping camp. The killer flow almost carried away the cook and two packers, but they managed to hang onto sturdy structures. The other packers—eleven of us—scrambled to the mules' picket line to retrieve the fifty packsaddles. The instant river was too swift for us: seven of the packsaddles and two saddles were swept away.

Packmaster Hickle issued his directions: saddle up and head for Marfa at once. The mules, some still eating, thought we were loco to be saddling them so soon after retiring. In no time, we were off on the thirty-five-mile trip to Marfa in the middle of a rainy night.

Our usually rigid formation deteriorated after a couple of hours of travel, so tired were we and the mules. At four in the morning of

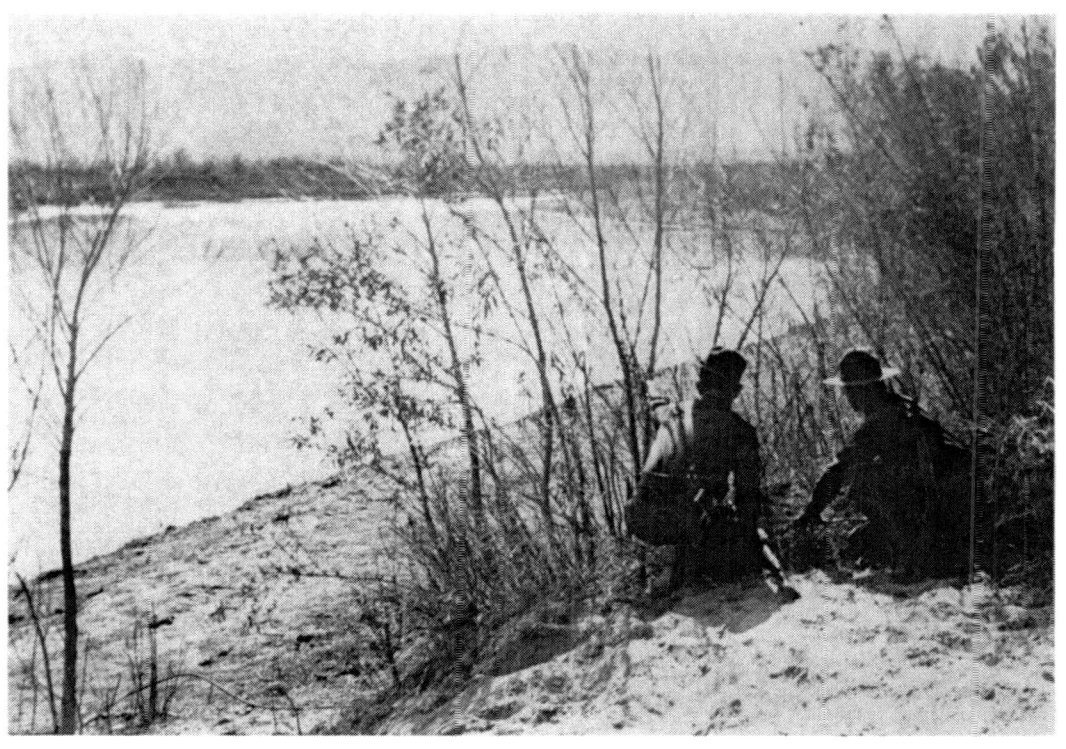

Above, Border Patrolmen watch for smugglers on the Rio Grande near Presidio, Texas. Below, liquor smugglers emerge from the Rio Grande near Presidio.

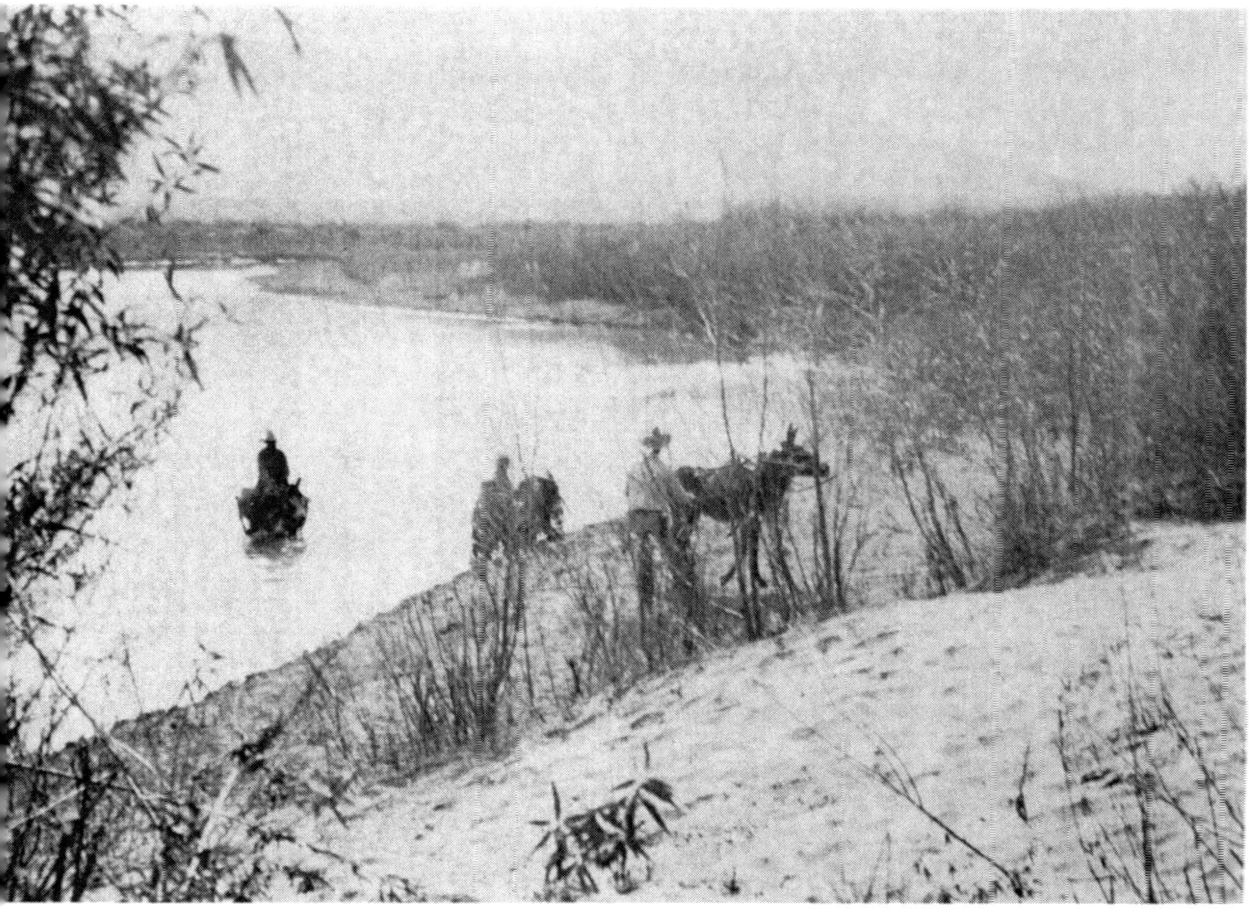

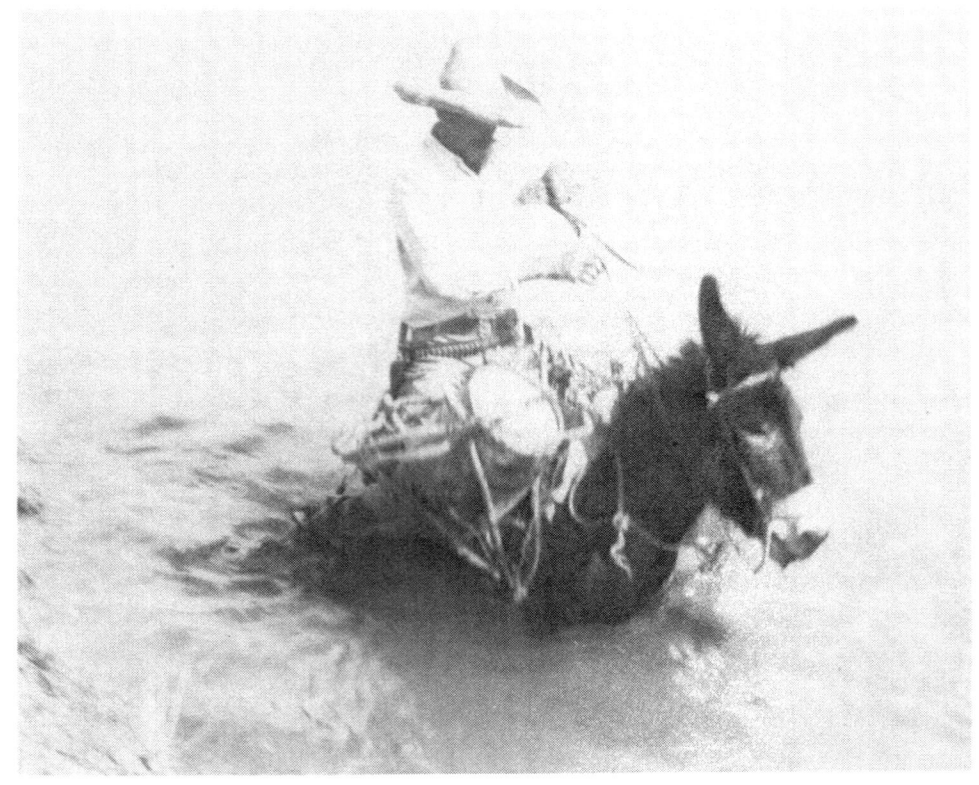

A smuggler (above) crosses the Rio Grande with two five-gallon kegs of sotol tied onto his burro. Behind him, three pack burros carry four kegs each. Below, smugglers caught by the tipped-off Border Patrol near Nogales, Arizona in 1926. The runner, scheduled to rendezvous with the smugglers, was not caught.

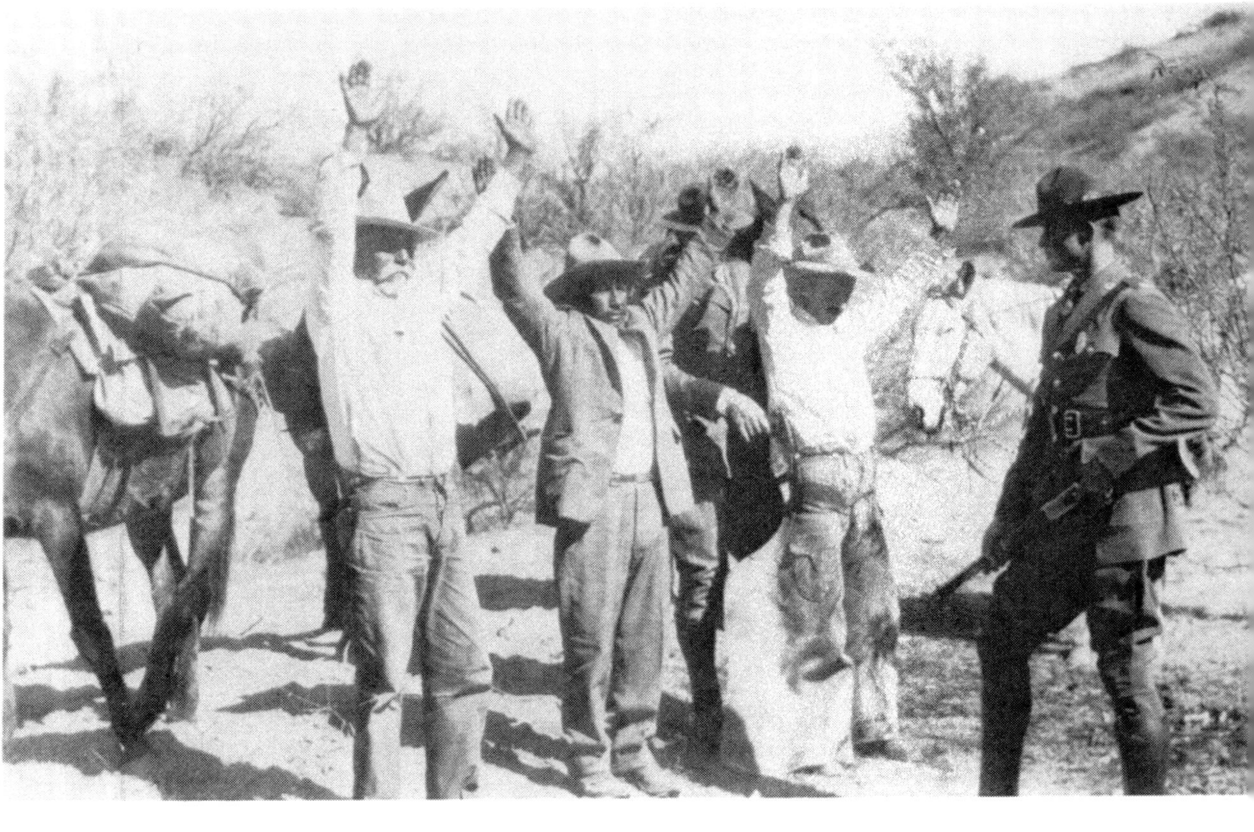

August 31, I wished myself a happy twenty-fifth birthday, feeling more like sixty.

We reached Marfa, single file, about eight o'clock that morning, and Packmaster Hickle led the way, not to our regular camping place at the railroad stockpens but to the cavalry corral. He told us to un-saddle the mules, line up the aparejos, then take off for the rest of the day. There was much refreshment in store: baths, shaves and haircuts, dry laundry, hot meals.

Before we left, a cavalry major came over and demanded to know who had given us the authority to put our mules in the corral. Hickle told him what had happened and said he would file a report to the quartermaster, but the indignant major barked orders for us to get our mules out of the corral. Hickle said, "Major, those are govern-ment mules needing special care for what they have been through, and if you want them out, you put them out." The major made no move to evict the mules.

After a big meal at the Longhorn Cafe, and a shared bottle of bootleg tequila, we tried to loaf around the town, but soon dis-covered that we weren't very good at it. None of us could remem-ber a holiday in more than fifteen months, and we were awkward at leisure. So we wound up back at the corral to work on the mules and check on the condition of our waterlogged personal belongings and equipment. During this lull there really wasn't much to do—I told George Hickle that I wanted to hand in my resignation, that I was ready to return to San Antonio. He agreed that I was making the right move, and he even offered to take my place as packer until the new man arrived.

On September 1, 1920, I collected my August pay, my last as a packer, and turned in my saddlebags and the Colt forty-five issued me fifteen months earlier. I hated to leave the pack train, but I knew it was the only sensible move if I was going to develop as a photog-rapher. Everyone agreed that most cavalry and pack trains would be withdrawn from the border in a few months, and that is exactly what happened. Most troops left in 1921, although a cavalry unit was as-signed to Marfa.

On September 2, I caught the early morning train to San Antonio, having been escorted to the station by my colleagues. The twelve-hour train ride was somewhat melancholy, and I wondered several times if leaving was the best thing. But the Big Bend was much in my future. My plan, as I trained eastward, was to return with bed roll, chuck box, and camera, finally to photograph the spectacular places I had seen or heard of over the last several years.

The Healers

My experiences with and exposure to curanderos—Mexican healers—literally began at birth, as I was brought into the world by a curandera in 1895. Then, as I have also told, I was cured at age seven by the same curandera, Maria, of a raging case of typhoid.

In later research, the first mention I found of such healing was Cortez's cure of a serious fever by his curandera, Marina—also his mistress, counselor, and interpreter. He was stricken in 1519, while the Spaniards were fighting their way from Veracruz to the Aztec capital. Cortez later wrote, "The noise of the brief battle had hardly died when I was attacked by a chill, well-nigh rattling my bones, and high fever followed fast. I sent for Marina. She looked at me, laid her hand on my brow, felt the leaping artery under my jaw, bade me be patient, and brought back a drug—a white powder—which she put in a cup of water. She warned me that it would be bitter as chicken gall, as it was made from the Quina tree."

I can only surmise that this powder Cortez spoke of was quinine, made from the bark of the chichona tree growing in Central and South America. The discovery of quinine is attributed to two French pharmacists, Joseph Pelletier and Joseph Bienaime Caventou, in 1820, but the Indians of Mexico and South America had used it and many other medicines years before the Europeans. The Spaniards, after conquering the Aztecs, conceded that their enemy was far more advanced in medical knowledge than they.

Cortez continued, "The drug caused my head to swim and I fainted away, but when I awoke, my whole body was wet with sweat. The worst of the fever was over. Marina gave me a dipperful of water to replace what I had lost, removed my clothes, and covered me. When I asked her where she had learned such wonderful healing skills, she told me the methods and secrets were passed on through her family."

It is obvious that Marina was curing Cortez of malaria—and the drug she used—quinine—was used later by modern man to cure the same illness. She, taught to heal as a child by her uncle, illustrates how Mexicans passed on knowledge to sons, daughters, nephews, and nieces.

As Marina had learned to heal, so did the Mexicans throughout their country and the Big Bend. This fact of passed-along knowledge was as fascinating as the Mexicans' innate sense and skill in selecting those plants with the strongest curing and nourishing powers.

More than techniques were learned from the elders; the ethics of the trade were handed down as well. Kind-heartedness, community spirit, patience, and a desire to help were the real motives of the curandero and curandera. Payment was only in gratitude—all the dedicated curanderos would want or expect.

Once again in San Antonio, Texas, after my return from the pack train, I found it impossible to get away to the Big Bend as regularly as I wished. My new photography shop was too successful; I couldn't break away. I went often to the border country nearer San Antonio—Laredo, Eagle Pass, and Brownsville—and learned much, but these trips were no substitute for the Big Bend. And Mexicans in all these areas treated me with caution because they suspected me of being a Prohibition agent.

There were several Mexican families living on the Burke ranch, a few miles from Cotulla, Texas, who became my friends. Mrs. Amanda Burke (nationally known as the "Queen of the Old Trail Drivers") owned La Mota Ranch. She was in her seventies when I knew her between 1921 and 1928. Living on the ranch with her were her son-in-law and daughter, Mr. and Mrs. Joe Bell, and their two daughters, Amanda and Nancy.

Seven-year-old Nancy made possible my friendship with Mexican families who had been suspicious of me. A grandmother in one of the families living near the Burke ranchhouse was one of the old-time curanderas, and she must have had a cure for every ailment known to man. I learned much from her. Her prescriptions ranged from a tablespoon of white granulated sugar for hiccups to complex, days-long treatments for serious illnesses. Some modern-day American physicians have been known to prescribe her hiccup remedy.

Throughout South Texas there were many qualified curanderos, and most of the small grocery stores in the villages and cities sold medicinal plants that were imported from central and southern Mexico. One of the most famous curanderos in the United States was Pedro Jaramillo, known as Don Pedro. In 1881, he came from Guadalajara to Los Olmos Ranch near Falfurrias, and soon became a noted figure. As his fame spread, many persons of various races came long distances to be cured by him. Although Don Pedro lived before my time, having died in 1907, I have known many Mexicans in San Antonio and South Texas who knew him. Odd how so many curanderos, like Don Pedro, have come from the Mexican states of Jalisco, Guanajuato, San Luis Potosi, and Queretaro.

Mexico, because of its variety of altitude, climate, and soil, must have the largest assortment of medicinal plants of any country. The cactus plants of Mexico and the southwestern United States are wide-

El Viejo, "the old man," of Pachuca, was one of the old-time curanderos and avisadores.

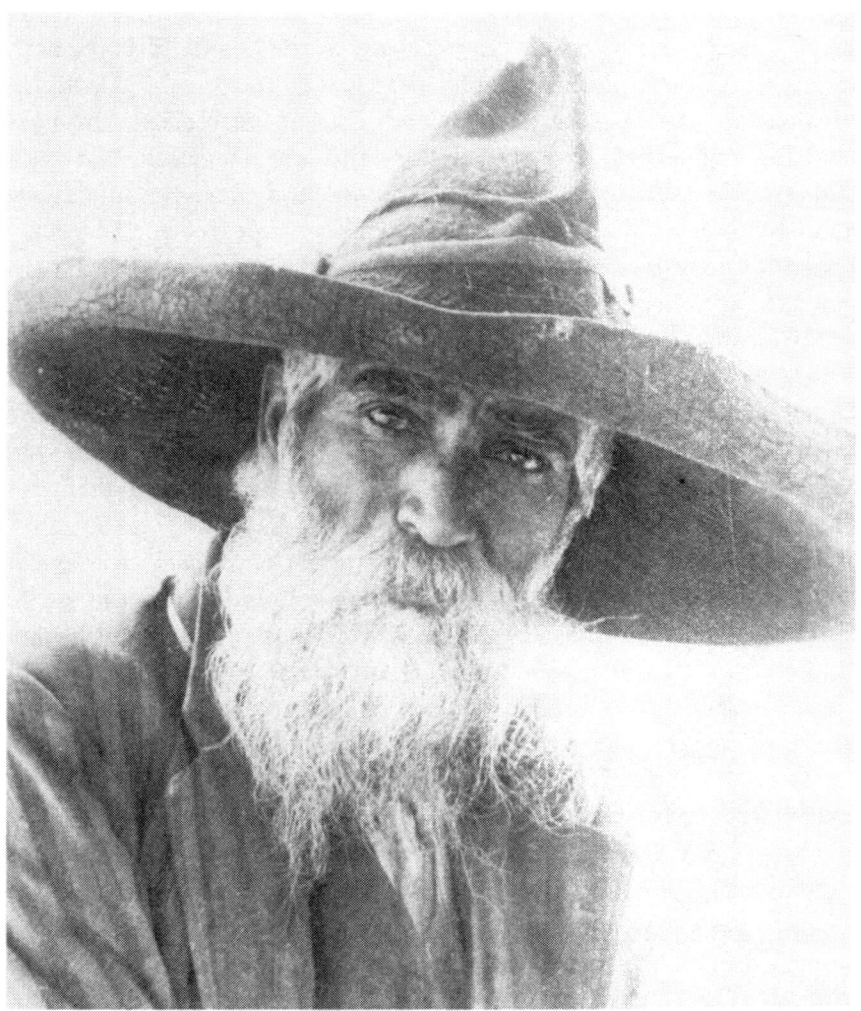

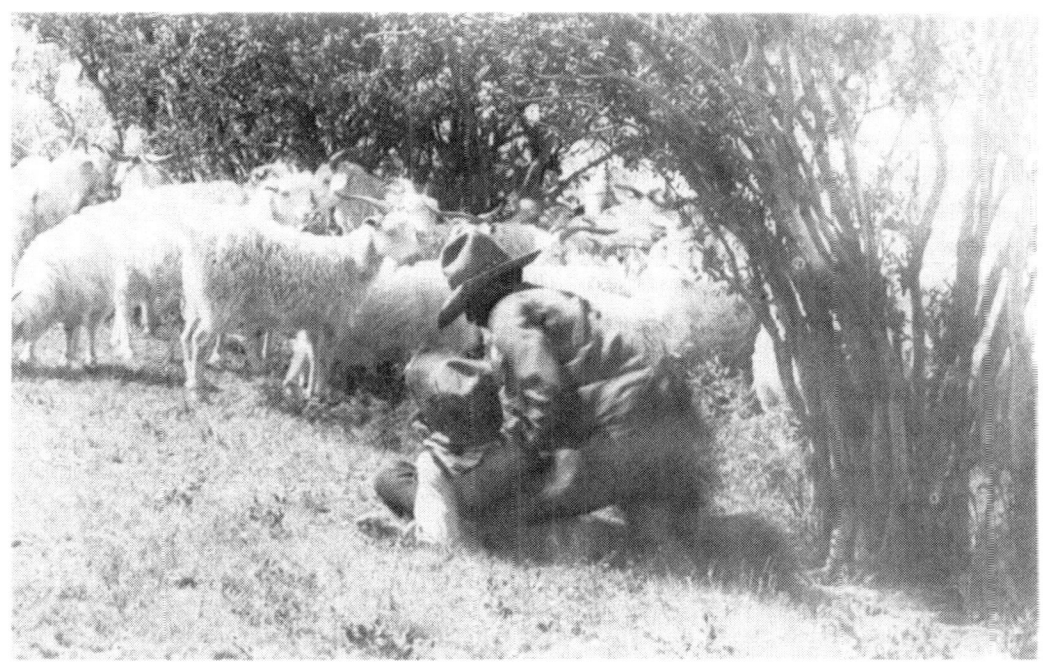

Rattlesnake bite! The boy's father (above), a curandero, carries him to shade and begins emergency treatment of tying tourniquet, gashing wound, and sucking venom. At home, the patient's curandera mother continues the cure with poultices of nopal cactus blades and goat tallow. A goat is killed so the boy can drink several cups of its warm blood to replace what he has lost. Below, a Mexican family, having tried Texas, moves back to Mexico.

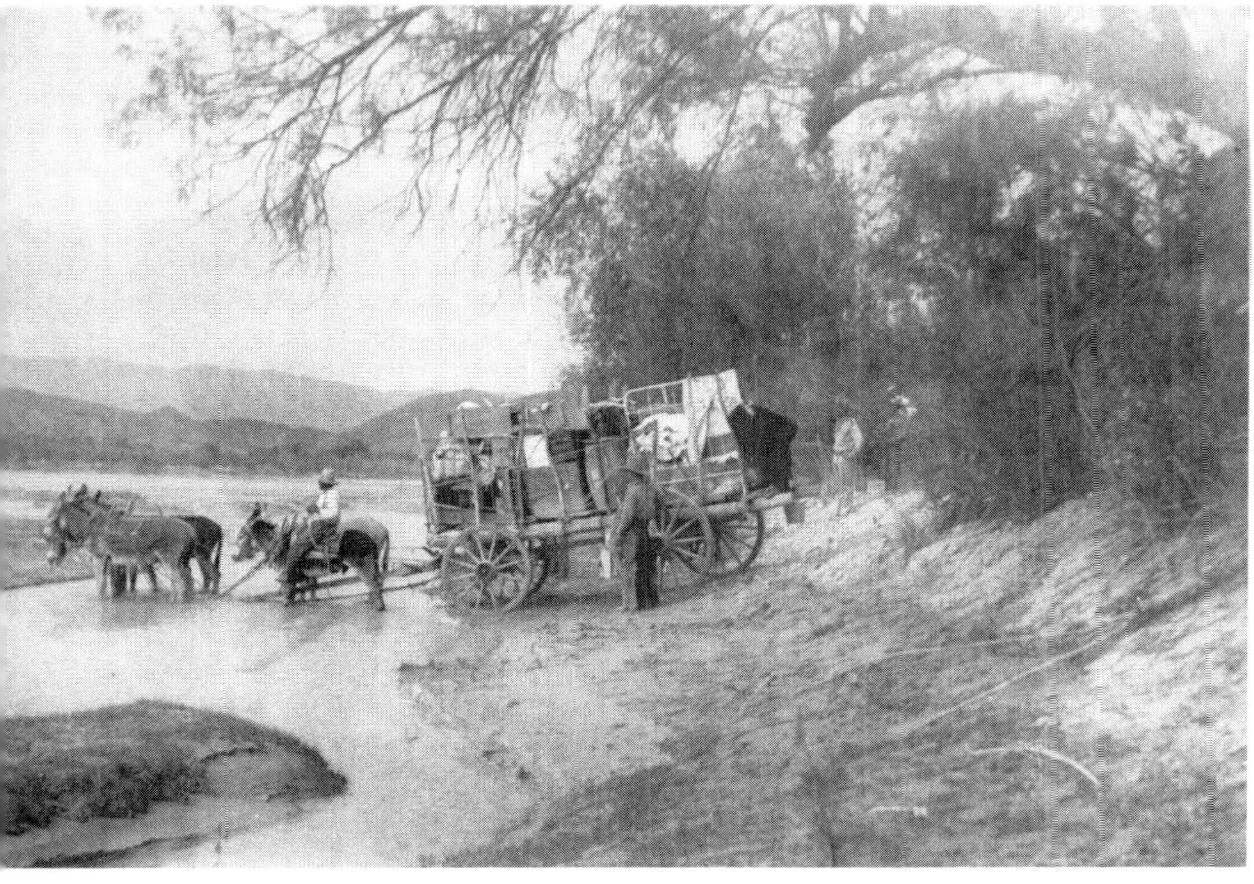

ly used as foods and medicines by curanderos, peyote (*Lophophora williamsii*) and "living rock" (*Ariccarpus fissuratus*) chief among them. People usually refer to both plants as peyote, but they are similar only in that both are used for the same cures, and both are hallucinogens. Both plants grow in a light, chalky soil that is inhospitable to most other plants. The turnip-shaped roots of peyote and living rock are larger than the plants above ground, and it is in the roots that medicinal substances are found. Medicines distilled from plants can be extremely potent, and arriving at the precise mixing, distilling, and combining methods requires the most sophisticated judgment. Tarahumara Indians of Chihuahua use the peyote and living rock plants as medicines, and also in a splendid concoction to give energy for their famous endurance treks across mountains and desert.

I recall one peyote potion of incredible simplicity that was used to treat kidney and heart ailments. A few drops of a solution of fifty grams of peyote roots, soaked in one hundred grams of alcohol for forty-eight hours, are taken in a glass of water three times a day. Stronger dosages may be fatal to the patient.

Aloe vera and zabilas (*Aloe mexicana*) were brought to Mexico by the Spaniards who knew the curing power of both plants. Since then, however, Mexican curanderos have discovered more uses for aloes. There is also the pitahaya, a cactus with a dozen species ranging in size from small clusters of *Echinocereus stramineus* to the forty-foot-tall *Lemainocereus weveri*. The word "pitahaya" also refers to the strawberry-like fruit that each plant bears.

Chia (*Salvia arizonica*) is the Texas species of a desert plant that grows only in the southwestern United States and Mexico. Its tiny black seeds have long been used by American Indians and Mexicans to correct stomach disorders. Ingested as a cereal, mixed in liquids, or added to stews and soups, chia seeds have a nutty flavor and the puffed look of tapioca. A glass jar of chia seeds was a staple item in any curandera's kitchen.

In 1924, while camped in one of the most isolated parts of the Big Bend, I was stricken with a severe case of yellow jaundice. I was 118 miles south of Alpine and the nearest doctor or drugstore, but only two miles from the home of Alejandro Domingues, a curandero, and his curandera wife, Lisa.

I should have gone to their home immediately, but I assumed that the weakness and chills I was feeling were symptoms of the flu, although this was unlikely for July. The problem was compounded by my diet, which consisted of a lot of greasy food. Bacon, sardines, and

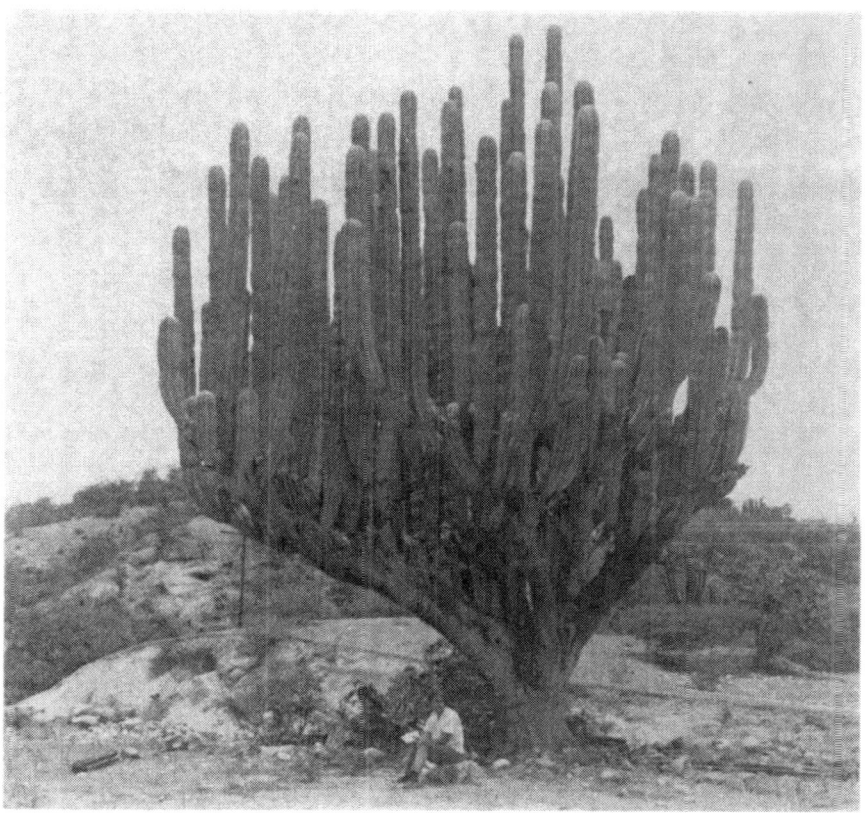

A pitahaya cactus.

pork were taking their toll on my liver. My therapy was to eat fruit—
as it was about the only thing that tasted good—and to walk as much
as possible. When the slightest bit of walking exhausted me, and
nothing in the chuck box appealed to me, I knew I had something
more serious than a cold or the flu, but never guessed it could be
jaundice.

I decided to go to Alejandro's house, but I wanted to wait until
the next morning, before he left to tend his goats. I got everything
ready in my Dodge to make an early start for Alejandro's, but the
next morning I overslept for the first time in my life—until ten o'clock.
I would have to wait another day. It was in the bright midmorning
sun that I first noticed my unusual coloring. My arms and hands were
yellow and, when I walked to my car, I saw a yellow face and eyes in
the rear-view mirror.

There was nothing I could do, though, except nourish myself on
canned and dried fruit, and wait until daybreak to meet with Alejan-

dro. That night brought a full moon and, even through sick eyes, I took in the Big Bend's beautiful splendor. Mule-Ear Mountain, about ten miles north, was clearly visible that night, as were the Chisos Mountains to the east. The lower mouth of Santa Elena Canyon also was visible. The jaundice began to manifest itself more violently: nausea, increasing chills, diarrhea, and fever. But I was determined to "get out of myself," to concentrate not on my body but on the beautiful night and the desert's creatures. So I walked about in the moonlight, stopping occasionally to sit on a boulder and rest.

During this stroll of three or four hours, the night life of the Big Bend paraded before me in sight and sound. Twice, as I rested on a boulder, a fox came within ten feet of me, stayed several minutes, then strolled away. Foxes, skunks, and kangaroo rats, grotesque little creatures with their disproportionately short front legs, all scurried across my path while I was walking. Scattered packs of coyotes took turns howling a serenade. Pondering their reasons for howling, I sat and listened and tried to place the different packs. The closest set up its howl from near the river, possibly on the Mexican side. When its chorus died, it was taken up by another pack, farther away, seemingly quite near the Domingues house. Various others followed in relay, and I placed them as being six to twelve miles from my camp.

The idea that coyotes howl at the moon had never made any sense to me and, sitting and walking and listening to the night sounds, it occurred to me that these animals are more active on moonlight nights because that's the time the rodents on which they feed are out in the greatest numbers. The sound of a pack howling in concert stirs the small creatures into motion, making them more visible prey. Owls use similar tactics, hooting to rouse their prey, then swooping to the attack, and this night their hoots rang from the cliffs around the mesa and the cottonwoods lining the Rio Grande. These hoots and howls also communicate a message to others of the same species, giving notice of territorial claims.

Finally able to sleep, I awoke between four and five the next morning, in relative comfort. After the last can of peaches in my box had served as breakfast, I loaded the last few items into my Dodge and headed for Alejandro's.

As I drove toward his house, he and his eldest son, Alfredo, were at the goats' bedding ground, ready to begin their day's work of tending the animals while they grazed. Having heard of my whereabouts by avisos, he wasn't surprised to see me, although he was startled by my condition.

Preparations for my cure began immediately. As Alejandro went off to gather plants, Mrs. Domingues and her three other children—Juanita, twelve; Jose, ten; and Maria, eight—escorted me inside. Diagnosing my ailment on sight, Mrs. Domingues asked what I had been eating the last few days. She sent the children to the garden for vegetables. Juanita went to gather a few *nopalitos* from the nopal plant from Central Mexico that grew in their front yard. The blades of the Central Mexican nopal are much larger than the ones native to the Big Bend area.

Alejandro soon returned with an armful of popotillo stalks (*Epbeda trifurea*), and one large stalk of ojazan (tarbush, *Flourensia cernua*). The stalk of ojazan, chopped, went into one of two large clay pots of boiling water. Once boiled, the tea was cooled by straining, and Lisa gave me a glassful to drink. Bitter but effective tonic for my stomach and intestines.

Lisa then began to boil the popotillo as she had the ojazan, but the popotillo was much different looking. Instead of leaves, it has clumps of yellowish-green straw-like growth from its wooden stems. Much medicinal substance resides in those brushes of straw, and it is often used for liver and kidney ailments. (In fact, popotillo's common English term is "kidney weed.") The popotillo tea was quite tasty, unlike

Ben Cobos, curandero, selecting medicinal plants near Alpine, Texas.

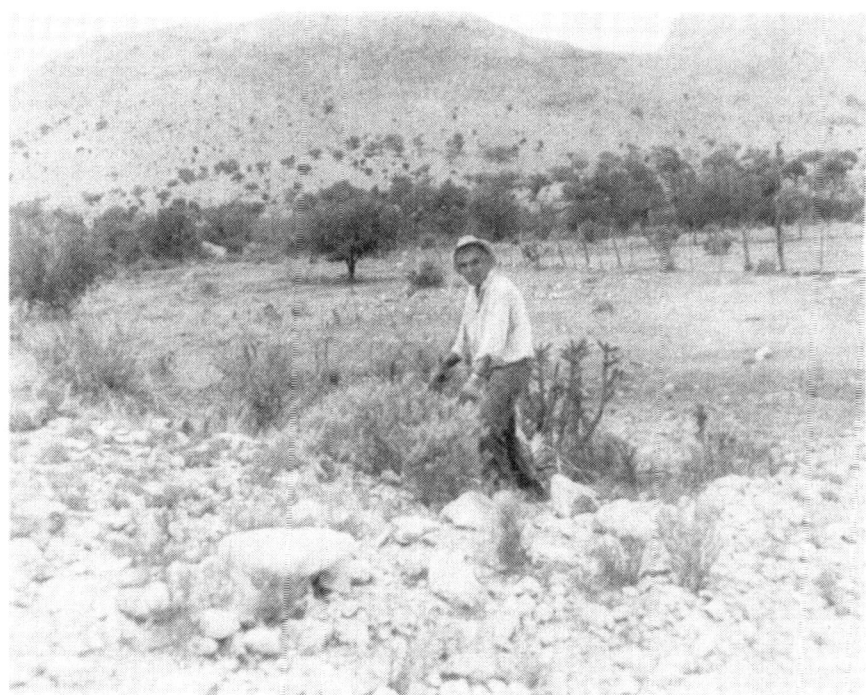

the ojazan brew, and many people along the border drink it regularly as a tonic and beverage. The popotillo tea was a mainstay of my cure, and for nearly a week I drank two glasses daily.

The foods, beverages, and Mexican hospitality were the substance of Lisa Domingues's cure for me, and her children did their share of attending as well. Whether gathering vegetables, carrying buckets of water from the river, chopping wood for the stove, or cleaning up, they were always eager to do what they could for me. Each tried, in a contest among themselves, to be the first each morning to greet me.

The menu for the first three or four days was meatless, and Lisa prepared various salads, vegetable stews, and fruit deserts. Okra, squash, carrots, turnips, small onions, *nopalitos*, lettuce, and corn were my foodstuffs. Garlic cloves, besides giving everything a good flavor, were effective liver medicine.

Green alfalfa was a main ingredient of the stew, with all sorts of garden vegetables, corn on the cob, parsley, mint leaves, and pita-hayas. Mexicans have used green alfalfa for years, mixing it with *masa*, or corn dough, to make tortillas, or cooking it like spinach and other greens. All of the ingredients, gathered moments before cooking, not only made proper medicines for yellow jaundice, but began to build my strength until it was soon evident that I was recovering.

Breakfast consisted of a glass of popotillo tea, a canteloupe, two soft-boiled eggs, and two slices of toasted bread.

During the course of my cure, I tried to help around the Domingues household as much as possible, but my limitations were obvious and Lisa recognized them. When Alejandro and Alfredo came in each evening, I would assist in getting the goats into the bedding area, but I soon grew tired. Besides these meager attempts, I provided the family with bread from my food supply—fresh baker's loaves. But mostly, I rested and recuperated.

After my cure, Lisa Domingues invited me to stay on, so long as I was happy with their accommodations. I thanked her, giving assurance that the lodging was fine, that I could roll out my comfortable sleeping bag right outside their house. We agreed that I should sleep under the arbor at the front door. They had a small house, and she felt badly that she could not offer me a room of my own. There was, in fact, only one bed in the house. All four children slept on goat skins on the floor—the two girls in their small room, the boys in the kitchen during cold weather and under the arbor when it was hot.

The house was of the typical two-room type scattered along both sides of the Rio Grande. Constructed of materials growing near the building site, it cost very little to raise. Usually, the families did not

own the land on which they resided, but would take over any aban-
doned house until it was reclaimed, or until the family decided to
move on. This is exactly what the Domingues family had done.

The houses were simple: four cottonwood or willow corner posts
supported beams for the roof. Two uprights divided the kitchen and
dining areas. A fence-like network of ocotillo (*Fouquieria splendens*)
served as a thorny wall, which was plastered with mud on the inside.
The outside was left uncovered. The walls were usually no higher
than six feet. The ceiling, of carrizo cane, was a series of laced stalks,
topped with the large flat blades of sotol and yucca to turn water. A
layer of adobe then was applied on top of those two layers, to make
a solid, hard roof. I used such a roof on a photo darkroom that I
built in 1929. A year later, while I was on a long trip to Mexico, the
roof leaked and ruined many of my choice negatives—including some
I had made while at the Domingues home. Such dwellings as that of
the Domingues family required constant attention and repair, and I
enjoyed doing what I could for them and their home.

During that 1924 stay, while I was being cured of jaundice, Alejandro wanted to learn all he could from me about the new Border
Patrol. Being an illegal alien, he feared he would have to move his
family back to Central Mexico, where bandits would harass them.
Alejandro had a *ranchito* between Cuatrocienegas and El Pino, about
fifty miles from the Rio Grande. Bandits frequently had harassed
him and his family there, demanding livestock and food. Many families like theirs, after enduring years of such treatment, gathered their
belongings and headed toward Texas. Those who settled in the upper
sections on the Mexican side of the river soon learned that their new
homes were in areas where Mexican bandits also had relocated. Alejandro Domingues was fortunate in having chosen the central section
of the area on the Texas side, where there were no ranches for the
bandits to raid and hence no cavalry patrols.

I explained to Alejandro that the new officers were going to en-
force the established immigration laws and there probably would be
new laws added go curb the number of Mexicans moving into the
United States. Though he would most likely be questioned, I told
him that, since he was making an honest living in a peaceful area, he
surely would be allowed to stay.

He didn't choose to do so. Even though he could have secured a
legal right to continue living in Texas, he and his family eventually
returned to Cuatrocienegas, leaving their place, much nicer than they
had found it, for a new family of squatters. In retrospect, the move
seems a good one for all of them, for the children could attend

school. (The first school in the Big Bend, at the Elmo Johnson ranch, was not started until 1934.)

While I was with Alejandro and Lisa, other patients, all of them Mexican, came by from time to time to be cured. Since Mexicans rarely went alone for a cure, these sessions at Alejandro's often were big social events, enjoyed by the patients' families and the curandero household. Food, stories, laughter, and faith were exchanged and, most importantly, health was regained by the patient.

Curanderos were remarkably successful at obtaining from wandering traders needs such as seeds, cuttings of rare plants, dried herbs, and other ingredients not available in their native areas. A substance much in demand was *Quassia picrasma excelsa*, a tree that grows only in southern Mexico and Central America whose dried bark is an effective tranquilizer.

The traders, "go-betweens" for the curanderos and *yerberos* (herb vendors), were nomads, unfazed by the long hours of horseback travel their jobs demanded. Most of the *yerberos* were at Sierra Mojada and Cuatrocienegas, the two railroad towns nearest the Big Bend, and the traders would journey from those Mexican communities to curandero families like Alejandro's, scattered along the Rio Grande. Curanderos depended strongly on the traders' valuable inventories of special herbs and healing potions.

Later in the 1920s, I was staying at Elmo Johnson's ranch, 120 miles south of Alpine, doing a lot of photography. The Johnsons had bought the old Grady and Williams trading post and surrounding property, part of which was used by the army as a landing field. Since the post was located on the bank of the Rio Grande, most of its clients were from Mexico. Elmo Johnson, introduced to me by rancher Wayne Cartledge, was quite a rascal whose tall tales once sent a cavalry patrol and armed troopers on a wild chase of bogus revolutionaries.

One blazing-hot summer day, a small Mexican boy ran up to us and yelled that Mrs. Harloe, a Johnson neighbor, had been shot. I told Ada Johnson that I would grab a first-aid kit and see what I could do for Mrs. Harloe, not knowing the first thing about the extent or nature of her wounds. This meant a journey on foot, for I had lent my Dodge to Elmo that morning, so I set out over two miles of blistering trail. I maintained a trot the entire way, over a series of mesas covered with rough gravel, rocks, cactus, and creosote bushes. The temperature that day was close to 110 degrees.

My headlong flight to the Harloes was thoughtful, I guess, and appreciated, but it was unnecessary. Less than a quarter of a mile

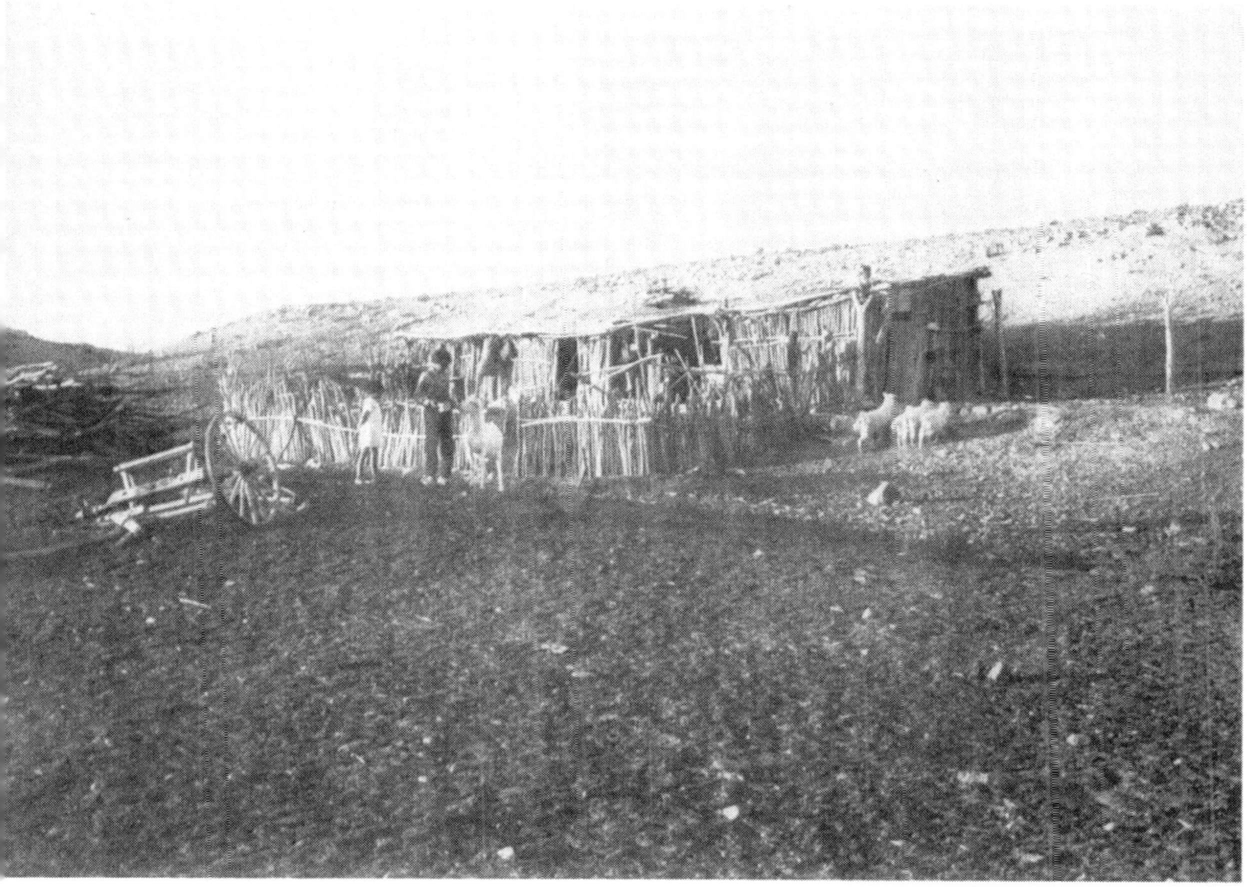

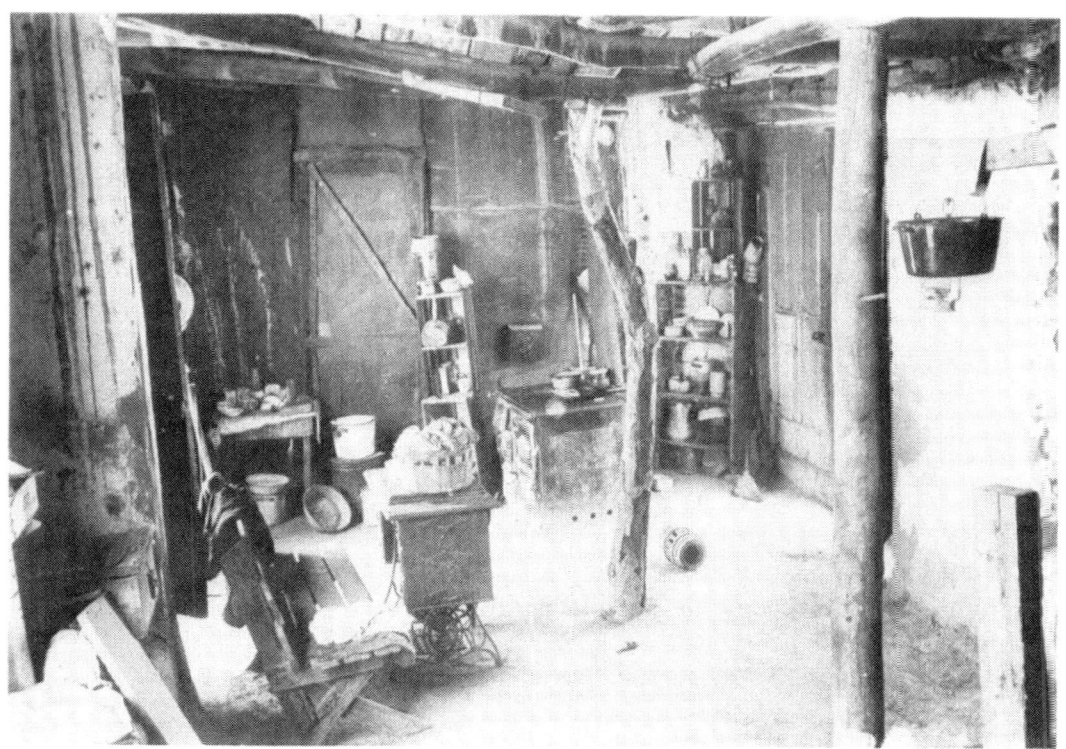

Juana Holguin's home (above), where I was cured of sunstroke in 1930. Below, the interior of a typical Mexican home in the Big Bend in the 1920s.

from the Harloe home lived the Holguin family and Juana Holguin was a wonderful curandera. Her treatment was underway when I arrived, panting and exhausted. Mrs. Harloe's wound, a painful gash in the lower right arm, was bleeding profusely. To stop the flow, Juana had applied soot from the cookstove, then wads of spider webs. This is an effective remedy, and I know of no case of infection ever having been caused by such a treatment.

The shooting had been completely accidental, and much less serious than it might have been. Her children had been playing with their father's twenty-two rifle, and when Mrs. Harloe cautioned them, they left the gun lying on the bed. When she picked it up to put it away, the hammer caught in a quilt and the weapon fired. If Juana had not been near, the shock and loss of blood could have been severe.

What a relief it was to see Juana there as I entered the house, gasping from my hour-long jog in the sun. After a cool drink of water, I opened the first-aid kit but found no aspirin, which Mrs. Harloe needed to ease the pain. Juana was preparing a tea of quassia and amara, which was as effective as aspirin, but it would require a long time to brew. After making a sling for Mrs. Harloe's arm, I decided, foolishly, to go back to the Johnsons' for aspirin.

I took a slightly different return route, nearer the road so the Johnsons could see me if they came along. I did not run but, always having been a fast walker, soon had to slow myself down. I began to have dizzy spells and my face and arms had a burning, prickling sensation. I thought that only something in the Holguin's water was causing my discomfort, so I kept up my pace.

As I was climbing one of the mesas, I blacked out. My last recollection was of ebbing strength and dizziness. I never knew how long I was out, but when I came to, my arms, face, hands, and clothes were wet, muddy, and torn, like my skin. A broken bump protruded from my forehead.

Mysteriously, I was in a sitting position, not knowing how in the world I had managed it. I stood, trembling. It seemed long minutes before my vision returned; all was blurry, but finally the south end of the Chisos Mountains came into focus, and I knew where I was— five hundred yards from the Johnson ranchhouse and one hundred from the road. My hat had blown away, and while looking for it, I heard my Dodge. I rushed to the road, hatless, to find Elmo and Ada Johnson, who needed only one glance to know that I had been sunstruck. Mrs. Johnson asked me how I was feeling. I told her all that had happened with Mrs. Harloe, her wounds, Juana Holguin, and my bid to fetch the aspirin. Ada Johnson had the aspirin bottle with her and wanted to take me to her house to recover. Mr. Johnson disagreed, saying that I should see Juana for a cure.

Juana was still with Mrs. Harloe when we returned and, after giving the patient some aspirin, we took Juana home. Her attentions then turned to me.

She brought out several goat skins, spread them in the shade of her house and asked me to remove my shirt and shoes and lie down. She sent her children to the bank of the nearby Rio Grande to gather the largest leaves of the elephant ear, or wild tobacco, plants.

While waiting for the plants, Juana prepared some large sunflower seeds by grinding them in a *molcajete*, a stone bowl, with a large stone masher. She mixed the mashed seeds with a little cottonseed oil to make a paste, which she spread thickly on the leaves. As soon as she had the leaves covered, she placed them on my forehead and temples.

A curandera arranging her medicinal plants for display and sale in a Guanajuato street.

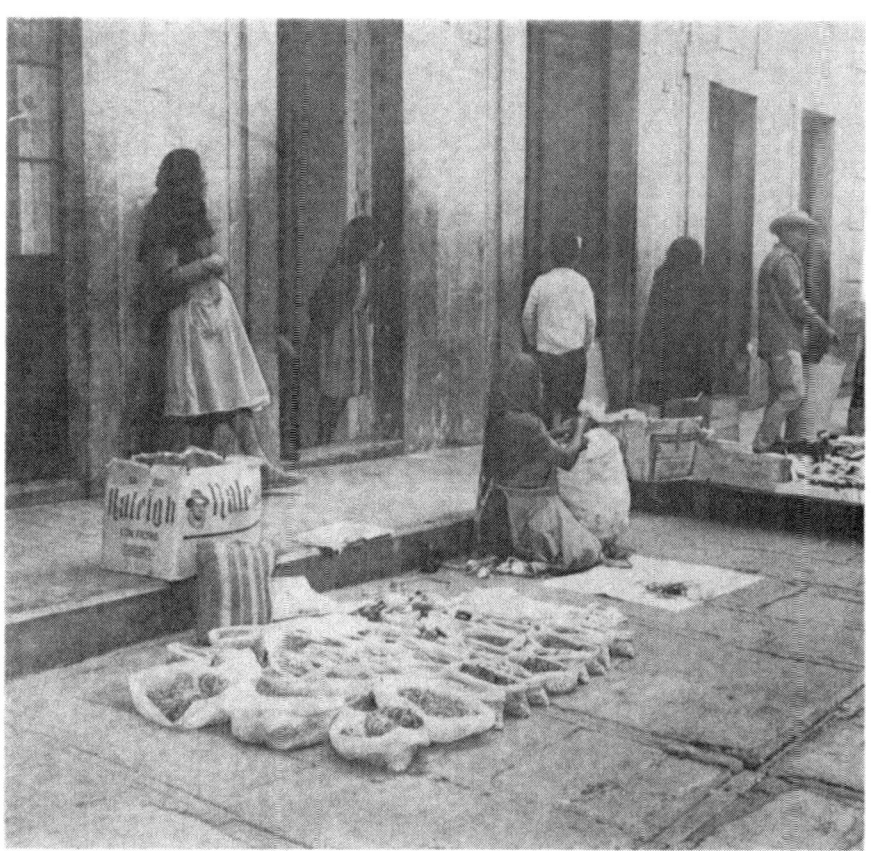

Half an hour later, a second batch of leaves and paste replaced the first. With this second application, I felt miraculous relief from the intolerable burning in my face.

During these applications, Juana and Mrs. Johnson cleansed my wounds and spread a salve on my cuts and scratches. It felt good on my skin, drawing the awful heat from my body. The salve was made from the thick blades of yucca and yucca elata, mashed and mixed with the fat from goat kidneys. Several times during the afternoon, she asked if I had pains in my heart, which I did not, although my stomach was very sick.

There were three treatments of the leaves and sunflower seed paste and the last one was removed near sundown. Juana told me that there would be one more treatment, a different one, the next morning. It was to be a shampoo of sorts and would require a lather to be left on

Fresh and dried medicinal plants sold in most Mexican markets such as this one in Juarez.

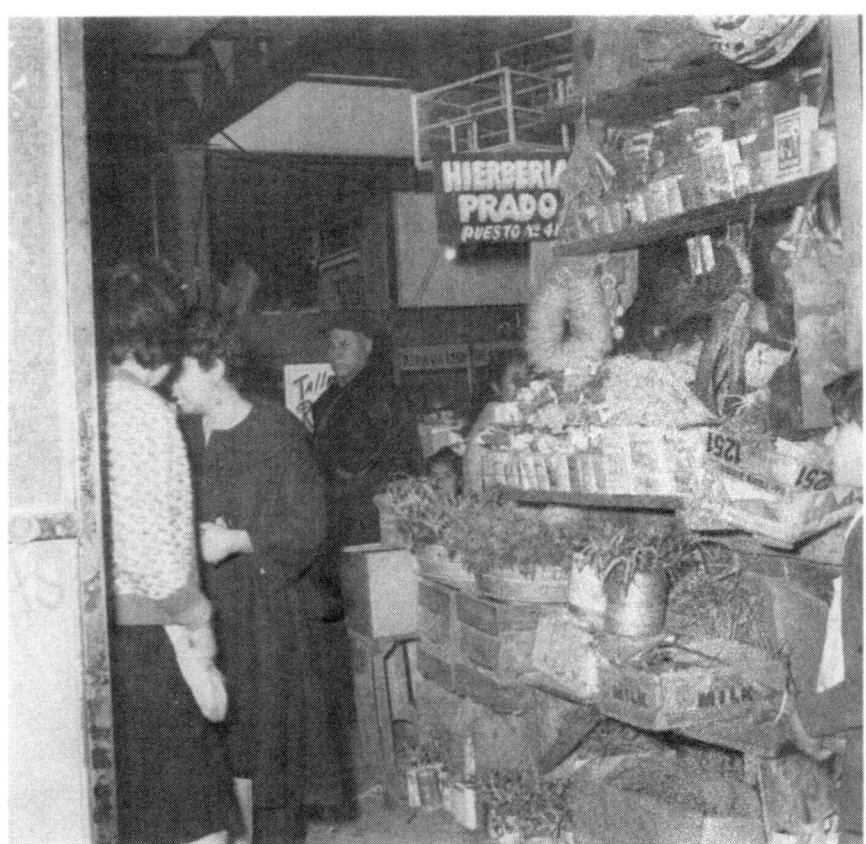

my hair and scalp for several days. As I left that evening, Juana instructed Mrs. Johnson not to give me any heavy food, suggesting that two eggs poached in beef broth would be the best meal for me.

The brew that Juana boiled during the night was of the small wild sunflowers, *Hilianthua annus*, and it was made from the entire plant—stem, leaves, and all. I arrived back at her house at seven the next morning feeling much better, for the second and last of the curandera's cure of my sunstroke. She had me sit in a chair under her mesquite tree near the large crock of the cooled sunflower brew. Slowly, she poured a cup on my head and at the base of my neck. My shirt was off, my head down. After the second cup was poured, she waited thirty minutes. My hair soaked up most of the first cups of brew. In her left hand, she had a small sponge soaked with the brew and used it as a swab on my brow, temples, and neck.

The process for the second pouring was much slower than the first, and the brew was gently massaged into my hair and scalp. The thin, slimey, yellow-green liquid had a surprisingly pleasant taste as it trickled into my mouth, and it carried only a slight trace of the sunflower's fragrance. After three hours, Juana announced my cure. No more treatments were necessary, and she urged me to go home and have a hearty meal.

My sunstroke, which could have been terribly serious, was cured in less than twenty-four hours. After this dramatic and totally effective remedy, I thought about the Mexican tradition of sipping a bit of sotol as a sunstroke preventive. Considering how few Mexicans suffer sunstroke, and how much time they spend in the sun in these parts, one wonders if it is not effective.

A few years after the sunstroke episode, I had a chance to repay Juana Holguin's kindness when she, her family, and her neighbors all were stricken with food poisoning. Nineteen persons in all, including children and two curanderas, were in need of medical attention.

One of the Holguin children who had not eaten the poisoned food came to the Johnsons' to get help for the others. I drove to the Castolon trading post to call a doctor, and I had a good idea of what to tell him about the case. I figured that the poison was the cotton-dusting chemical, used on ranches, that one of the Holguin boys had mistaken for lime used in tortillas.

While I made the thirty-two-mile round trip to call Dr. Joel Wright, Mr. and Mrs. Johnson went on to the Holguins' to see what they could do for them. Wisely, the curanderas there, Juana included, had all the afflicted ones drink a solution of lard and vinegar to make themselves vomit. When Dr. Wright arrived ten hours later, they were still extremely ill but out of danger. And even curandera Juana was grateful for the medicines he had brought with him. Both doctor and curandera agreed they were lucky that the chemical had been mixed with *masa*, thereby avoiding a full, perhaps lethal, dose of the poison.

Mexican Grapevine

When the Spaniards invaded Mexico in 1519, they knew nothing of the Aztec methods of sending messages. Nor, according to early documents that I have read about their time in Mexico, did the Spanish conquerors ever learn anything at all about avisos except that a secret, coded communication system was used among the Aztecs. In several early documents attributed to Cortez, he mentions several times that he and other Spaniards were aware that the Aztecs and other natives had a rapid communication network. The efficiency of this network was manifested when Montezuma, a four-day journey away in the capital, knew of Cortez's landing in the Veracruz area minutes after it occurred. Marina, Cortez's curandera, probably never explained to him the secrets of the avisadores, but she did tell him that Montezuma had placed "spies" all along the coast to Tabasco.

I have been in the states of Veracruz and Tabasco several times, and must conclude that the Aztec avisadores were extraordinarily skilled. The country is jungled, mountainous, and volcanic, posing formidable obstacles to avisos, which could have been sent only in relay. To flash messages in code over such distances and such terrain, with accuracy, is quite a feat. I've never seen contemporary avisadores show such sophistication in their craft.

The first avisadores—in any time, any culture—are not known. It is recorded that in 400 B. C. the Greeks had developed mirrors—thin disks of bronze, slightly convexed and polished on one side. The oldest ones were large and equipped with handles, but later ones were completely round, small enough to be held in the hand. The more elaborate mirrors were obviously for vanity purposes, but the smaller, simpler ones are intriguingly like Indian message senders.

The notion that aviso communication was developed from observing animal behavior has some followers. The animal in question is the pronghorn antelope, *Antilocapra americana*. The shape of the antlers gives this group its name. These horns are about seventeen inches high on the mature male, a bit smaller on the female. Both bucks and does are tan in color and have two white bands on the throat and an oblong white spot on the lower side that blends into a white underbelly.

Two white spots on the buttocks have given rise to the aviso speculation. The spots are a series of hairs arranged in a concentric pattern—short hairs in the center, longer ones radiating outward, filling a ten-inch circle. When the animal is startled, flanks tighten and all the white hairs in these spots spread and stand out. In the sunlight, this creates a "flash" that can be seen for several hundred yards. Antelopes graze in groups of ten or twelve—does, yearlings, fawns, and a single buck. The buck is keenly sensitive to danger, but it often is the doe that "flashes" the first warning. The flashing is observed by the others, and soon the whole herd is blinking out *aviso con tiempo* among themselves and to other antelope herds. It is interesting to note that frontier soldiers and surveyors called the antelope a heliograph because of the similarity between their flashed warning signals and man's messages sent by reflecting the sun's rays from a mirror.

If man got the idea for avisos from observing animals, he has developed it considerably. The principle has been used for centuries, by message senders in many parts of the world. Probably the most outstanding features of avisadores are their secrecy and their wide distribution. While surveyors and the military in this country have employed the Morse code in heliograph communications, the avisadores' codes are assumed to have been arranged among the members of various families or clans. I never learned any of their codes, although I was told that they did send avisos that included words not ordinarily used in normal conversations. An aviso "dialect," then, seems a possibility. I recall an incident in which this construction of phrases and translation proved avisos as effective as speaking.

Elmo and Ada Johnson decided, in 1929, to have an American Christmas for all the Mexican families in the area. Dinner was to be served and gifts given, and Santa Claus was scheduled to appear. The Mexicans knew nothing about our Christmas traditions, and the preparations were on a grand scale. Maria and Andrea Holguin, who had worked in American homes and shared in such Christmas festivities before, did lots of sewing to make Santa's suit and fifty large stockings. Mrs. Johnson began the project in July, as she had to order most of the supplies by mail.

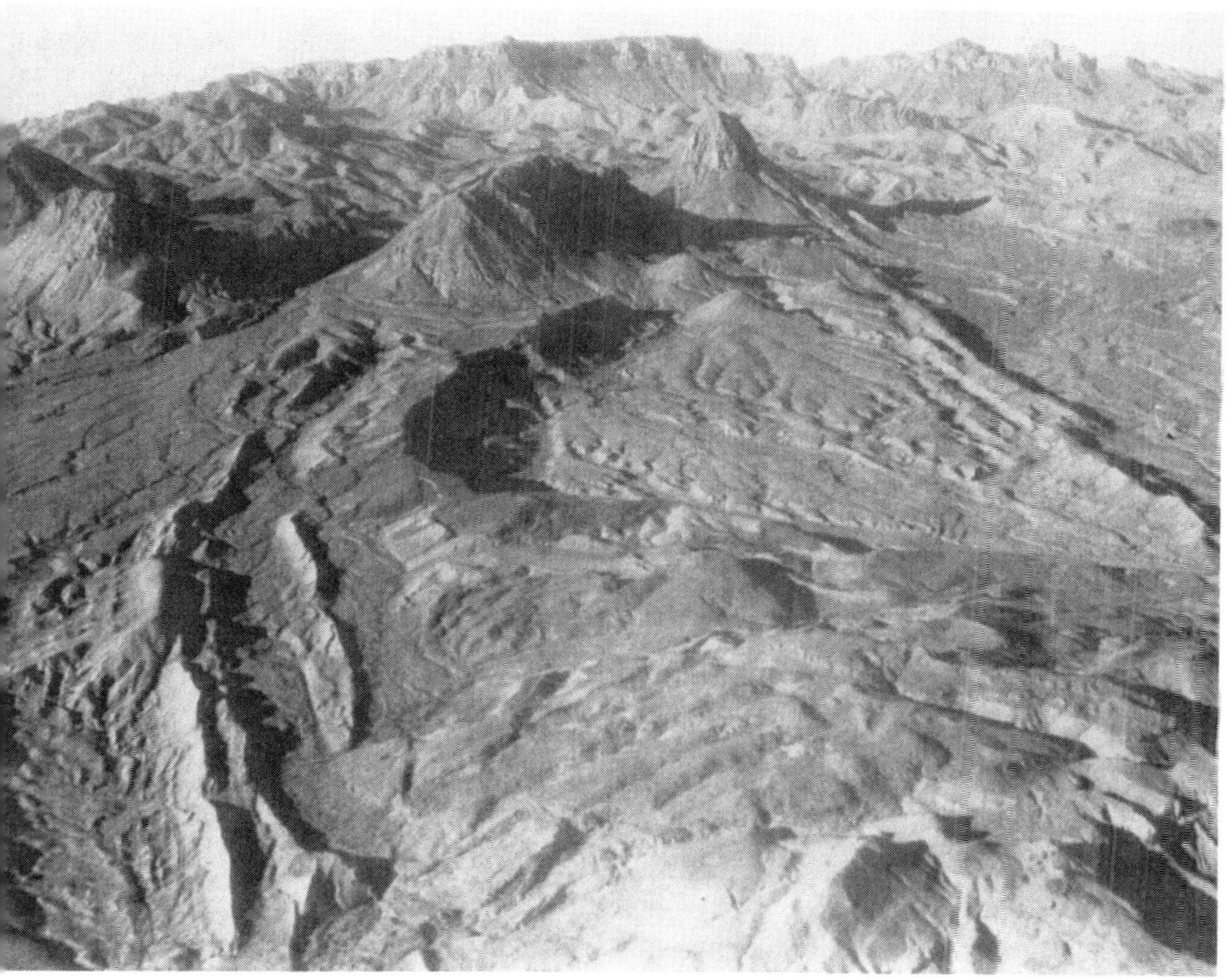

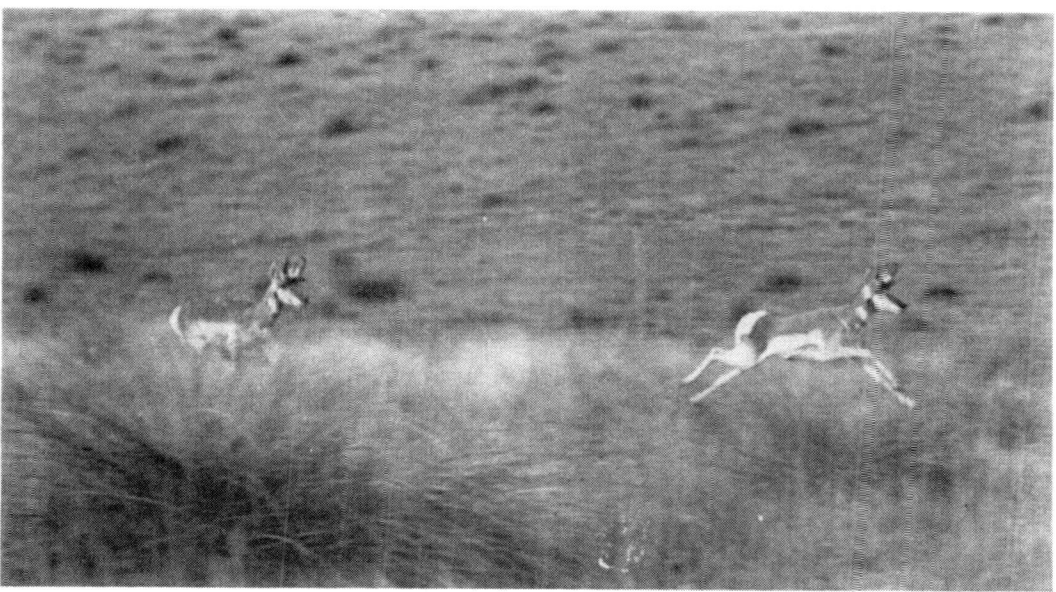

The Big Bend's rough country (above), bordered by the Chisos Mountains, made formidable obstacles to avisos. The cone-shaped mountain, called Elephant Tusk. is a landmark. Below, two pronghorn antelope "flash" warnings with patches of white on their rumps. The first avisos?

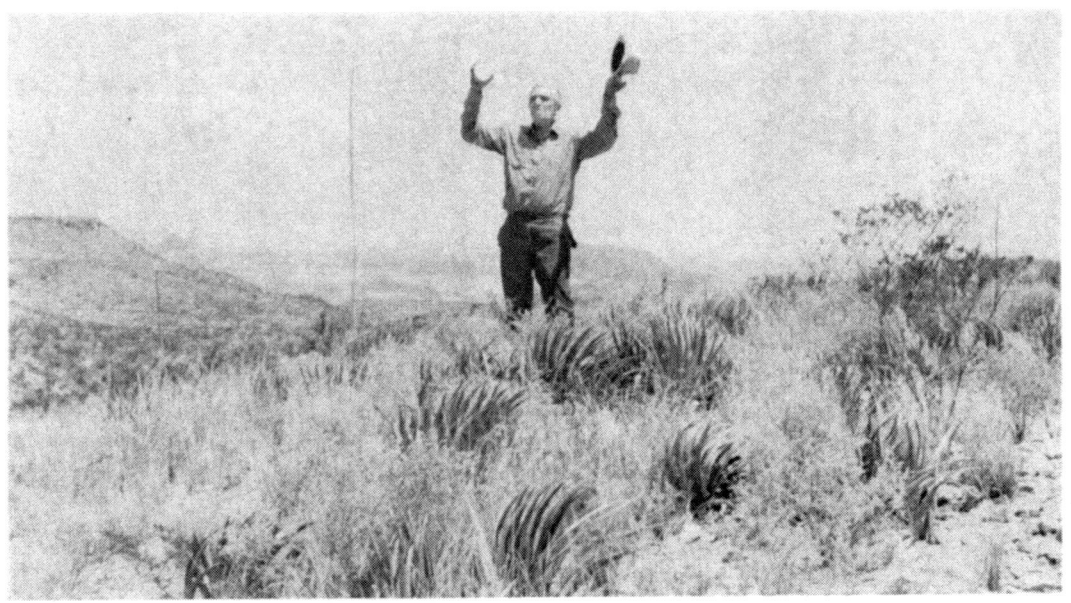

A Big Bend avisador, above, sends a message with a pocket mirror. The positions of the arms, hands, and hat often are important to the procedure. A home situated near a hill (below) was ideal for sending and receiving avisos.

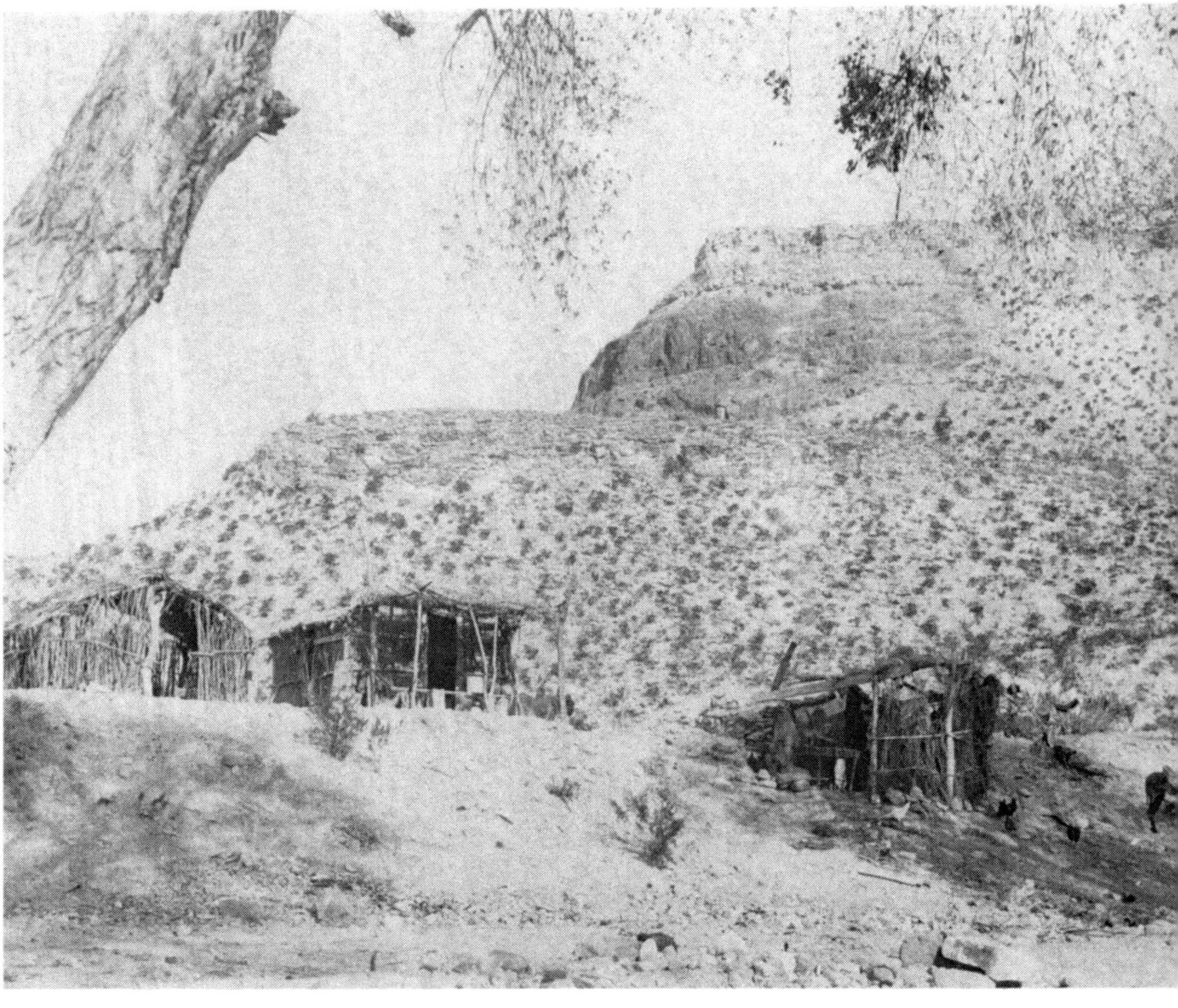

The Johnsons had a Delco power unit, so colored globes and all sorts of other illuminated decorations were ordered. Two days before Christmas Eve, I drove to Alpine to pick up last-minute items, and on the way back I chopped down an eight-foot cedar tree, which we all decorated. Lee Rackley, a young fellow from Boerne, Texas, was recruited to be Santa Claus, and he was eager to don the white wig and beard and the red suit, padded with a pillow.

It was time to send out the "invitations." Alejandro Garcia, who worked for the Johnsons, was to send an aviso to every Mexican family within twelve miles of the border. All were invited, but the aviso was to stress that children especially were to come, as Santa Claus wanted to meet every boy and girl. Dinner would begin at noon, followed by gift giving at two o'clock.

Most of the words of the message, such as *navidad* for "Christmas," or *regalos* for "gifts," were easily converted into avisos. "Claus," though, in "Santa Claus," was difficult, for the closest Spanish word is *clausa* ("clause"). I described Santa Claus to Alejandro as being rather like one of the three wise men who visited the infant Jesus.

Shortly before two on Christmas Eve, the large patio of the Johnson home was packed with children and their parents. I was near two boys, both about ten years old, when Santa made his entrance. One exclaimed, "Santo Claus walks just like Lee!" The aviso had been understood.

That the shrewd children detected the speaking and walking characteristics of Lee Rackley is nothing more than testimony of the attention those people gave to an individual's mannerisms. The important fact is that the aviso communicated all the specifics—save for that *o* displacing the *a* in "Santa"—of the Johnsons' gracious invitation.

Ada Johnson must have made more people happy that Christmas Eve than any other person in the Rio Grande area. Months after the celebration I was in Cuatrocienegas, 180 miles from the Johnson ranch, and several people, upon finding out where I was from, said that they had heard of the Johnsons' *feliz navidad.*

There was a bit of spillover from Alejandro's aviso, for, several days after the party, some Mexicans would come to the Johnson ranch asking about gifts and "Santo Claus." Although Alejandro's invitation was the first aviso I ever asked to be sent, it brought me no closer to understanding avisador codes than I had been before. One of the few specifics I learned was that, in most avisos related to me, I was referred to as *el fotografo* (the photographer).

Subsequent experience with avisadores proved further that their skills were diligently developed and no casual matter. In 1930, I asked Alejandro Garcia to send an aviso announcing that I would buy fifty or more deer antlers of the three species found in the Big Bend area—the mule, whitetail, and flagtail. I told Alejandro to explain that I wanted no horns that had been shed. The aviso had no distance limits and, in the following weeks, antlers were brought in from as far as sixty miles away. All were according to my specifications.

Alejandro sent another aviso for me in the spring of 1932, this time with a much more intricate message. It was delivered to boys between ten and fourteen years old living within three or four miles of the river. The project behind the aviso was wildlife photography, made possible by my having worked a year in St. Louis, Missouri, saving enough money to buy twelve lenses and shutters and a supply of film and flash powder. I also had devised a system whereby night-feeding animals, such as deer and antelope, would trip the shutter of a camera while nibbling food I had put out for them. The other subjects of my wildlife photography were birds, and I was having trouble finding enough variety. Thus, my avisos to the Mexican boys were calls for research assistance.

The aviso was specific: many nests were needed, and none was to be disturbed. Rather, I asked that each boy who found a nest take me to it. For each nest, I gave the boys a Boy Scout knife and, if the nest was rare, a coin or two. Such rewards were really appreciated by the boys, and the response from them was strong. So strong, in fact, that several days after the project began, I asked Alejandro to send another aviso telling my researchers not to include the nests of road-runners, white-wing doves, and several others of which I had more than enough specimens. I also had Alejandro reiterate the three-mile boundary stipulation, for I could cover only so much ground. It was clear to me that much could be said in aviso communication—its two-way signaling a simulation of spoken dialogue, with messages that could be corrected or amended. Even reprimands could be given.

Several amusing and educational incidents occurred during the bird project, like the time a boy ran up to me with the news that he had found a night hawk's, or bull bat's, nest. When he tried to re-locate it, there was no trace of the bird's eggs, since night hawks do not build nests but move their eggs from place to place. Once we found the eggs, I tied a strip of cloth onto a nearby bush, but the hen moved her eggs by the very next day.

One eight-year-old youngster, for whom the avisos had not been intended, knew that his older brothers were getting pocketknives and wanted to get in on the action. Discovering a hummingbird nest with two babies in it, he proceeded to break off the branch that cradled the nest and bring it to me. He wasn't aware of my stipulation that nests were not to be disturbed, so I did not scold him harshly. But those young hummers had to be cared for. I took the nest to Ada Johnson, who was happy to feed them a sugar solution through a medicine dropper. From their nest in one of the Johnsons' patio ferns, the young birds soon began to fly—around the yard and garden, and in and out of the house. They stayed around the Johnsons' until their first migration, from which they did not return. I never secured proof that hummingbirds return to their hatching place, like swallows and some other birds.

By marking swallows' legs with a bit of aluminum paint I discovered that even after lengthy migratory flights the birds returned to their former nesting sites at the Johnson ranch.

It was amazing to watch a swallow build its nest of mud, requiring of the male at least a thousand trips to and from the river bank, and of the female many hours of padding the damp mud with the fluffy blossoms of cottonwood trees.

During one of many periods spent at the Elmo Johnson ranch, I had a number of lively experiences with avisadores. Johnson, as I have told, had a trading post on the bank of the Rio Grande, and most of his customers lived on the Mexican side. There was, therefore, ample opportunity to make frequent trips over the border. One of Johnson's customers, Juan Hinojos, told me about a large canyon some twelve miles into Mexico where he had seen old petroglyphs and writing on cave walls. He said he would be happy to take me there, but no date was set. Two days later, while having breakfast with the Johnsons, I decided to go to Juan's and ask him to guide me to the canyon. I saddled up and left for Juan's house before it was completely light outside. When I arrived, he was standing by his saddled horse, ready to go. When I asked what he was doing, he replied that he was waiting to take me to the canyon. It was obvious that avisos had given him advance word of my coming.

About two miles from Juan's home, riding toward the canyon, we saw a mounted man on a high ridge. Looking toward us, he made no move, except to extend his right arm in salute. Soon we saw another man, sitting on his horse atop a ridge, who gave a similar greeting. Juan confirmed my surmise that avisos were being relayed the length of our journey, hence the welcome we received as we progressed toward the canyon. Had mischief been our intent, the avisos would have worked against us.

There is a peripheral quality about avisos; they are by no means privileged communications. Anyone seeing these flashes, if he were familiar with the codes, could have known what we were doing in the area. Usually, though, codes are sufficient to protect aviso messages, and often their contents of strategy and tactics.

From eight miles away, Juan flashed a message to his friends, the Jesus Martinez family, which was received "loud and clear." When we arrived at the house, lunch had been prepared for us.

As Juan and I left the Martinez home, Mr. Martinez sent an aviso and the two riders again appeared on the ridge as we rode past them. Juan's family knew exactly when to expect us and, later that evening, the Johnsons had dinner on the table for me when I rode up. It

Juan Hinojos in the Canyon of the Dead, which we explored and found old burial grounds and ancient carvings on walls.

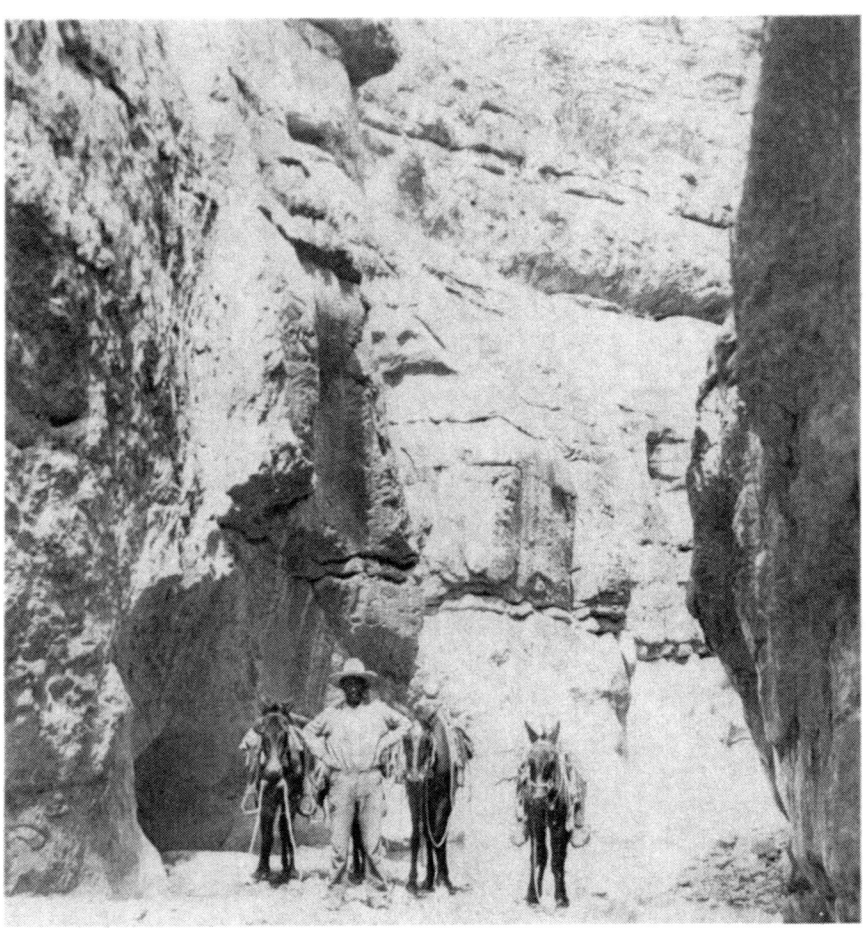

turned out that Maria, the Johnsons' cook, was the instigator of the aviso network that day, for she had heard me say at breakfast that I was going to Juan Hinojos's. She told Alejandro Garcia, who flashed first word in Juan's direction. Telephones could not have done it better.

Despite my close relationships with Juan Hinojos, Maria, Alejandro Garcia, and many other Mexicans on both sides of the river, they would never divulge to me the secrets of the avisadores. The one fact they would admit was that avisos did indeed exist as an established, secret communication system. But this was acknowledged only after I discovered that they had uses for mirrors other than as looking glasses.

A U. S. Cavalry outpost from 1916 to 1920, Castolon was one of the few such stations with buildings intact. In 1921, Wayne Cartledge bought the buildings to establish the largest trading post in the Big Bend. He also ran a huge cotton farm and cattle ranch near Castolon. It was there in 1928 that I saw one of his ranch hands flash an aviso.

I was on one of my monthly two-week trips to the lower end of the Big Bend district. Castolon was one of my regular stops, as were the homes of most Mexicans and the two Americans who lived in lower Brewster County—Mr. and Mrs. Woodson and Det Walker. The Woodsons had a small farm about three miles above Walker's and both lived on the bank of the Rio Grande. A man named Derrick operated the trading post at Castolon for Wayne Cartledge.

Standing near my Dodge roadster, talking with Mr. Derrick, I was about to leave Castolon when we heard a car coming up the hill. A Border Patrol vehicle topped the rise and stopped, and Shelly Barnes and Oscar Stetson got out. Paying little heed, I was facing the opposite direction still talking with Derrick when I saw a sudden flash of light from a rocky hill at the foot of Castolon Peak—less than a mile away.

It was an aviso, warning all Mexicans in the area of the Border Patrol's presence. You can bet that numerous other avisos were sent during the next few days, while the patrolmen were en route from Castolon to Glenn Springs.

About a minute after I saw the flash, I drove away but stopped at the edge of the hill where the road started down and got out of the car. With my binoculars I could see the Mexican ranch hand standing where I had seen the flash, but he was no longer flashing. I figured that he was waiting for the patrolmen to leave, and perhaps me as well. That would require two avisos—one of warning, regarding the Border Patrol, and another of "friendly gossip," about my whereabouts.

So it was that I got firsthand proof that mirrors, or other shiny objects, were used to flash messages among avisadores. Elated, I left Castolon and stopped at the home of Juana Ramirez, an elderly widow. Her house was a Big Bend landmark—a small structure on top of a hill overlooking a big stretch of the Rio Grande. Below the hill was a large stone dyke extending across the water. Juana's home was a perfect spot from which to send avisos, and the best possible relay station. An avisadora, as well as one of the best curanderas in the region, Juana often would pick up avisos and relay them.

Between 1922 and 1934 I frequently visited Juana, and not once did she fail to appear in her front yard as I approached, obviously having learned of my coming and awaiting my arrival. She tried to conceal the fact, but she must have known I knew about the aviso, as all the Mexicans were a little weary of my curiosity about their secret communications.

Noticing a bulge in Juana's dress pocket, I suspected it was a mirror. She was the only woman I knew who always carried a mirror, a fact supporting my conclusion that most aviso senders were men, who were never without their pocket mirrors. Although Juana never offered me much information, I surmised much by studying her behavior and her person.

Perhaps the most mysterious and inexplicable aspect of this aviso business is how avisadores know when an aviso is being sent their way. Avisos gave no audio warning of their arrival, but I have seen many avisadores look up, change directions, and drop whatever they were doing to read them. Many times these messages were sudden warnings, so their receipt could not have been prearranged. Some uncanny sixth sense seemed to tell avisadores when avisos were on the way, and they would then turn to receive and relay them. Even during work that required constant vigil, such as irrigation, avisadores knew precisely when they should look up to catch a message. Mental telepathy? Supersensitivity? Whatever, this special sense rarely failed the avisadores.

In 1935, I found evidence of the widespread use of avisos when I made a two-thousand-mile border trip from the mouth of the Rio Grande below Brownsville to the last monument on the edge of the Pacific in California. I was sworn into the U. S. Immigration Service to check on the condition of markers along the border and to make photographs, including aerial ones, of the borderlands. My reputation as the photographer of the Border Patrol secured the job for me, and part of my assignment was to photograph officers of the various border subdistricts. Allowed to travel on either side of the boundary, I

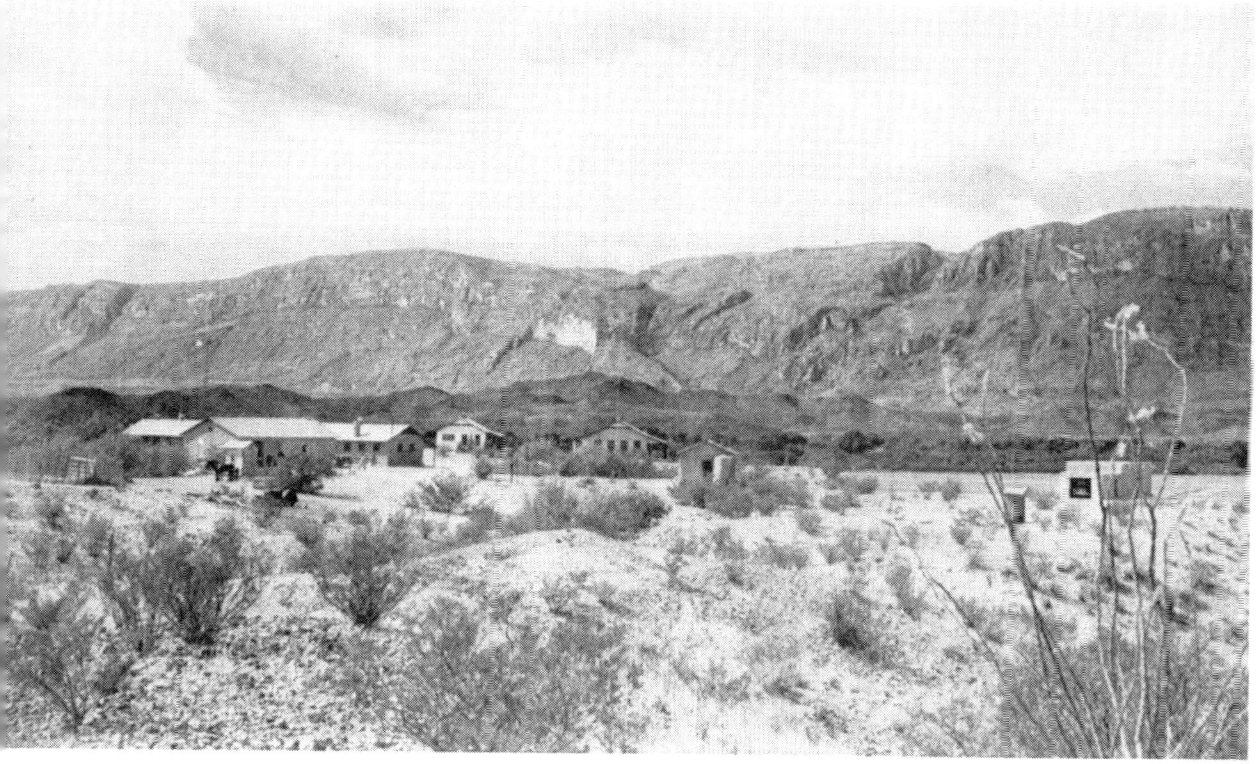

Above, Castolon Trading Post in the mid-twenties. Before Wayne Cartledge bought it, it was a cavalry outpost. Santa Elena Canyon loops in the background. Bottom, the Mexican side of Monument 139, ten miles southeast of Sasabe.

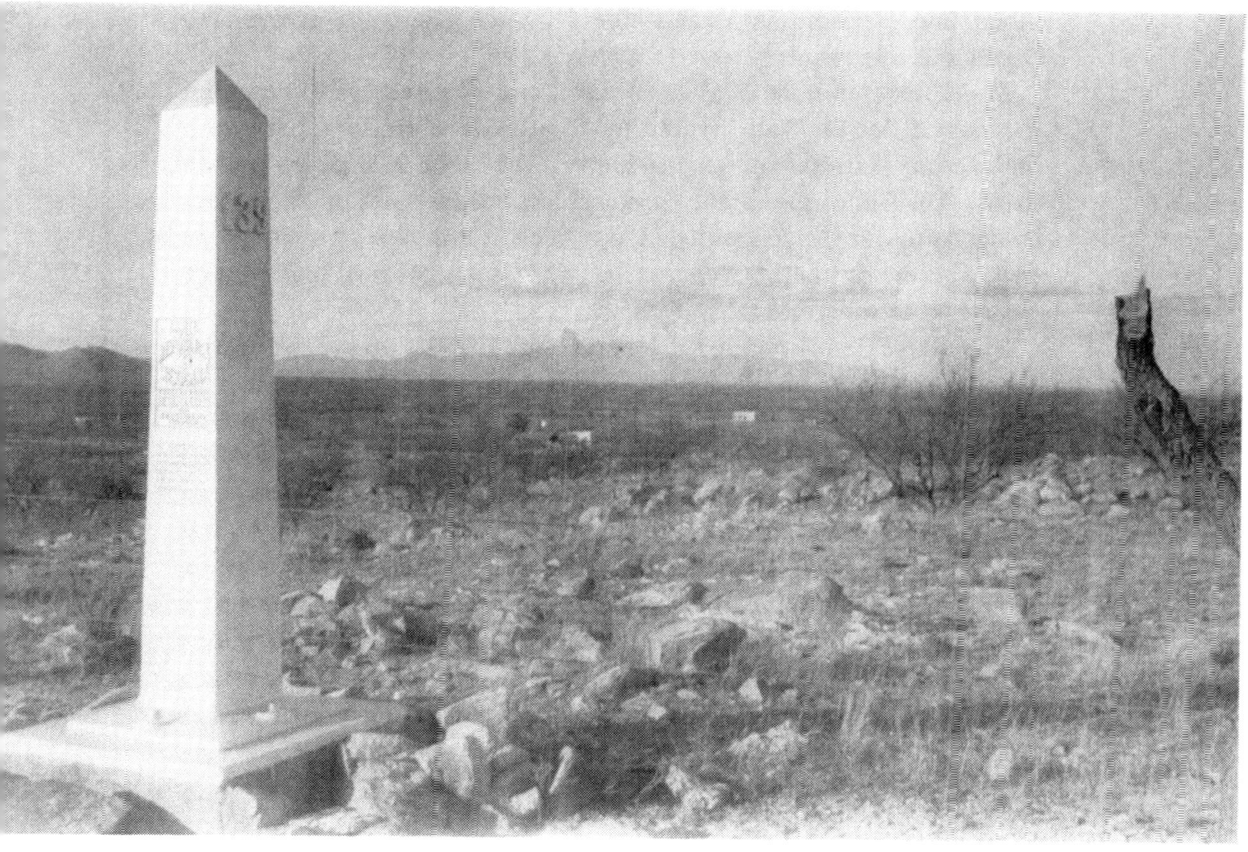

enjoyed ready cooperation from the Border Patrol, U. S. Coast Guard, and Mexican *fiscales*. In each of the eight border subdistricts, two patrolmen were assigned to show me the markers and familiarize me with the countryside. The subdistrict headquarters were Browns-ville, Laredo, Del Rio, Marfa, and El Paso, Texas; and Tucson, Ari-zona; and El Centro and San Ysidro, California. The three districts were located at San Antonio, El Paso, and Los Angeles, where super-visors commanded the eight subdistrict chiefs.

The terrain I crossed during that trip was varied—from deserts to fields of snow. For instance, near El Centro, the border line lay across a hot desert and up a range of high mountains where the snow was more than four feet deep. I had to wear skis and dig out this monument, number 247, to make a picture of it. An hour later I was on the hot desert again, traveling west on the boundary line to monu-ment 258, right on the coast.

The 258 border markers ranged in height from 6 to 12 feet and most were made of iron, some of stone, and one, the last, of marble. Each had two bronze plaques, one in Spanish, facing Mexico, the other in English, looking toward the United States and reading, "This is an International Boundary marker of the United States and Mexi-co. Defacing is punishable by law." Theoretically, the markers are in direct line of vision with each other, but the geography of the area makes this impossible.

Monument number 1 is in El Paso, and number 258 is near San Ysidro, California. Both, visited by thousands of tourists, have been replaced as souvenir-scavanging has eroded them. A high iron fence finally was built around the first and last border markers, the others being somewhat inaccessible. These iron fences were virtually the only ones along the boundary, except for an occasional barbed-wire perimeter of some border-snuggling ranch.

The assignment provided me a great opportunity to see the border areas I had missed on other trips. The task, which netted close to two thousand photographs, required nearly four months. From my home-made camera, I developed photographs along the way, using a motel bathroom as my darkroom and, when I returned to El Paso, the facili-ties at the Border Patrol headquarters. All during my journey I was welcomed by Mexicans who had received avisos about my mission. Every Mexican and Indian I encountered was friendly, and knew why I was in their area. I was always quick to tell them that I was not an officer, which was plain to see since I did not carry a gun or wear a uniform. The avisos concerning *el fotografo* must have increased in frequency and amiability as my trip progressed, for the farther I went, the more friendly the natives were.

I managed to conduct a bit of research while on assignment, talking to avisadores and curanderos, and studying plant life. I found it interesting that the avisadores' techniques, ethics, and hardware differed little from Texas to California. Chief among my contacts were the Papago, Yaqui, and Apache Indians along the Arizona border, and other Yaqui in the state of Sonora, Mexico.

Not everyone knew as much about avisadores as I. In New Mexico and Arizona, in fact, I educated patrolmen who were baffled as to how the Mexicans knew so much so soon about intruders into their areas. But avisadores were not new on the scene. I'm sure that most Indians of North America at one time had some sort of aviso system. Only some of them, because of necessity, topography, or tradition, have retained this marvelous mode of communication longer than others.

The Border Way

Everything about goat herding is interesting to me, but perhaps the most fascinating aspect is the herder's practice of serenading his goats. It was a tactic that Big Bend herders would use when goats had to be moved to new grazing or bedding grounds. Owners of small to medium-size goat herds did not make such moves—they could provide for their animals at their home sites. But herders with many goats, like Librado Iniguez, who herded for Elmo Johnson, had to move the animals regularly to other pastures. Such mobility was unsettling to the goats and, when they were restless, Iniguez would calm them by walking among them, imitating the song of the whippoorwill. The whippoorwill song was familiar to the goats, as the night birds were always around the bedding grounds where they fed on the many insects attracted to the goats. When a herder imitated the whippoorwill, the goats felt like they were back at their old bedding ground.

Scattered around the hill where the goat herd grazed were many little goat houses, made of two large flat rocks standing upright with another on top for a roof. These simple structures provided shade for the young goats. The children of herders made pets of baby goats, calling them *sanchos*, a word whose dictionary meaning they stretched to include both orphaned kids and small animals.

Virtually every Mexican family in the Big Bend raised goats, and everyone over six years old got involved in caring for the herd. I think the hardest workers, though, were the goat dogs. The dogs began their training for the herd at about two weeks of age, when they were taken from their mothers to be nursed by a gentle nanny goat, preferably one that had been a *sancho*. The children gladly saw to it that the nannies nursed the pups at the proper times.

When the dogs were nearly grown, they were taken with the veteran goat dogs on the 12-hour grazing periods. The average goat herd, such as Alejandro Domingues's, consisted of from 150 to 200 goats, and about 5 dogs. The dogs were truly essential to herding, for they saved the herder much labor and allowed him to work alone or with just one other man.

When the goats started off each morning, Alejandro, on his burro, was at the front to lead them to the range where they would graze that day. Two dogs worked each side, keeping close watch on the goats. A fifth dog brought up the rear. When the goats reached the range where they would graze most of the day, they were allowed to spread out. Then the goat dogs would station themselves in a wide circle surrounding the entire herd. The two herders would position themselves on a small hill overlooking the scattered herd.

Herders and dogs were guardians of the goats, which surely needed protection from coyotes, eagles, and bobcats. When a large eagle swooped down on the herd to grasp a small kid in its talons, an alert herder could shoot at the predator with a rifle, but there was little the dogs could do. There was plenty the dogs could do in dealing with coyote attacks, however.

Coyotes were cunning. Their attacks on young goats were sly and methodical. But the dogs countered with their own clever defenses. You might say that both dogs and coyotes were equally matched, the outcome of the fray depending on other circumstances. A pack of six or eight coyotes would begin their attack by circling the herd, looking for a kid that might have wandered near the outer edge. One small lapse of attention by one of the dogs would afford an opportunity for the coyote that he was quick to take advantage of; some luckless kid became his meal.

A standard procedure was for one of the coyotes to attack a dog. While the fight was going on, the other coyotes would plunge into the herd with jaws snapping. Sometimes the dog-coyote fight would break up, and sometimes it would end in death for one of the adversaries, his opponent's fangs piercing the jugular vein.

No help came from the other dogs unless they were close at hand. So much was going on in a herd that a coyote could attack a dog unnoticed. Occasionally a coyote raid would be staged at night, but this was rare. The herd was more compact and controllable after the goats had bedded down, and the coyotes sensed the dogs' advantage.

Large bobcats also troubled the herders and their goats, and the cats were dreaded because they could function equally as well at night as in the daytime, so quiet and quick were their attacks. But the coyotes were the real terrors, simply because they required so

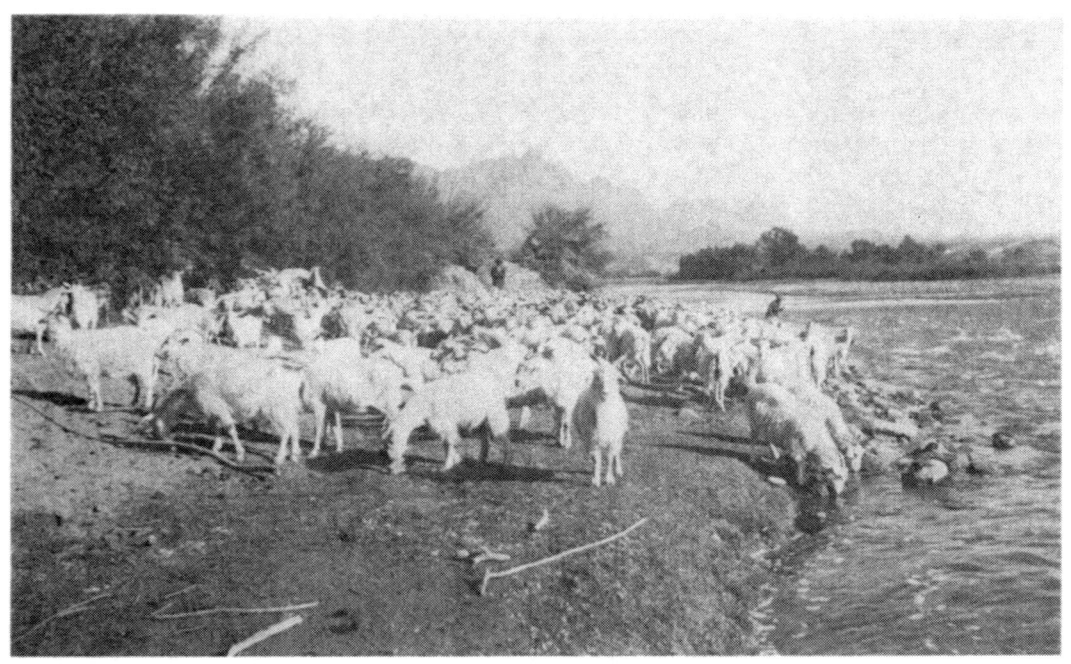

The Chisos behind him, Librado Iniguez (above) drives his goats; 1929. Below, one of goat herder Iniguez's children with her *sancho*.

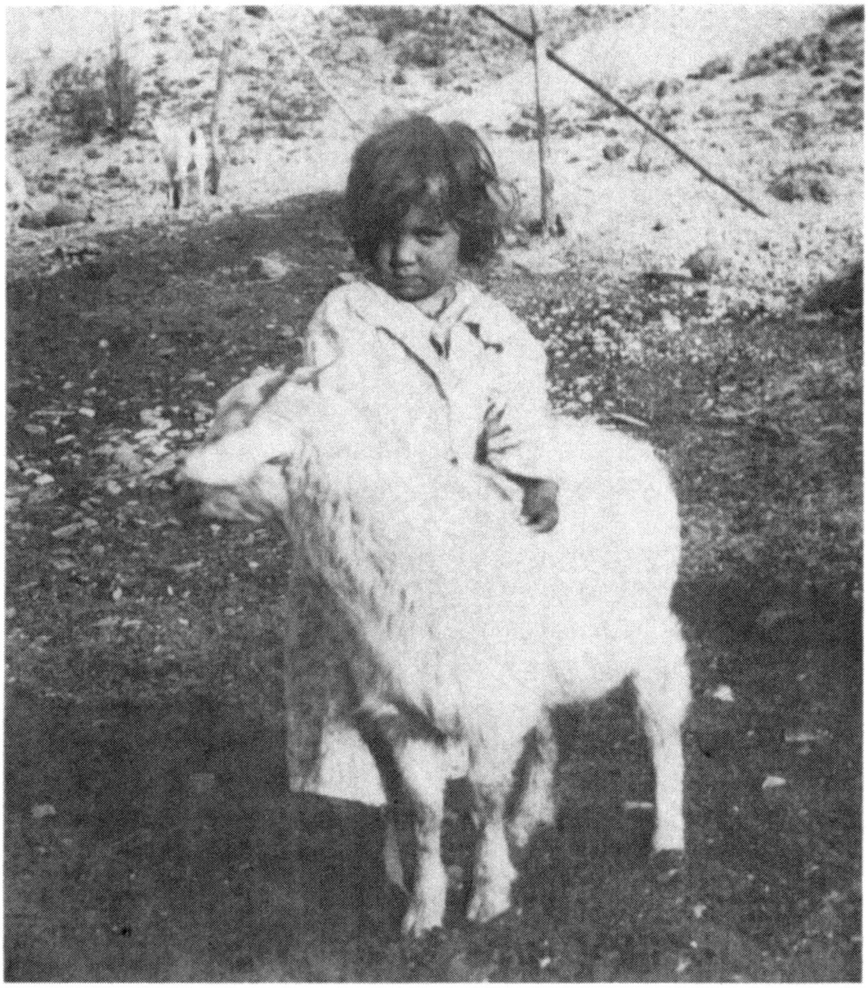

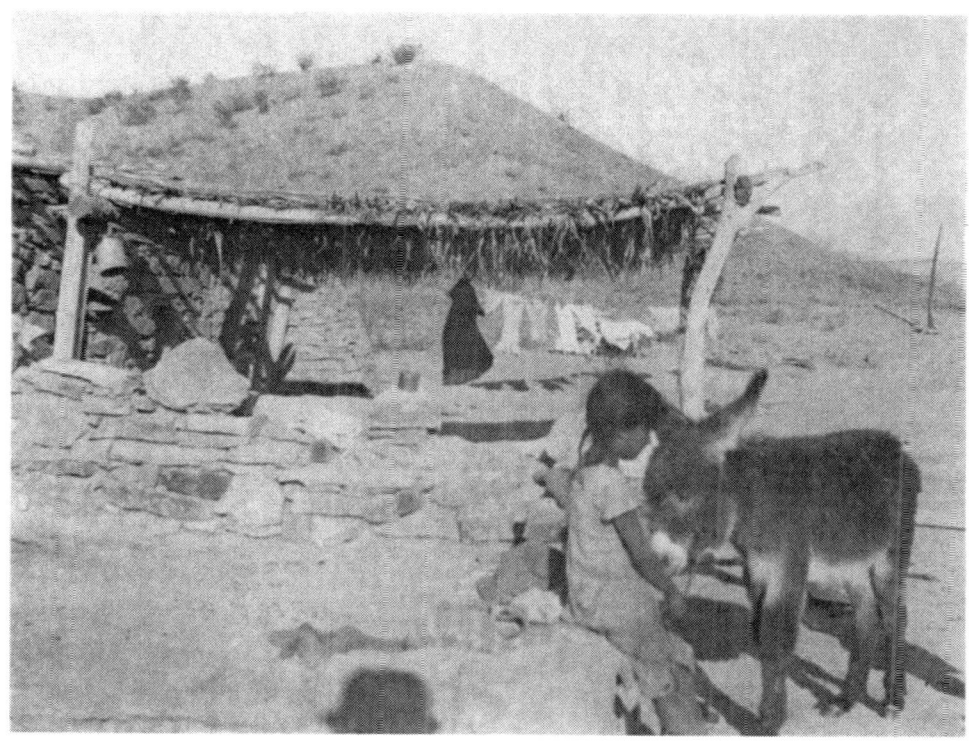

Above, a young girl with her *sancbo,* a burro colt. Below, at sundown, a goat dog is ready to guard his herd for the night. Bushes could conceal the goats' worst enemies: coyotes and bobcats.

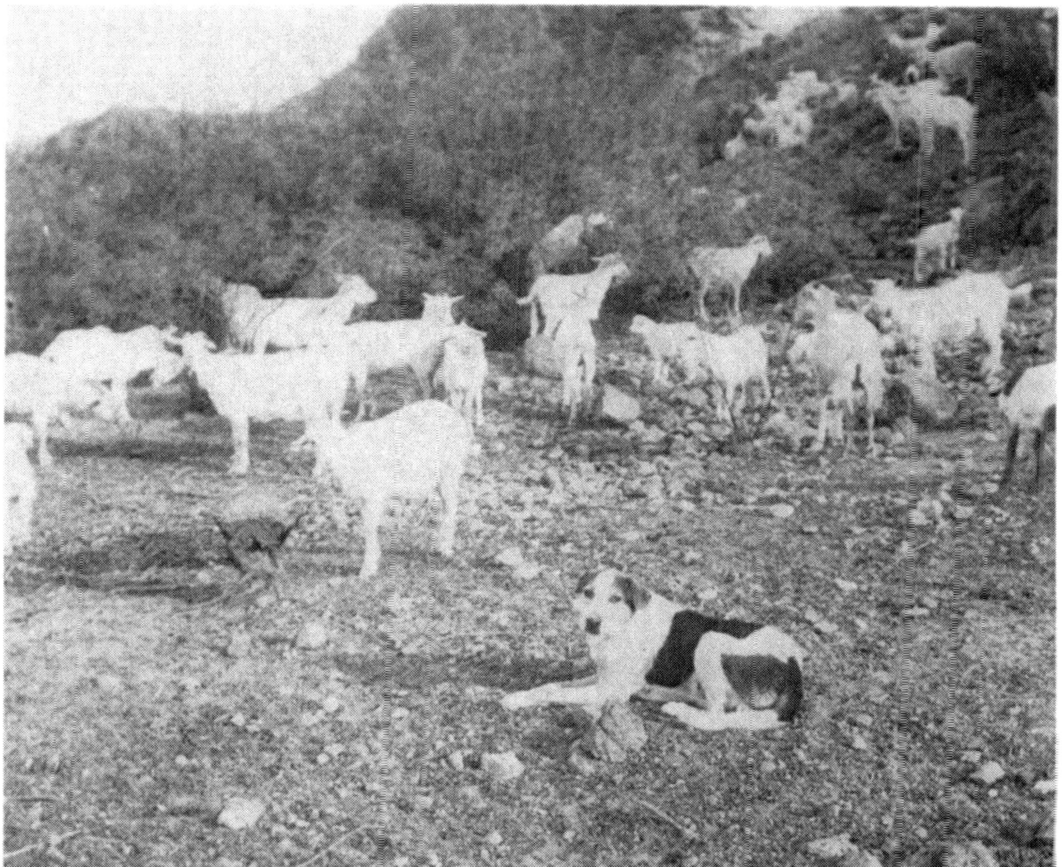

much meat, especially when a litter had to be fed. That so few goats actually were killed by coyotes is testament to the courage of the herders' dogs.

For their hard work, the dogs received few rewards. They pretty well had to provide for themselves, scavanging for food and protecting themselves against animal attacks. When possible, families would give the dogs table scraps, and in the winter months the dogs got more meat than usual. Herders would set a few steel traps and feed the dogs skinned carcasses of skunks, foxes, ringtail cats, bobcats,

This herd of Angora goats at Oak Creek Ranch on the north side of the Chisos Mountains was the first in the lower Big Bend.

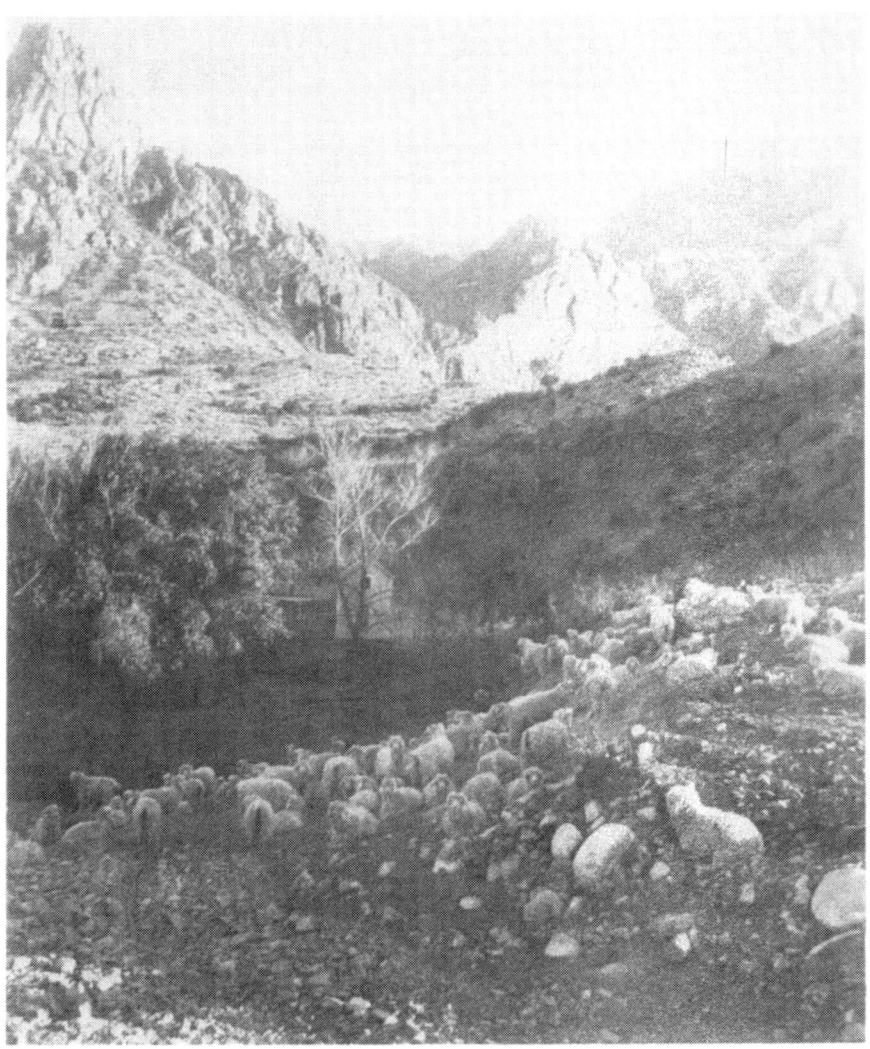

coyotes, and badgers. Even the goats sometimes provided food for the dogs, when they flushed out rodents while grazing.

Many herders told me that no more than one dog ever left the goats in search of food at a time; each took his turn, going out for meals only when the others were there to protect the herd. The herd-ers wanted the dogs to kill most of their own food, saying it made better fighters out of them. That may be so but, during my ten years around goat dogs, I never saw one that did not look hungry.

One of the best goat dogs in the Big Bend was El Vagabundo. He got his name from his habit of wandering, and I saw him with at least eight herds. No one knew where he came from. He joined each herd on the range and left it the same way. After a few weeks he would move on to assist another team of dogs. El Vagabundo made friends with all the other goat dogs, and he was gentle with children, but there was no mistaking that he was a fighter. After about a year of wandering from herd to herd, he disappeared. It was considered like-ly that he had been killed in a battle with coyotes.

Many have a notion that the Big Bend is a desert area, but that is far from true. There are parts, of course, that are dry, without rain for much of the year. But there is no area completely without vege-tation. Of the hardy, dry-weather plants, one is ocotillo (*Fouquieria splendens*), which sheds its leaves during hot weather but produces fresh growth and leaves when the rains begin. Leafless, ocotillo looks like a cluster of old stalks, but it is far from dead. Reaching a height of twenty-five feet, the plant is used by curanderos to make a medi-cine for reducing swelling. It also contains an excellent wax for treat-ing leather. Another plant in the dry regions is cenizo (*Atriplex cane-scens*). Its common name is barometer plant, for cenizo blooms right before a shower. The flowers have a short life, soon falling to the ground to provide splendid food for deer, rabbits, and goats.

The Holguins were typical of many families in the area who plant-ed only enough seeds to grow a little more corn and frijoles to last until the next year's crop. Some vegetables, though, were grown year round.

If at all possible, the gardens were situated so they would catch rainwater as it flowed from mountains, and a bit of primitive engi-neering diverted this water from dry creeks onto crops. During ex-tremely dry periods, water had to be carried in buckets from the Rio Grande.

It was easy to get liquids from certain plants that grew in abun-dance near family dwellings. The stems of the maguey (*Agave scabra*) and various others are not only tasty when roasted but also contain a

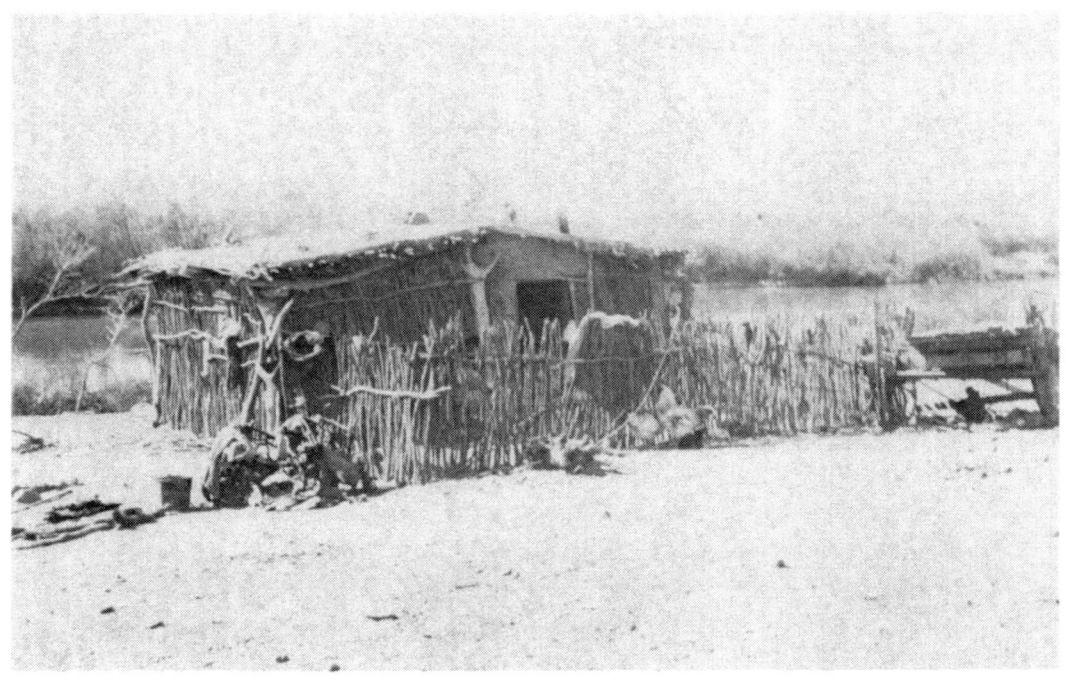

Above, a two-room house, handmade by its Mexican residents. Most of the house was of ocotillo stalks and mud plaster. Below, the unusual method used for transporting young kids whose feet were too tender to range all day over rocky ground. The best goat herders tied the feet together and suspended the youngsters from the mother's neck for a free ride back to the ranch at the end of the day.

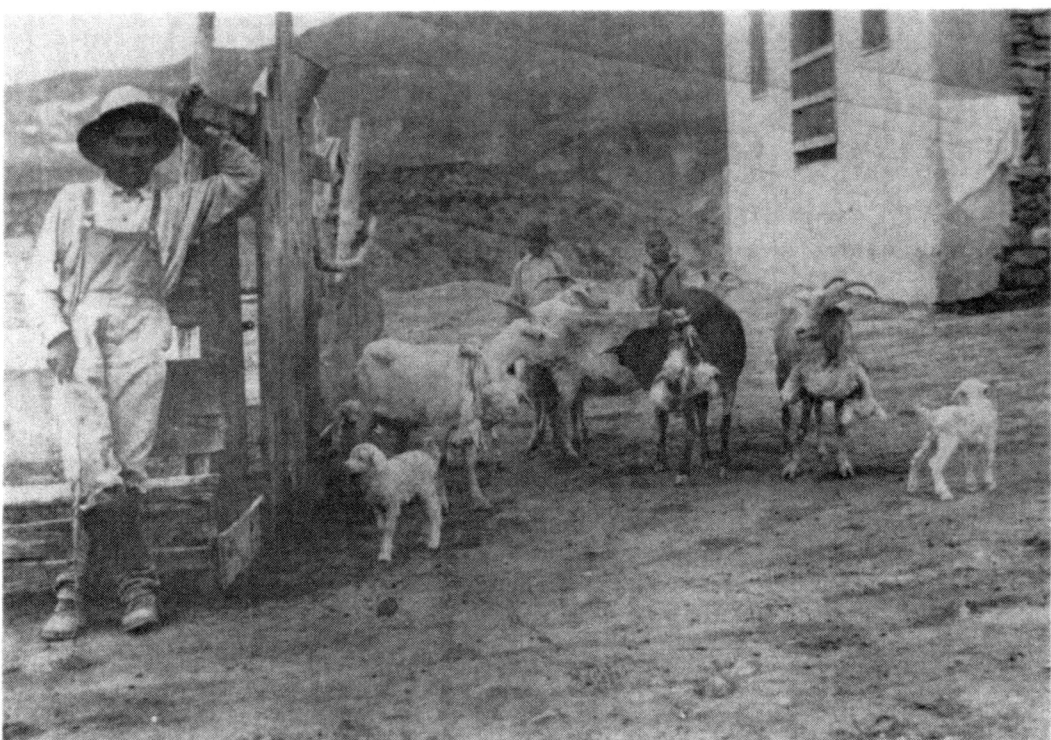

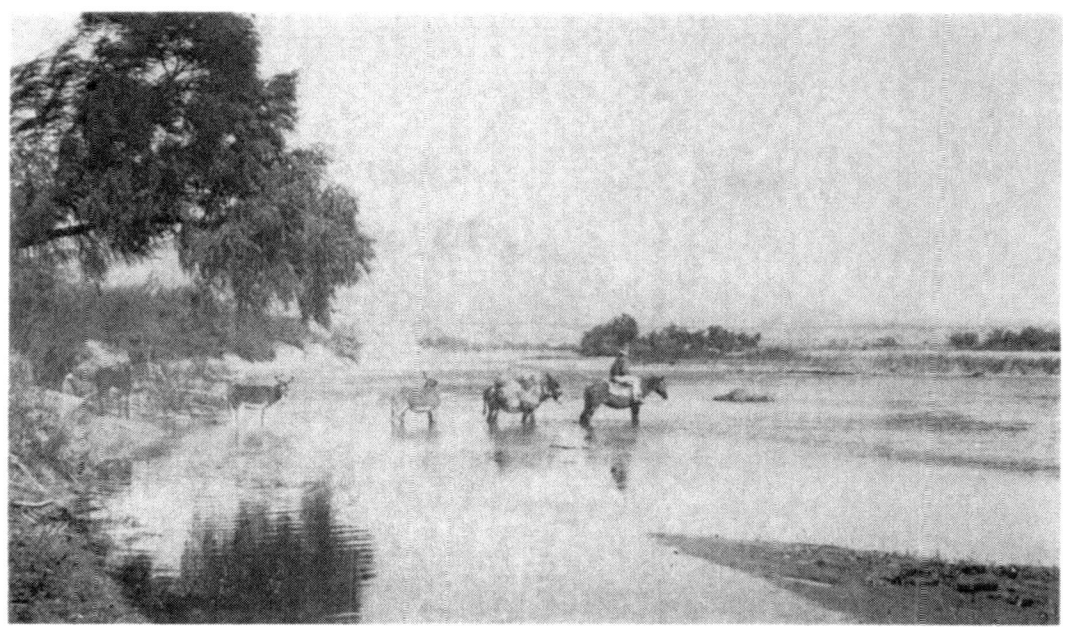

Above, a downstream view of the Rio Grande near Juana Holguin's home. Below, a Mexican boy fills canvas bags with water for delivery to homes in the Big Bend. The bags, waterproofed with candelilla wax, have cow-horn spigots.

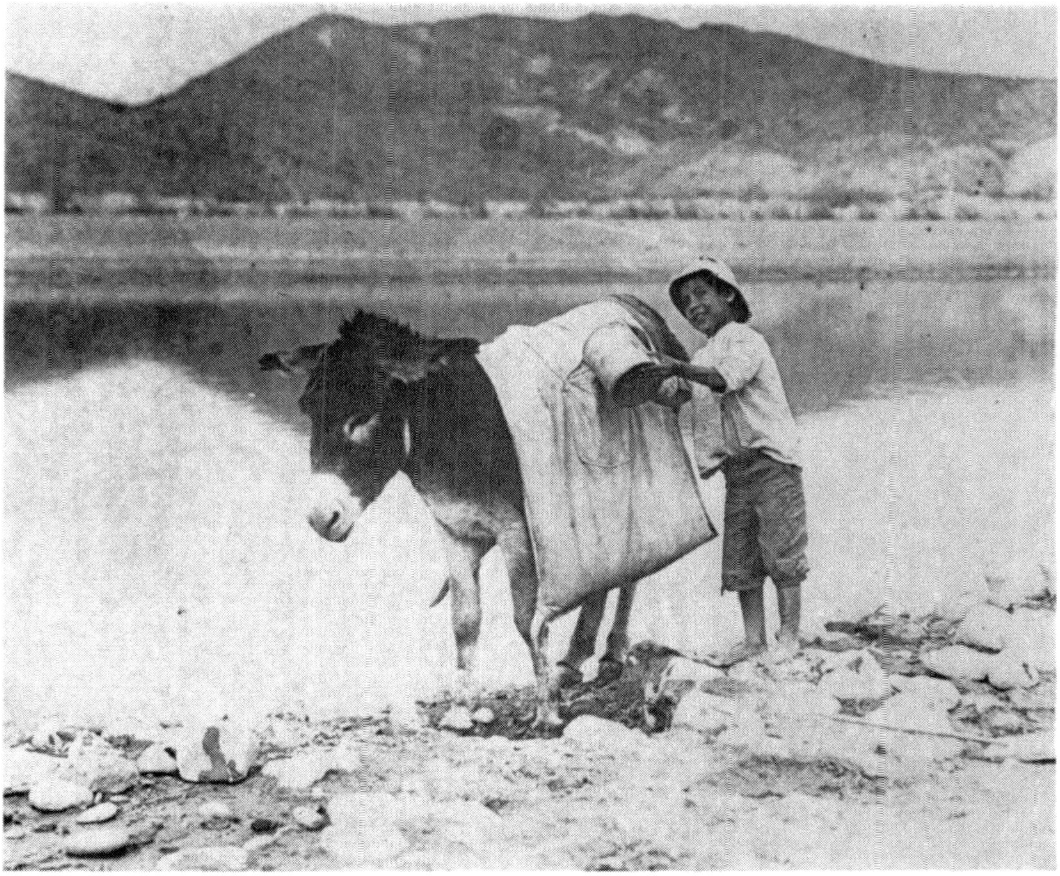

juicy, honey-like pulp. In fact, the juice of the maguey is called honey water. Throughout the land, there were and are several types of barrel cactus, which contain water. Desert people have always said that nature gave barrel cacti their bright red spines so that people in need of food and water could see them.

Another native plant in the area provided a supplemental income for many families. Brijador Holguin, eldest son of the widow Juana Holguin, offered to take me up the mountains to make some photographs of the gathering of the "cash crop," chino grass (*Boutoloca bicuiseta*). Chino grass grows only in the higher elevations of the rough, rocky places alongside lechuguilla (*Agave lechuguilla*). The fiber of the lechuguilla plant is used to tie the bundles of chino grass, then to secure them to the burros' packsaddles.

So Brijador, Jose Ramos (a neighbor of the Holguins), Ramon (Brijador's younger brother), and I left the Holguin's home at dawn one day in 1927, all on burros except the horsebacked Brijador. It was a good five miles to the grass fields at Pinnacle Peak, one of the Chisos Mountains. In two hours we were atop the peak, where the chino grass was growing among clumps of lechuguilla. I remember that the terrain was "wavy," the abundant chino grass growing in curly clusters of long stems.

The *zacateros* (grass or hay farmers) would pull up entire clusters by the roots and stack them in piles of about twenty pounds each. Then, blades of the lechuguilla were cut off at fourteen to sixteen inches, and torn into strips to tie the grass into bundles. Five bundles were hoisted onto each of the eight burros. The burros could have carried more than one hundred pounds, but we had to consider the balance of the load, and especially the narrow, cliffside trails leading down the mountain.

It took more than three hours to gather the grass, tie it in bundles, and pack it onto the burros. The grass was worth ten cents per bundle, or four dollars for the eight hundred pounds we harvested. Not much for a day's work.

If the grass was gathered near the market, two Mexican men with eight burros could earn four dollars in eight or nine hours. The two dollars per man was twice what he could have earned for twelve hours of work in the mines or on an American ranch or farm in that period.

The grass usually was sold to ranchers, as a substitute for hay and oats. Green or dry, the grass was enjoyed by horses. Cattle, deer, goats, and burros liked it green. Prior to 1920, the market for chino grass was quite large, as the Texas Rangers, U. S. Customs officers,

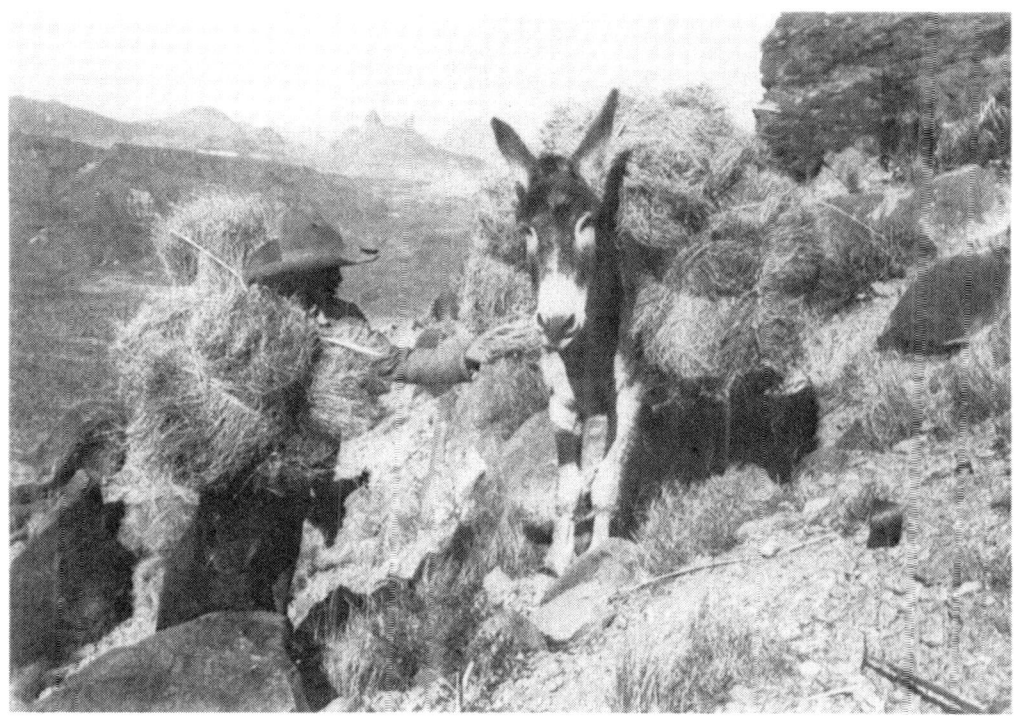

Pancho Holguin, above, offers one of his burros a clump of chino grass as they head down the mountain. Mule Ear Mountain, in background, seems almost to be the burro's shadow. Below, Brijador Holguin and his burros on their way to a trading post with their chino grass harvest.

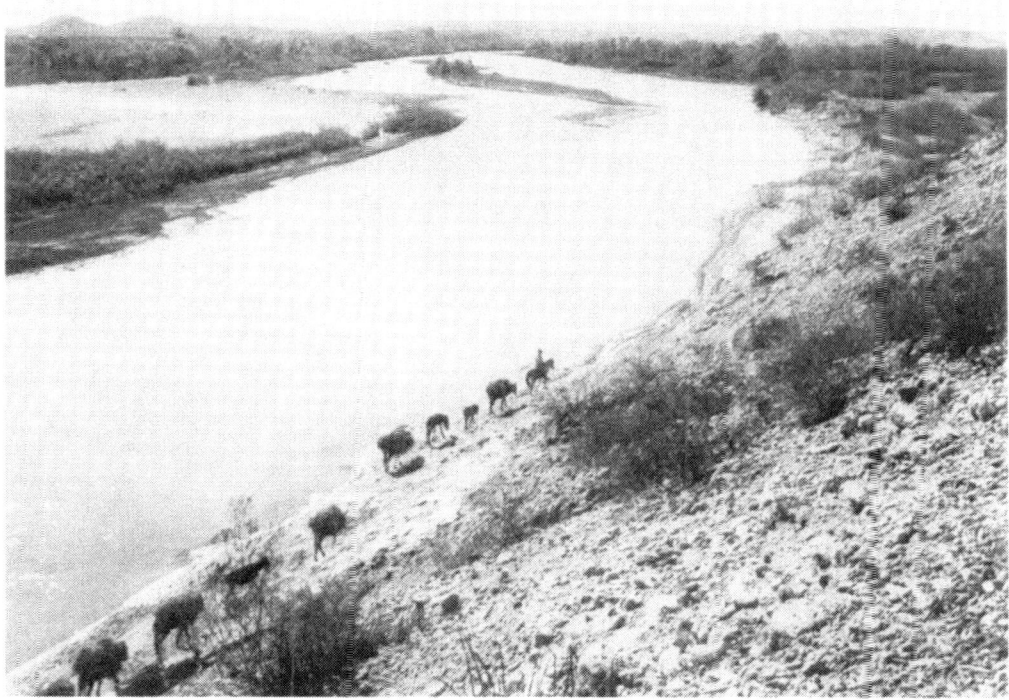

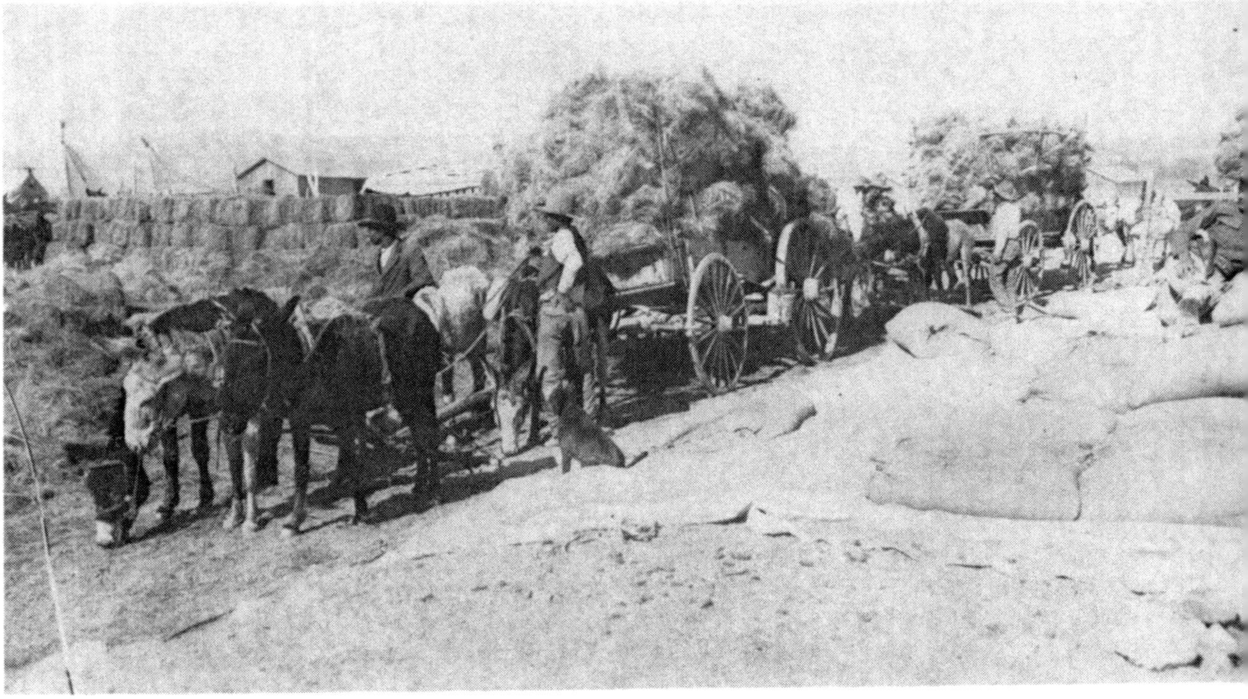

A big load of chino grass (above) is delivered to the cavalry. Below, one dollar is earned as the wife of a zacatero sells the two burro loads to cavalry officers at the going price of ten cents per bundle, fifty cents for a burro load of five.

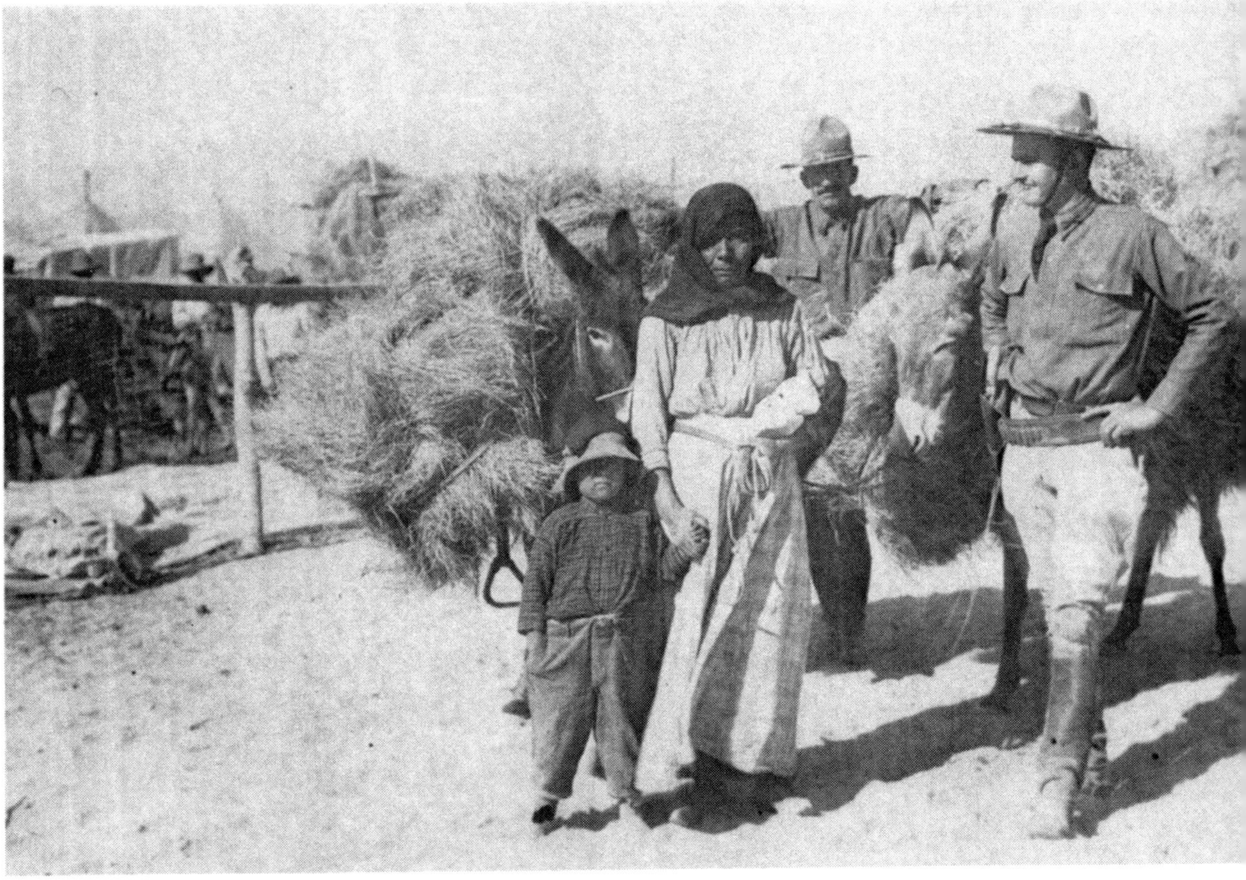

and cavalry troops purchased it regularly for their horses. Given the sometime scarcity of hay and oats, and the fact that the Rangers and customs officers had to furnish their own horse and feed it, chino grass was a practical, nourishing solution. The Texas Mexicans, in fact, could not provide all the chino grass needed in the area between 1916 and 1920, so Mexicans from Mexico were allowed to bring it across the Rio Grande one day each month, known as Port Day. With the chino grass, they also brought wagonloads of wood to sell to the cavalry.

During the twenties, the demand for chino grass dwindled to the customers on ranches near Castolon and the few on the north side of the Chisos. There were a dozen Mexican wagon trains at Terlingua, where Brijador could sell a full eight-hundred-pound load. But that entailed a sixty-eight-mile round trip to earn his four dollars.

Otherwise, the chino grass was used by the chino farmers themselves, their families, and their friends. It was hardly a lucrative business.

Brijador Holguin provided a good living for his mother and siblings. He owned seventy or eighty goats, valued at around one dollar each, a few cattle worth twenty-five to thirty dollars a head, and six horses worth fifty dollars each. His twelve burros really had no monetary value, as there were hundreds of the animals running wild in the Big Bend, many of them claimed by no one. Burros provided the basic means of transportation for Mexican families in the Big Bend; Brijador Holguin was the only Mexican I never saw ride a burro.

By the midtwenties, wandering traders in the area were decreasing, their craft and livelihood nearing extinction. Nonetheless, there was a good number of families living in isolated parts of northern Mexico who depended on the traders to bring them a few food items in exchange for furs, goat hides, and hand-woven woolen blankets and rugs. Such food items as coffee, salt, rice, sugar, and tobacco were needed. They also bought cloth for children's clothing, thread, and various other items, such as cheap earrings for the girls.

Mexican rural traders, like curanderos, came upon their profession through family ranks. But unlike curanderos, traders were in business to make money. Don't overestimate the profits of the trade, though: fifty cents per day was an average take-home earning for a trader. The trader saw his family only a couple of days every three or four months, spending most of his nights at the homes of his customers. He usually would have dinner and breakfast at his evening stop and arranged his next day to be at another customer's house by lunchtime. Always grateful, a trader brought small gifts to his hosts and hostesses: candy, cinnamon, a knick-knack.

Daily travel for the trader was about twelve miles, involving more than four hours in transit. Traders exchanged a lot of petty news and gossip with their customers—tidbits that avisadores did not waste their time on. Although some would joke that traders were a lazy lot, I think they were truly devoted workers, and lovers of the road. Not strongly family oriented, their personalities were such that they enjoyed company immensely.

Nor was the trader's work easy--he had to load and unload three or more pack horse, mules, or burros several times a day, and I surely know what that's like. The trader's pack loads remained about the same during the entire trip, as the weight of what was sold was replaced with what he traded for.

Their packsaddles were homemade of cottonwood, so that they did not cause blisters on the back of the pack animals, and the rigors of the trip for both man and beast were lessened. Avisos told families of the trader's approach several days in advance, and usually a quick aviso was flashed just a couple of hours ahead of his arrival. The family, prepared for the trader, could have its goods ready and be prepared to haggle with the trader over prices. The avisos, therefore, were important to both trader and seller. The man of the family usually handled negotiations with the trader.

When the trader arrived, the family brought out all the goods for trade that had been accumulated since his last visit. Carefully appraising each item, the trader kept a running tally in his head and could announce at any point the current subtotal. (The Mexican families shared this gift of rapid mental computation with the traders.)

Severe haggling over prices was quite rare, for the traders were fair and patient. Their prices were of course a bit higher than those at the trading posts, but they had to be. For example, traders paid an average of forty to fifty cents for a fur, which they sold at forty-five or fifty-five cents. Surely the service they provided warranted such a profit margin. If the trader misjudged the quality of a fur, he lost money on the deal, for the family could evaluate merchandise expertly. This did not happen often, but when buying in quantities, as the traders did at the trading posts, it was difficult to scrutinize every item purchased.

In buying from a trader, a family first sought food and other necessities. The essentials purchased, they then used any money left to purchase other needs, weighing their decisions carefully. But there

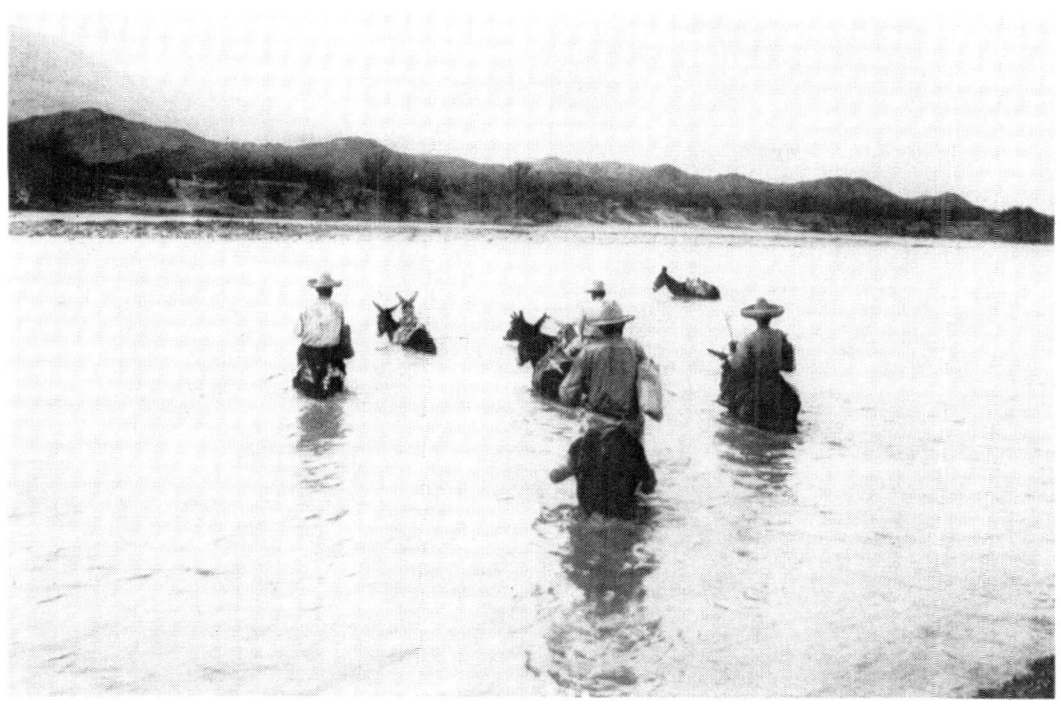

After selling their chino grass to Wayne Cartledge, these traders (above) return to Mexico with their burros at Santa Elena, opposite Castolon. Below, Mexican traders on their way to the Lajitas trading post, wagons loaded with lechuguilla fiber ropes, goat hides, and furs.

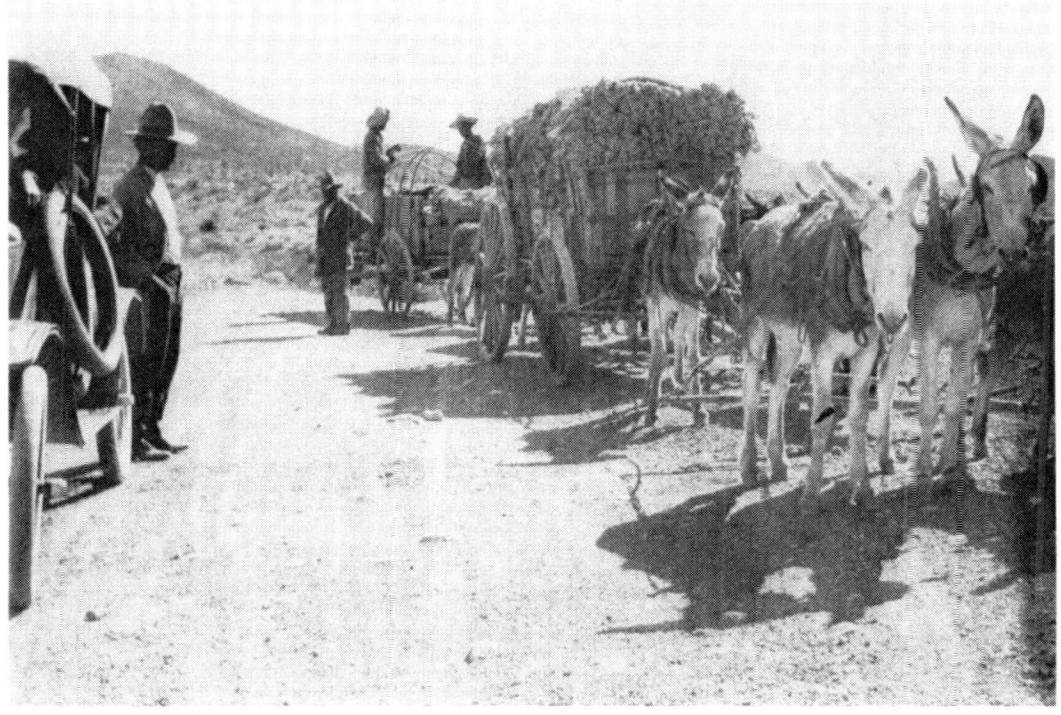

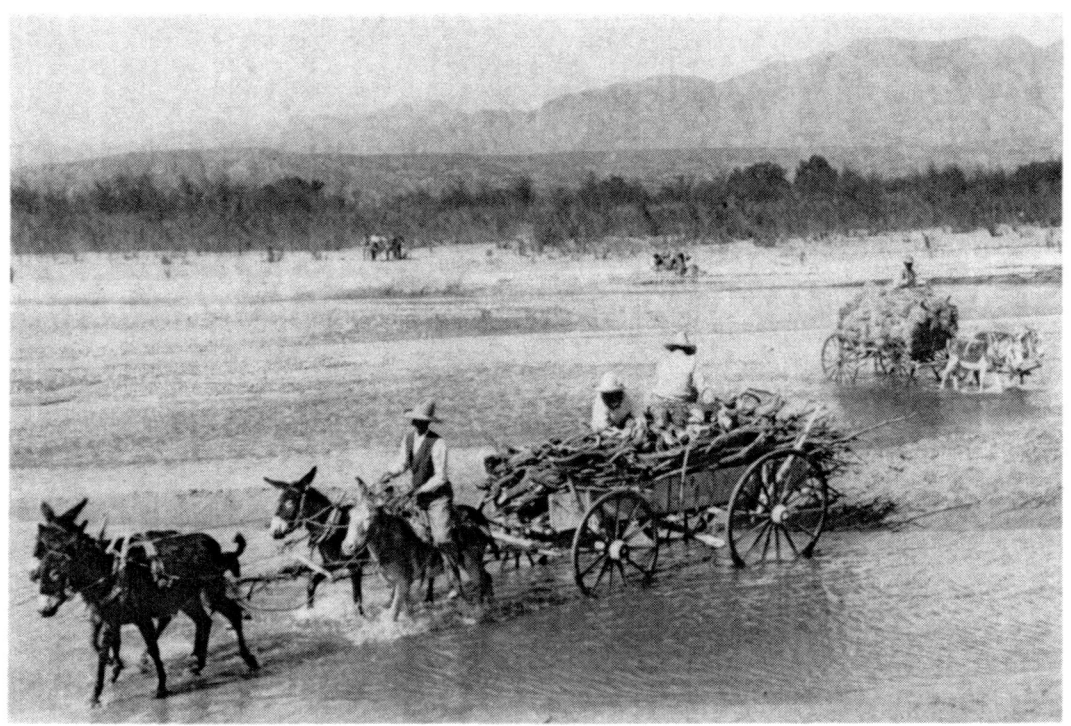

On the first day of each month during the Mexican border trouble, Mexican citizens were allowed to cross into Texas to sell such items as these loads of stove wood and chino grass (above). The cavalry troops were their best customers. Lajitas, 1916. Below, zacateros and burros at Castolon about to cross toward home.

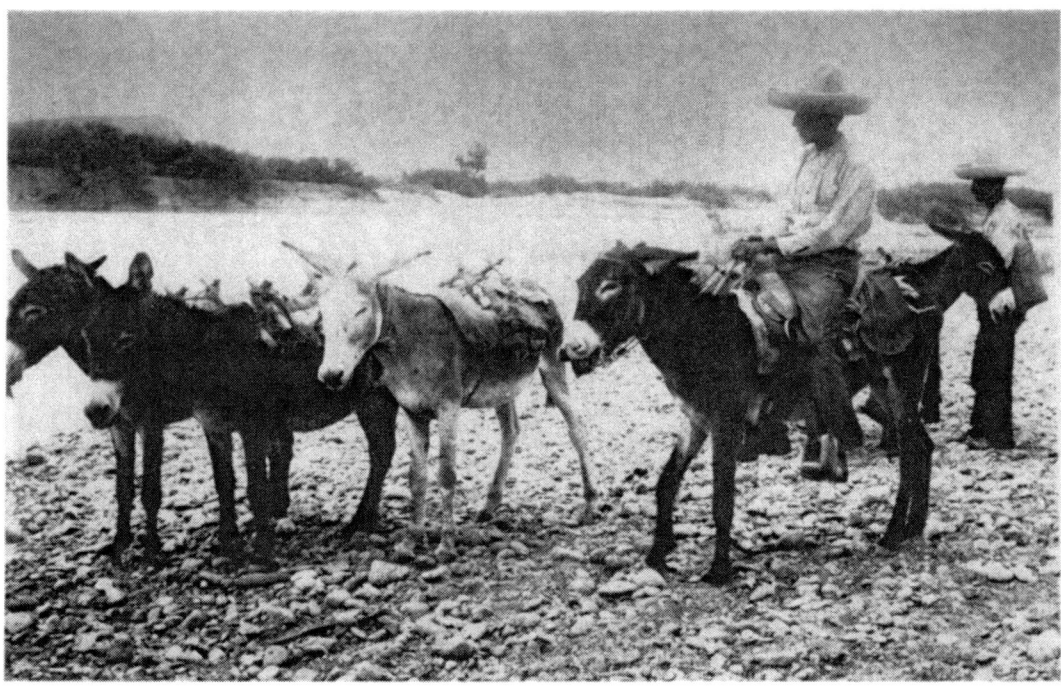

was little fretting when they had to do without a needed item; they d
get it later.

The women and children had important roles in the trader business too, although they usually did not do the actual dealing. The
bulk of what the family had to sell—woolen blankets, rugs, saddle
blankets, trinkets—was made not by the father, but by his wife and
children. His job was to shear the sheep. The women and girls washed
the wool and dyed it and spun and wove it into cloth. The men did
make rope from lechuguilla fiber, and gathered sotol and other plants
from which the women wove mats, bags, and baskets.

Finished clothes seldom were traded in the Big Bend Mexican
families, since the mothers made their daughters' clothes and the
younger boys got hand-me-downs from their older brothers. Some of
those boys' shirts and pants had so many patches that it was hard to
tell which part was the original cloth, but the garments were always
clean. Shoes were bought for the women and girls, but the men and
boys wore sandals made from pieces of auto tire and strips of tanned
goat or deer hide. When a discarded tire was found, it was split up
among friends to be made into several pairs of sandals.

The trading activity was just one indicator of the busy family life
in the Big Bend. Gardening and irrigating were important as well to
support fruit and vegetable patches and small fields of corn and
beans. Livestock, too, required tending, for it was the goats, chick-
ens, and sometimes catfish that provided protein at mealtime. When
a deer was killed, there was meat enough for a family to share with
several friends.

Bread was made for almost every meal. Corn, boiled with a bit of
lime or ashes, was ground on a curved stone (metate) into a dough
for tortillas.

In the hot months, venison and cabrito were cut into thin strips
and dried in the sun. It was tasty uncooked—jerky—but much better
when boiled with vegetables. Deer hides were not for sale at the trading post, or anywhere else, as Texas law was very strict about selling
or buying any part of a deer. Goat hides, though, were sold at an
average of twenty-five cents each—a substantial portion of a family's
income when many hides were purchased. One of the few luxuries af-
forded was tobacco for cigarettes, which most men and women
smoked. The most popular brand was Lobo Negro ("Black Wolf"),
and the strong, dark weed was sold in small five-cent bags.

There was always a bit of lively bargaining going on in the trading
posts at Lajitas, Castolon, Grady and Williams, 120 miles south of
Alpine, and at the Johnson ranch. The owner appraised the items

that the shopper—usually a matron, since the woman knew her family's needs best—had brought in to sell, and both would agree on a final value for the goods. The dickering usually was friendly, no one trying to cheat the other person. Sometimes, besides the hides and furs, the families brought hand-woven goods, including ropes and bags made of lechuguilla fiber. If salable goods were lacking, a family would have to sacrifice some livestock to buy what it needed for the trading post.

The selection of groceries available at a typical trading post was impressive: a variety of coffee beans, sugars, dried peaches, apples, and prunes and several kinds of flours and candies.

During my long visits to the Johnsons' ranch, I often served as their storekeeper when a shopper came in. If he had only a few goat hides to sell, I paid the usual twenty-five cents for each. But if the customer had furs, saddle blankets, or other items to sell, I called in either Ada or Elmo Johnson to make the deal. A trading post was a perfect place to learn much about the native peoples' habits, abilities, and personalities, and I was quite impressed with the caliber of person I encountered there.

The Mexicans, mostly illiterate, were whizzes at arithmetic. While the trading-post manager was laboriously figuring the sum of their purchases, the Mexicans kept a mental tally of their expenditures. Computing various quantities of differently priced groceries is not easy, but the shoppers always matched totals with the traders. Indeed, some of my first friendships with those living on the Mexican side were made in the trading posts and, during the early days of prohibition, when every stranger in the Big Bend was mistrusted, these friends were helpful to me.

Alejandro Domingues was one of the first Mexicans to offer friendship, and through him I met many others. On our first or second meeting, he told me that he and his friends had noted the fact that I was always alone, and that I never carried a gun. Still, the popular suspicion was that I was an informer for the Texas Rangers or U. S. Customs, or that I was some sort of prohibition officer.

Not until I had made several trips from San Antonio to the Big Bend was I trusted by the local people. The credibility I finally had achieved was threatened when I started filing stories with the *San Antonio Light*, 350 miles away, by carrier pigeon. The people of the Big Bend thought I was sending intelligence about smuggling to the authorities. I finally was "cleared" when Wayne Cartledge, owner of the Castolon Trading Post, read aloud my news story in Spanish before releasing the bird. One pigeon, shortly before this episode, had

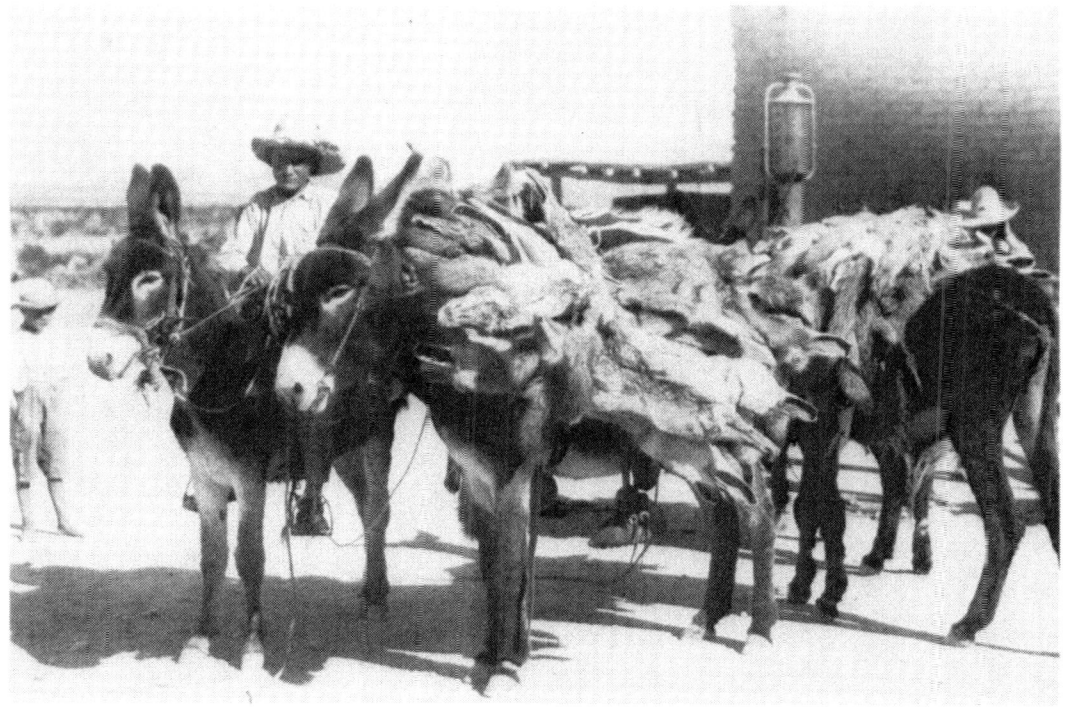

Elmo Johnson bought furs from neighboring families (above), providing them a source of income during the winter months. At his trading post, he also bought furs from Mexican traders (below). The trader's merchandise usually was obtained from families living too far from trading posts to bring it in themselves. Johnson, who was fair, paid from forty to seventy-five cents per fur.

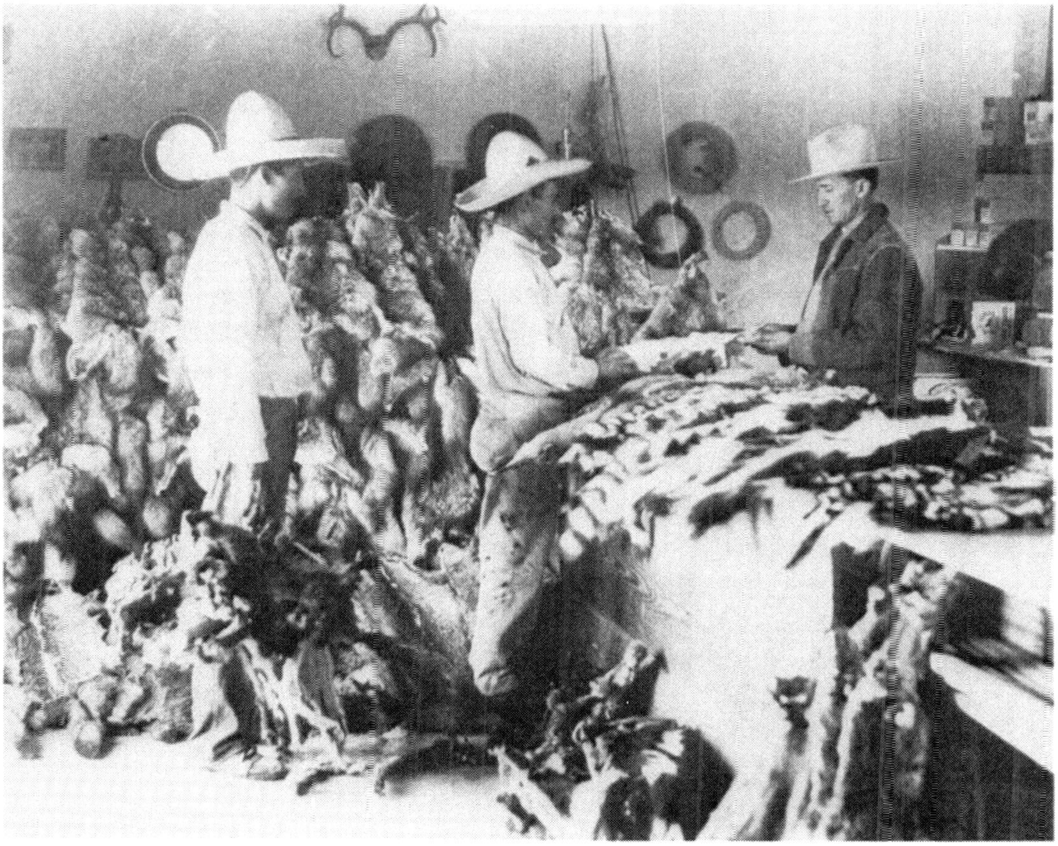

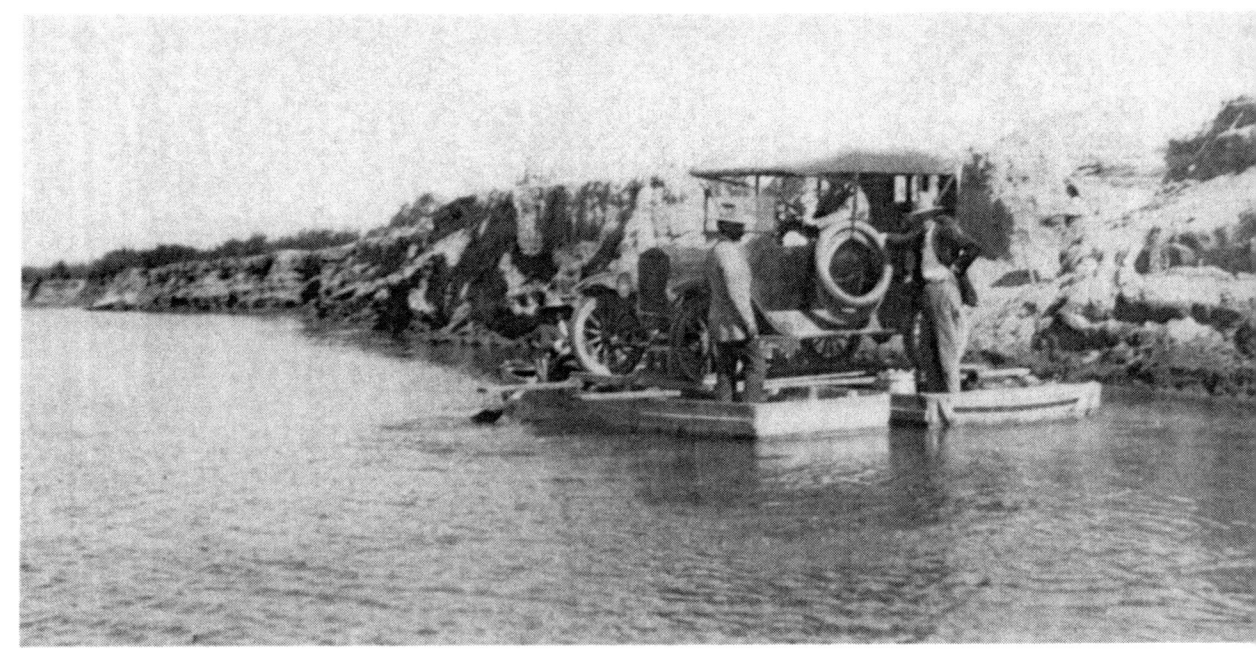

Above, the ferry at Lajitas, 1916-1920. Below, clusters of candelilla wax plants, in foreground.

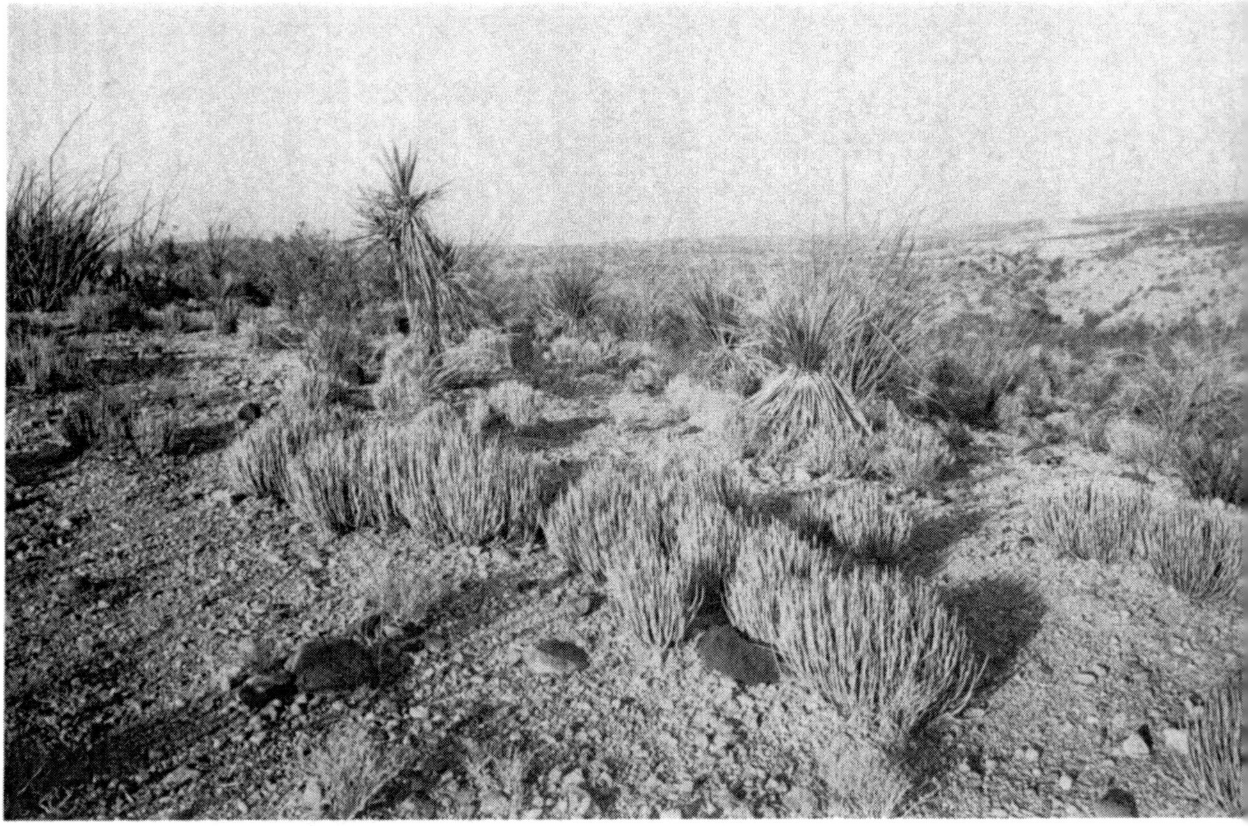

set a record for carrying the longest story—a full 8½ x 11-inch page—although he took 10 hours and 15 minutes to get to San Antonio, by no means a speed record. I could certainly understand the Mexicans' suspicions toward the carrier pigeons, for their experience with them was limited. Perhaps that system seemed as mysterious to them as avisos did to me. The pigeon-carried stories were a popular feature in the newspaper, reporting all sorts of news from the Big Bend, and specially tagged, on the front page, with "Special by Carrier Pigeon." The birds sometimes were pictured alongside the articles.

So I visited my good friend Alejandro Domingues and his family for a long while after my yellow jaundice cure. I enjoyed bringing gifts to them all, especially tablets and pencils and earrings for the girls. Mrs. Domingues most appreciated kitchen gadgets—wire strainers, graters, or large wooden spoons and forks. The grater was particularly helpful in making cheese, as they did, from goat's milk.

Nor did I forget my American friends when I made these regular trips to the Big Bend from San Antonio. The most cherished items I could bring them were issues of the San Antonio papers and the *Alpine Avalanche*. No one had radios in the Big Bend until 1929 and, even then, the only stations they could get were in Juarez and Del Rio. They were fairly starved for news.

My two-week stays in the Big Bend varied, of course, but I always tried to see familiar sights and friends. After leaving Alpine, I would usually go to the Domingues home. I stayed only a day or two, to their disappointment, but we made the most of our time together. As I had done during the last days of my convalescence from jaundice, I took Juanita, Jose, and Maria to see the Garcia children on the Grady and Williams farm. I'm sure that part of the thrill for the Domingues children was riding in my Dodge, the only car they ever had been near. While the children of the two families played, I spent about an hour at the trading post. Once I was through with my business, we headed for the Holguin home, for more relaxed visiting.

I loved the children as photo subjects—and they loved to receive pictures of themselves. It was a real delight to give the parents photographs of their sons and daughters cuddling a favorite pet goat, burro, or puppy. Before I built my darkroom at the Johnson ranch, the families would have to wait a month to get their photographs—a month of excitement, waiting to see what *el fotógrafo* had taken with his camera. Today there are several Mexican men and women living in Alpine, Texas, whose children are older than they were in the early twenties when I made photographs of them.

From 1915 to 1920, Captain C. D. Wood had a candelilla wax

factory (where wax was made from candelilla plants [*Euphorbia antisyphilitica*] growing all over the Big Bend) that I liked to visit. Wax-making was a profitable business, the substance selling for eighteen to twenty-five cents a pound up to 1920. Workers in Wood's factory were paid a dollar a day, about standard for the Big Bend. Candelilla plants were bought from Mexicans who also had large wagons needed to haul them—fifty thousand plants for one thousand pounds of wax—to the factory.

They were paid $2.50 per ton for the plants, and three men were needed in the operation of gathering, loading, and unloading the candelilla. The man who owned the wagon could clear about $5.00 per day, after his investment in the wagon, two helpers, and a team of mules.

Tom Miller (Uncle Tom) and his son, Ray, had a home and a small farm at San Vicente, where I always stopped on my trips. Pioneers of the Big Bend, both men knew the area better than anyone else. Several times during my monthly trips, Sam Woolford, an editor of the *San Antonio Light,* spend his two-week vacation at the Millers' with me. Sam eventually bought Uncle Tom's farm and home and allowed his friend Tom to stay on. I believe that Sam intended to live there after retirement but, when the Big Bend National Park was created, everyone had to move out.

After spending the night with the Millers, my next short stop was Hot Springs, where the Langford family ran a small trading post and operated the local mineral baths. The baths attracted a lot of people, from across Texas and from other states, hoping to cure arthritis and other bodily ailments. Other hot springs I knew of were at Ruidosa and Sierra Blanca, Texas, and at San Antonio de Bravo, in Chihuahua. The water from these hot springs was used for both drinking and bathing.

Between stops, I passed by many cave areas, where primitives had lived, with petroglyphs etched on cave and canyon walls as the only evidence of their once-exclusive presence.

From Hot Springs it was a slow ten miles to Boquillas, with two stops between—Ogles, with a small hot spring, and Graham's, the 1916 location of Jessie Deemer's trading post. As a rule, only an hour stop was allowed at Hot Springs, Ogles, and Graham's, to give friends in each place a loaf of bakery bread and tell them the news from the outside world.

The last four miles from Graham's to Boquillas was nothing but a rough gravel road over sandy stretches and a few hills. At many

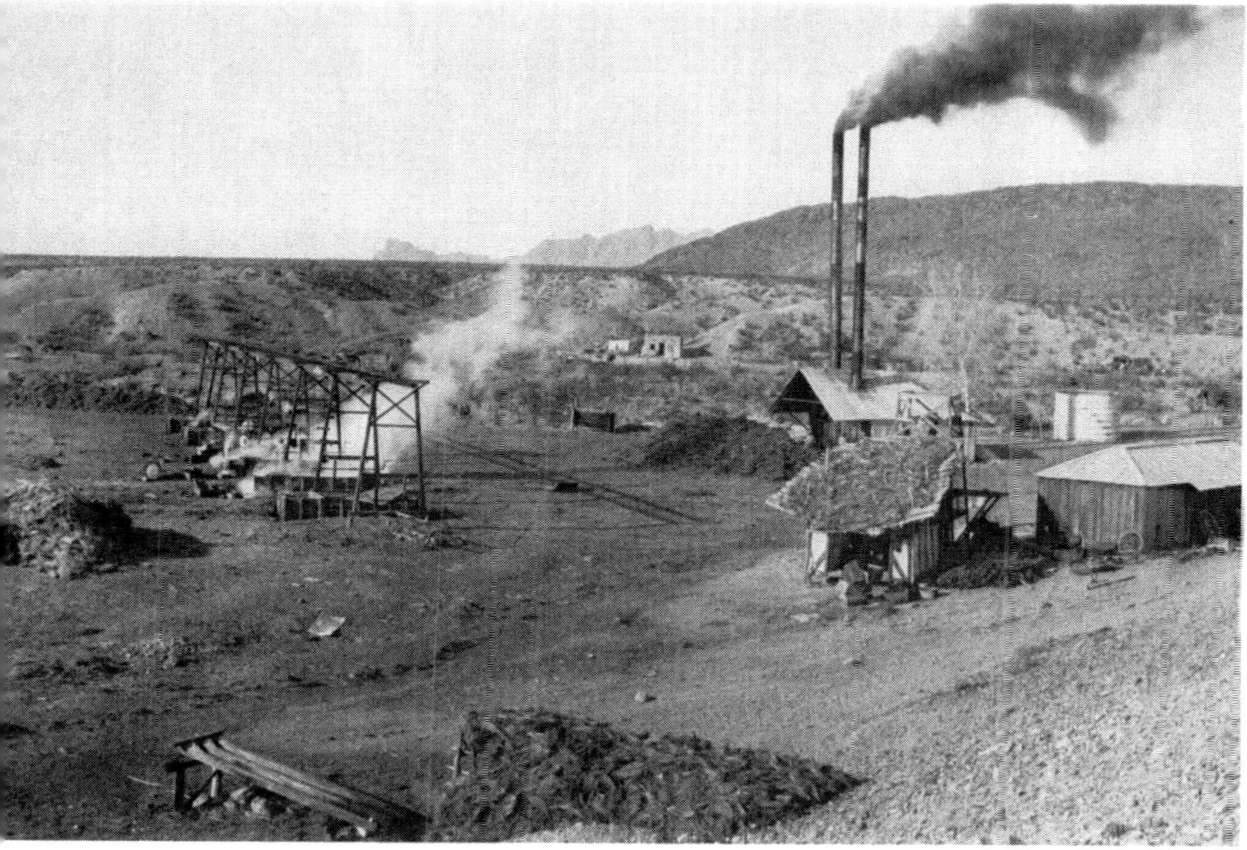

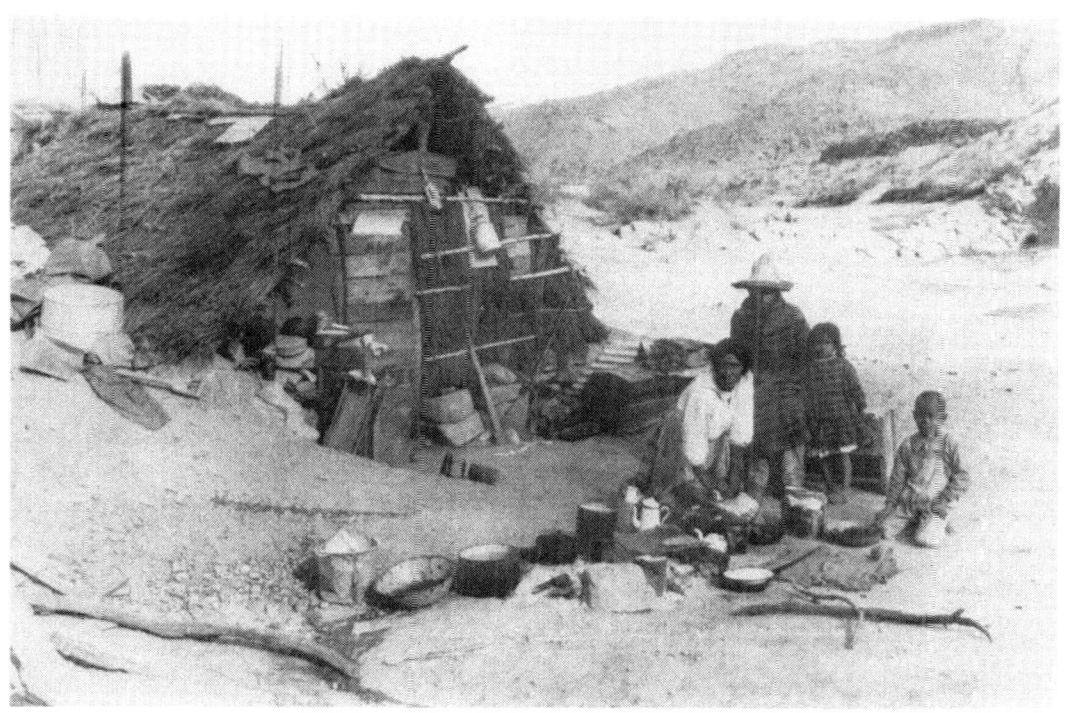

Captain C. D. Wood's candelilla wax factory at Glenn Springs (above), 1916-1917. Below, husband and children wait for their morning meal, which included tortillas. The man was an expert wax maker at the Glenn Springs factory in 1917 and had made the house of candelilla plants in a dugout in the side of the hill.

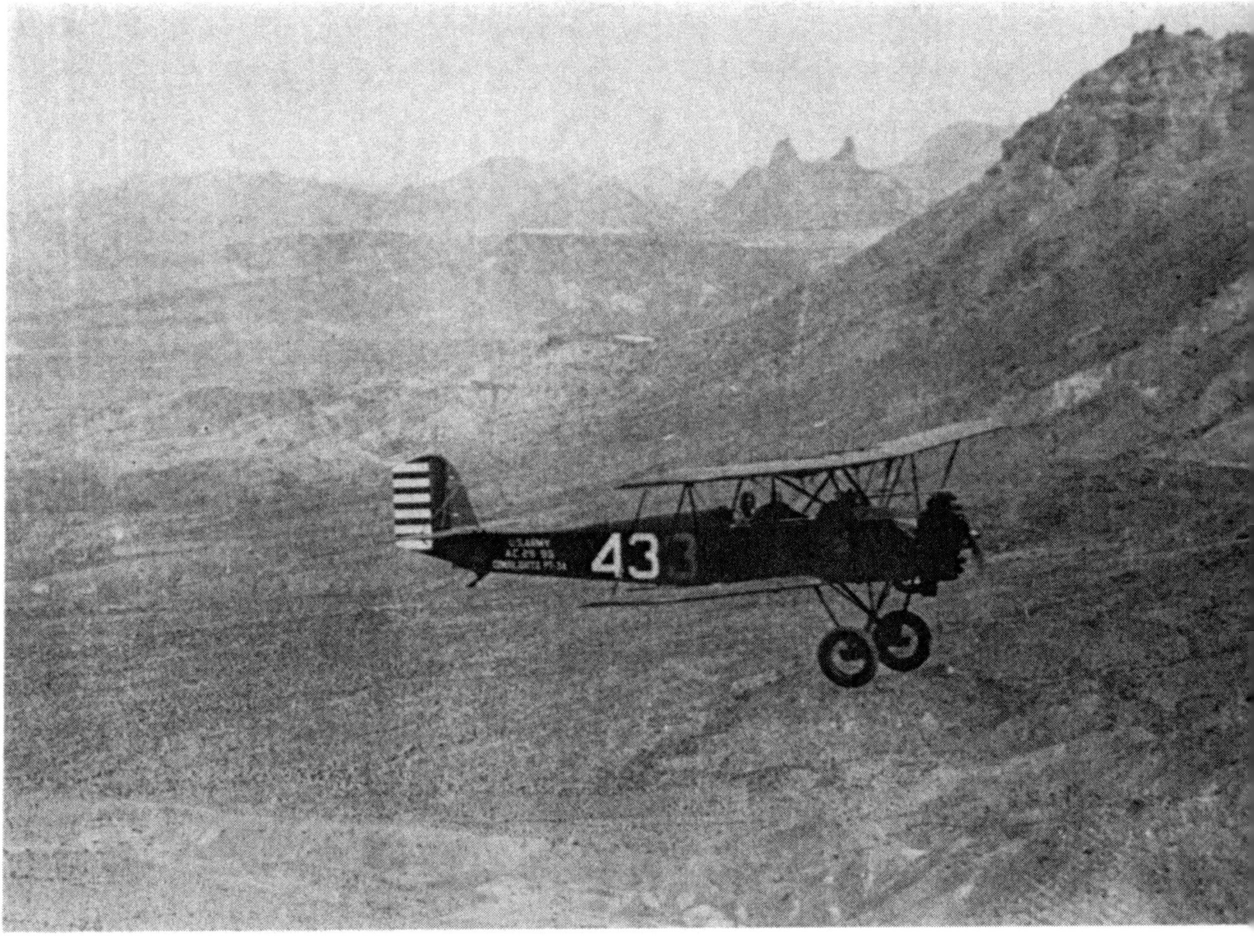

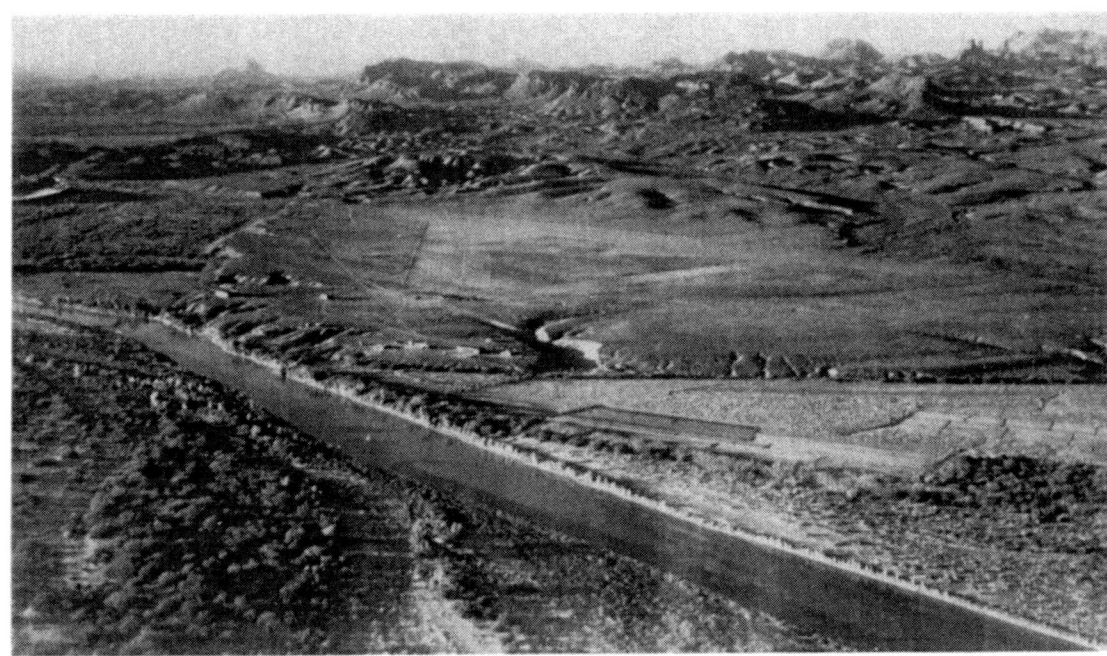

A P. T. plane flies over the Big Bend (above). Below, the Johnson Air Field is seen just above the small cluster of buildings at the left center, including my darkroom, the smallest structure on the right. Lying between the mountains of the Rio Grande, Johnson's was one of the more spectacular landing fields.

points, this leg was scenic, especially in view of the Sierra del Carmen.

The village of Boquillas, Texas, was at the end of the rough road. About a mile down the Rio Grande from the two villages is the huge Boquillas Canyon, its walls extending for many miles between Mexico and Texas. Both villages were called Boquillas. In the pre-twenties, the Texas Boquillas was the larger of the two, and an important connection in local silver distribution, but it now is gone, having been replaced by a trailer park called Boquillas Village.

In 1927, Juan and Chata Sada and their children were one of only two families in Boquillas, Texas. Chata's name actually was Maria, but since girlhood she had been called Chata, which means "Pugnose." She had no children of her own, but for several years had adopted numerous children, most of them becoming American citizens. Eventually Juan and Chata opened a trading post at Boquillas, as the town became bigger and developed in importance as a connection point in the Big Bend. As Juan also ran a small silver mine in Boquillas, Coahuila, he was at the trading post only at night. Chata became famous for the meals she fixed for travelers, and her hospitality was a real relief from the rigors of the road. It seemed that the people who traveled the Big Bend in the twenties did so for a definite purpose—people from the International Boundary Commission, geologists, prospectors, naturalists (several rare-bird and mammal species are found in the area). All were prepared to rough it—fixing their own meals and sleeping on the ground in bedrolls—so you can see that Chata's simple accommodations and wonderful meals were welcome delights for such folk.

Juan was not a bootlegger or liquor smuggler, but he always had a small supply of Mexican liquors and beer. Chata had a kerosene refrigerator from which Sam and I enjoyed a few cold ones before her wonderful dinner. The Sadas treated all travelers royally, and they both spoke enough English to pass on lots of news about the latest developements in the area. A stop at their trading post was a real treat.

Away from the comforts and profits of my commercial photography in San Antonio and amid the hardships of those trips in the Big Bend, I never thought of discontinuing them. The trips never were rigorously scheduled; I just arranged them so they would not conflict with other assignments, such as aerial photography and various picture stories I did on traveling circuses. I just did not let other commitments hassle me when I was in the Big Bend—a relaxed attitude I learned from the Mexicans.

The commercial end of my photography business in San Antonio undoubtedly suffered when I was away on these excursions. Several other good photographers in town took business away from me, but I wasn't too concerned. Had I stayed and tended my shop at all times, I would have made more money. Somehow the trips seemed more important, and apparently my instincts were correct: I left San Antonio and moved to the Big Bend in 1929.

In July of 1929 an air field in the Big Bend seemed essential as the Mexican Escobar Revolution became more threatening to the border area. If nothing else, the mere presence of an air field would serve to deter invaders.

Selfishly, I had always wanted an air field so that aerial photography of the Bend would be possible. When I approached Elmo Johnson about such a project, he offered, without hesitation, as much of his ranch land as was needed.

I then went to see Colonel Fisher in the Fort Sam Houston Quadrangle and showed him how ideally the Johnson ranch was situated for an air field. He listened to my pitch, then asked, "How did you know that Washington wants a landing field in the Big Bend?" Of course I did not; the idea just seemed right. We discussed it further, joined by First Lieutenant Thad Foster, who was in charge of all landing fields in the Eighth Corps Area. The lieutenant and I were flown to the army air field at Dryden, twenty miles east of Sanderson. From there the sergeant in charge of the Dryden facility and I went by truck to the Johnson ranch (it was during this trip that my first home-made camera was crushed when it fell out of the vehicle).

Once at the landing site, we had only a few hours to prepare a strip for Lieutenant Foster's air arrival from Dryden. Clearing the area of rocks and clusters of pitahaya cactus, we set about constructing the "airport." With lime we marked a large arrowed "N" on the ground. Johnson's road grader was used to clear the greasewood bushes from a long strip for the runway. I put up a wind sock. High above, we heard the plane and set off two smoke canisters so that Foster could see the strip. We stood ready for refueling.

After landing, Foster said he had seen the large tin roof of the Johnson's house before he saw the smoke. He was delighted with the location and the serviceability of the field—and had the lease agreement in his hands. The army was to pay Elmo Johnson one dollar per year for the land.

Two weeks later, two Douglas transport planes carrying twelve infantry soldiers and full equipment loads landed at the Johnson field. Two enlisted radiomen soon were stationed there full time.

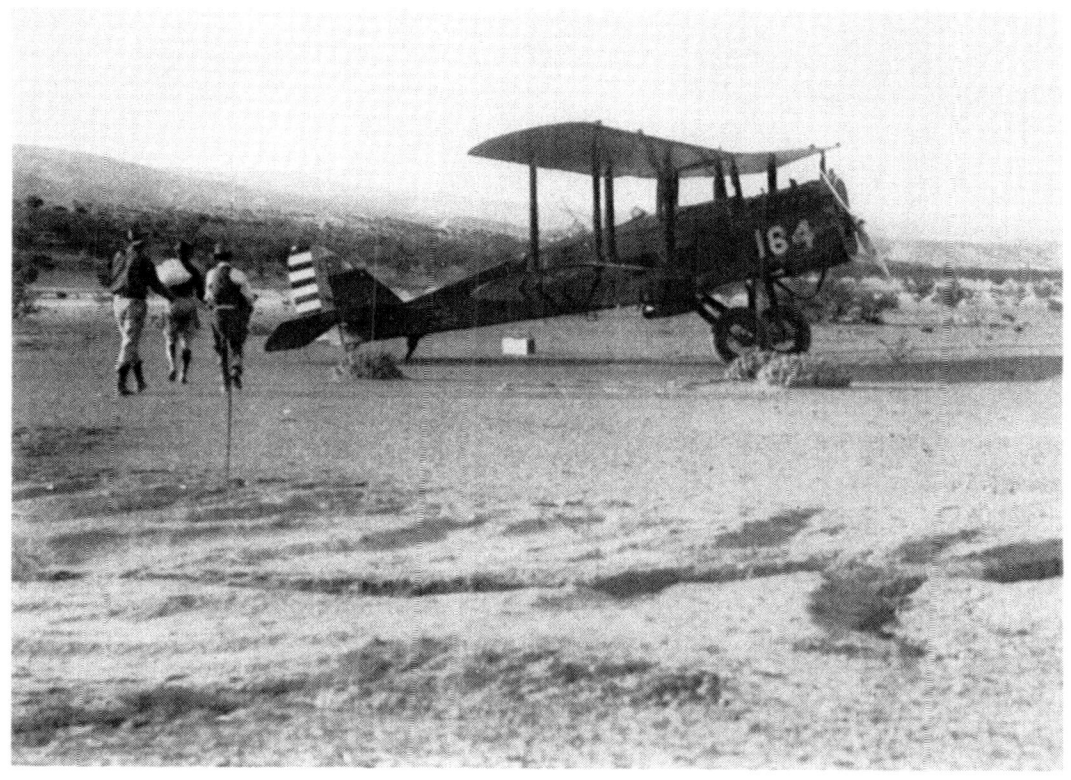

The first plane, a DeHavilland, to land at Johnson Field (above), is readied at San Vicente. Below, a plane is refueled at Johnson Field. Elmo Johnson stands over the fifty-five-gallon drum of gasoline.

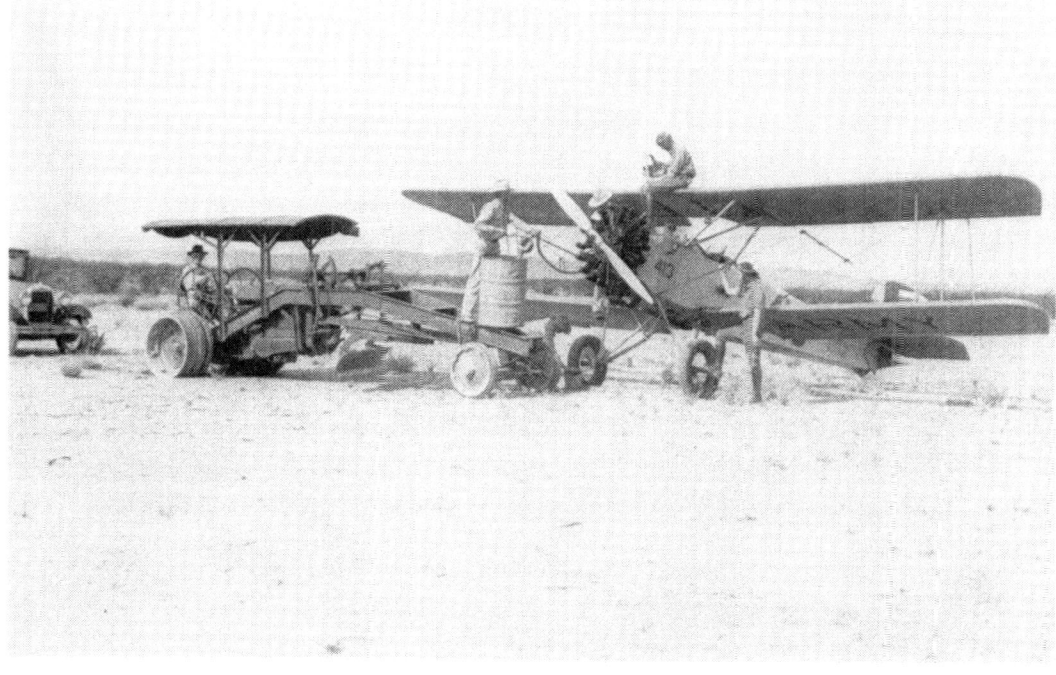

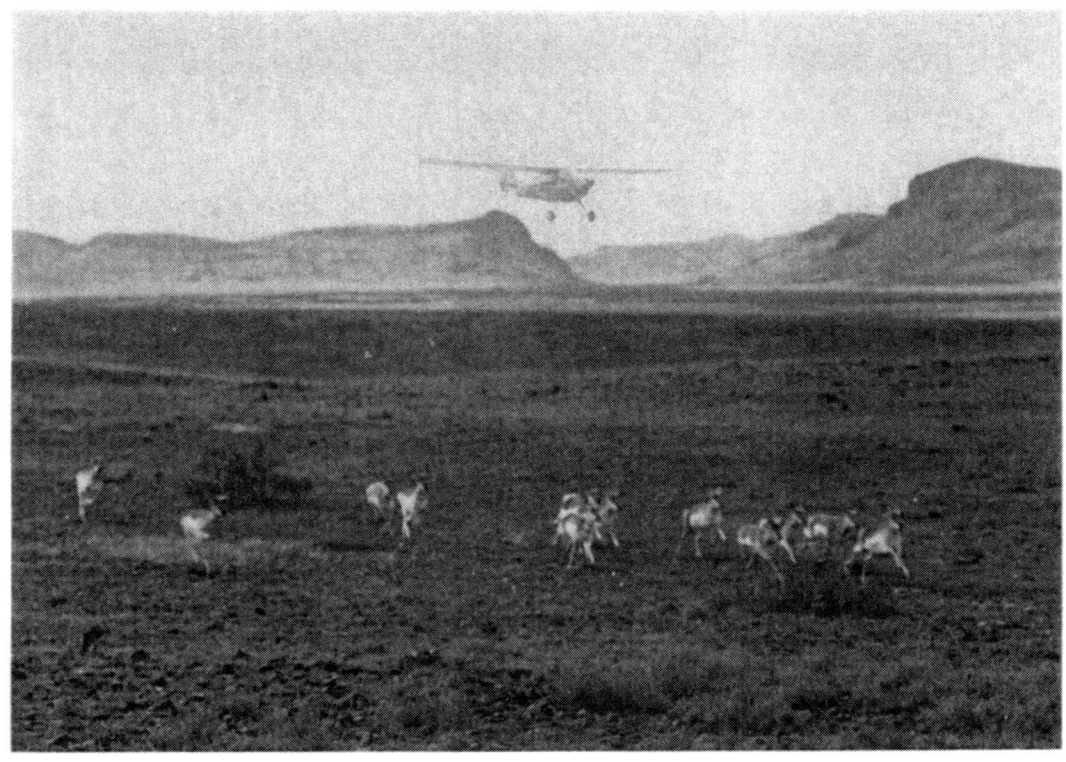

An airplane antelope roundup is seen above. Before ranchmen in the Big Bend engaged J. O. Casparis to shoot eagles from his plane there were few antelope. After he was through, the antelope population increased so much that many of the animals had to be shipped to other parts of the state. Here pilot Casparis drives the antelope into a trap. Below, two Douglas planes, part of the Texas National Guard, at Johnson Field.

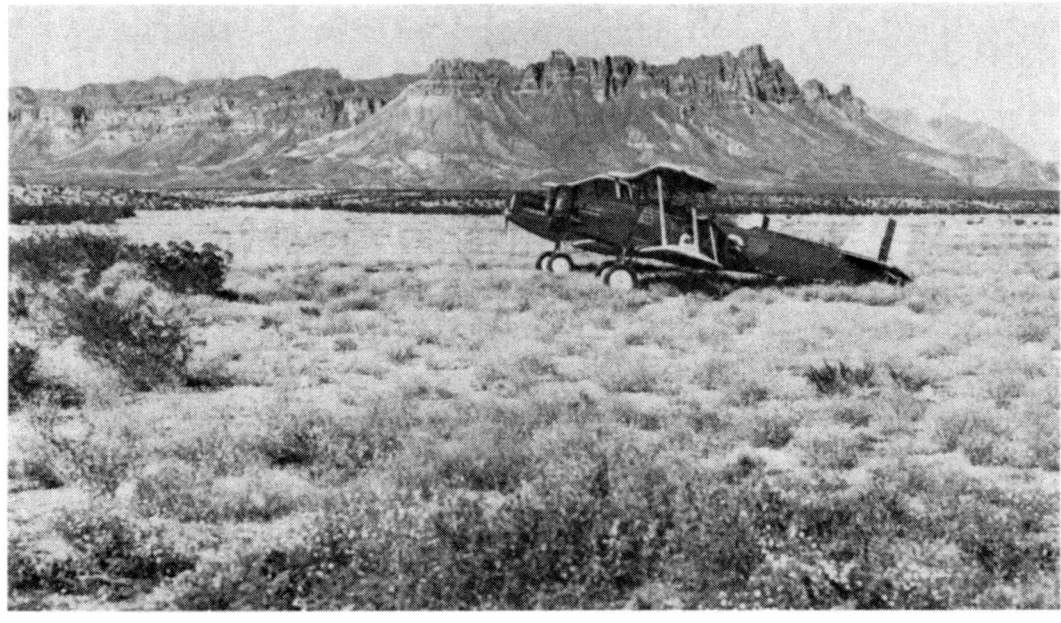

The field never was needed for border battle, but there is no doubt that it prevented incidents; it signaled to troublemakers the army's new capacities. Douglas attack planes made frequent flights from Galveston to the Johnson field, training for cross-country flights while practicing aerial gunnery. Each attack plane carried three fifty-caliber machine guns—two in front, and one in the rear. Shooting at oil drums and flying low, the planes and their fierce potential must have been the subject of many avisos, intelligence flashed to any would-be invaders on the other side of the border.

From 1929 until 1944, when the Big Bend National Park took control of all land in the area and closed it, Johnson Field was a popular place. (The Johnsons, like others, had been able to keep their land in 1933, when the area was designated Texas Canyons State Park.) The peak of activity was in the thirties, with planes in and out every day of the week.

Often some of the Brooks and Kelly Field instructors made flights with new cadets, and Johnson Field was perfect for these tests. They would arrive in late morning, chat and lunch with the Johnsons, then return to their home fields. Ada and Elmo encouraged these visits, and were always the most gracious hosts, issuing standing invitations to flyers to share meals with them, stay over weekends, and drink a toast or two. During Prohibition, the flyers agreed never to transport sotol or any other liquor from the air field.

In 1934 I renewed acquaintance with Lieutenant Nathan F. Twining, whom I had known in 1927 at Kelly Field. In late 1933, he was transferred to the Third Attack Group and made his first trip to the Johnsons' on December 8. His name is registered in the large book we kept in the patio. Twenty-five years later Twining was chairman of the Joint Chiefs of Staff, a four-star general. In 1958 I mailed him pictures of all the pages in the registry book with his signature, and he wrote back a wonderful letter recalling all the good times he and the other flyers had had at Johnson Field. He closed with, "I hope some day to go back and see the Big Bend National Park. It must be a very beautiful place."

When the field was closed in 1944, a way of life for the Johnsons came to an end, and a new era for the Big Bend began.

9

El Fotógrafo

I don't think a Kodak Instamatic could have survived the conditions my cameras endured. Fierce winds, the rigors of pack training, and the Big Bend heat demanded that my equipment be as tough as possible. Commercial equipment was hard to come by in the early 1900s in the Big Bend, and I had to have lightweight cameras that were easy to handle, packable, sturdy without tripod, and, especially, adaptable. Clearly, such a camera would have to be custom designed; so, just as I made my own enlargers, I constructed my first camera in 1913. To withstand the high winds during aerial photography, I used a wooden cone rather than a bellows. The focal-plane-shutter camera I made used 5 x 7-inch glass negatives. In 1930 I made a second camera from two wooden apple boxes that used 4 x 5, 3¼ x 5½, and 4¼ x 6½-inch film packs. I used this one until 1948. That's when I was given the commercially made Printex camera—developed by a manufacturer in Pasadena, California, from my own design.

After 1929, I used few glass negatives; they were too bulky and fragile. Kodak film packs were perfect for a roving photographer. I also mixed my own flash powder—an explosive combination of chlorate and magnesium—and set up darkroom equipment in my kitchen, to be used before dawn, or under the ground. Once, with the help of a construction worker from the McDonald Observatory project, I excavated a gravel pit to make such a darkroom. We straightened the walls, set in flooring, and installed a roof. Chemical trays were made by lining narrow wooden boxes with oil cloth. (In Mexico, I used *cazuelas* for my chemicals.) For enlarging, I cut a system of sun vents into the roof when electricity was not available. But I was trained to develop in total darkness, so the lack of light was not so much of a handicap. Even with the development of orthochromatic film, which can be used with red illumination, I preferred a lightless darkroom.

The subterranean darkrooms are among the largest, most efficient I have ever worked in, and were particularly good for making oversized enlargements.

There were hazards with such "tombs" of course. Most of the negatives I made at the Johnsons', including the wildlife series, were destroyed by rain seepage through the thatched roof. Otherwise, my dugouts were just about perfect, being impregnable to light, and you can imagine how my going into the earth enhanced my role as the local, enigmatic *fotografo*. More reliable, though, were my predawn kitchens, conveniently equipped with sink and water supply.

I did a lot of film developing on the road and I was able to improvise acceptable, though far from ideal, darkrooms in various Texas and Mexican inns. Harnessmaker's thread was strung across those rooms for drying negatives.

When I was doing the wildlife photographs, I needed to devise a way to cause the animals to trip the camera shutter, and this was accomplished quite easily. I connected the concealed camera to a covered wooden flash pan, which was lined with tin. When an animal disturbed the bait, the flash powder ignited, the pan's lid flew up, the shutter tripped, and the exposure was made. This device was even used once to nab watermelon and egg thieves on the Johnson ranch.

I didn't make all of my equipment. I owned a 120 folding Eastman camera in 1912 that was well-suited for packing. In 1916 I bought an 8 x 10 Eastman viewing camera with a tripod, and in 1921 and 1922, while running the photography shop in San Antonio, I bought over $1,000 worth of lenses, cameras, and other necessities.

For much of my livelihood, I devised all sorts of schemes for commercial photography. Back in El Paso for my long border assignment in 1935, I interested two Border Patrolmen in photography, and they helped me develop the many photographs from the trip. For their assistance, I made them a set-focus camera for making identification pictures of aliens and another for copying fingerprint cards.

On one occasion in the Big Bend, I got into a dispute that provoked me into what might be called "social" photography. In 1923, I went to Terlingua, hoping to photograph the quicksilver mining operations. But no sooner had I arrived than the mine owner, Howard Perry, and his manager, Bob Cartledge, ordered me not only out of the village, but also out of the entire lower Big Bend. They apparent-were afraid of the negative publicity that photographs of the miners' working conditions might generate. Since Perry owned Terlingua, I did leave, but camped nearby, used country roads, and took as many photos of the mining operations as I could.

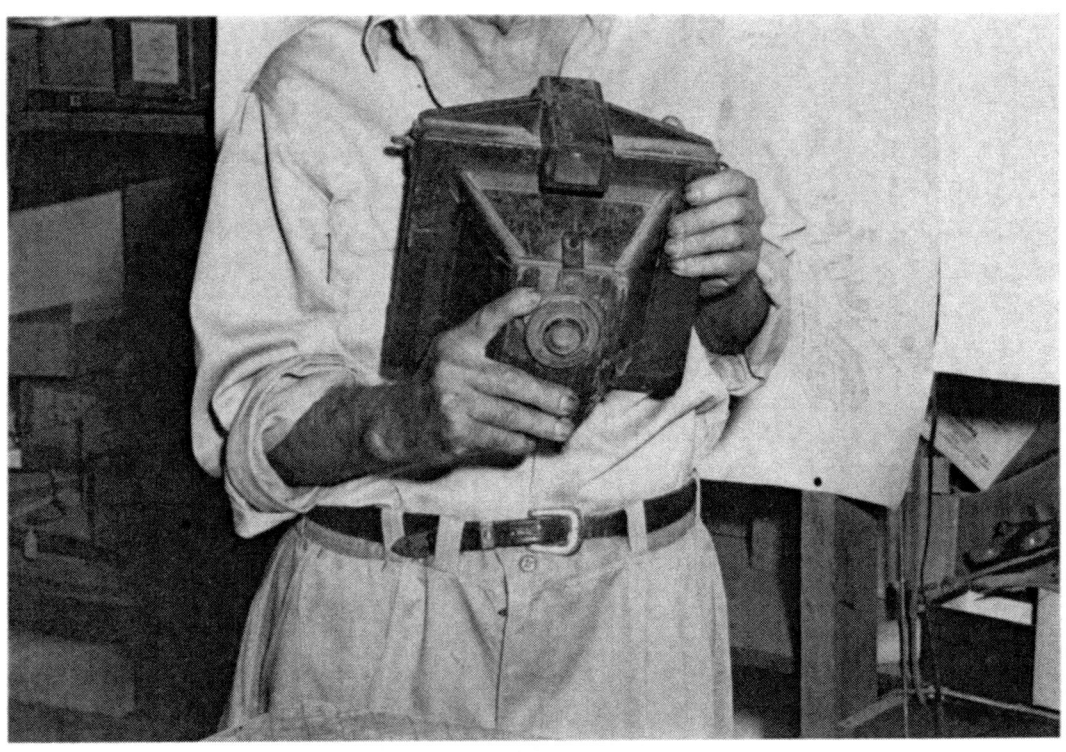

Above, a homemade beauty I used from 1929 until 1950. Below, an overnight camp. By igniting flashpowder on a sheet of paper, I got this whole scene near Mule Ear Mountain.

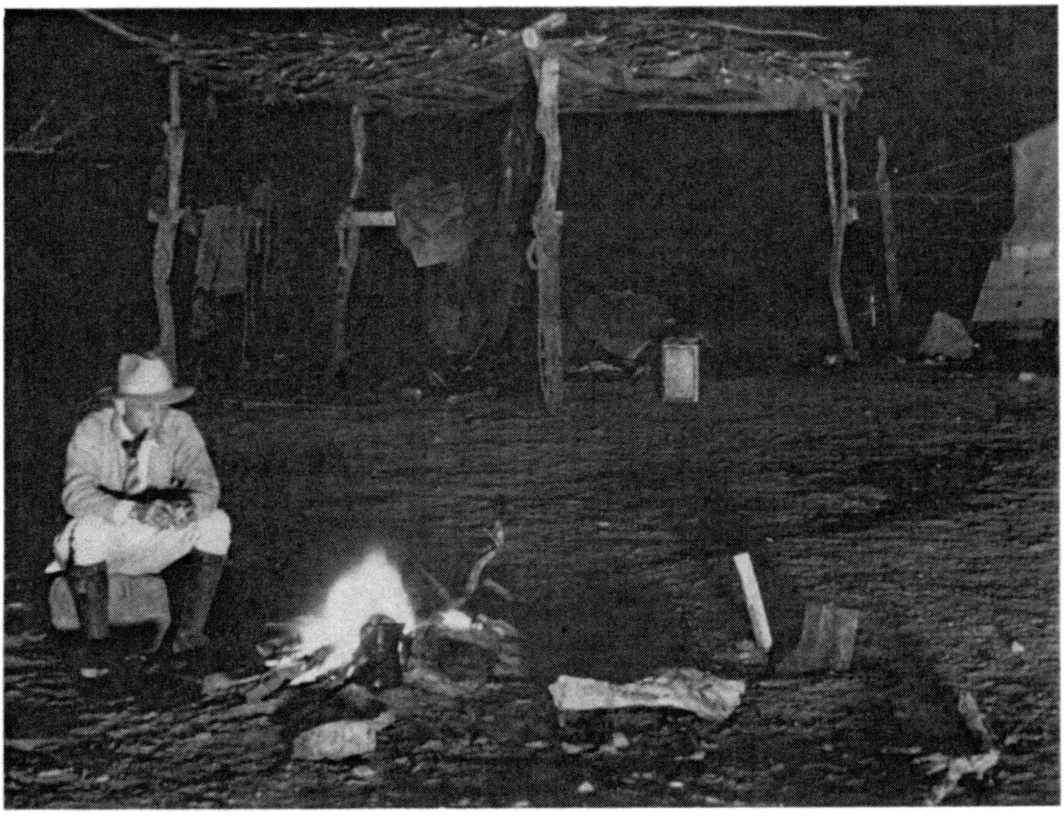

After the border assignment, I stayed in El Paso until August, 1936, then moved to Alpine and opened a photography shop. A year prior to this move, I began to receive letters from Dr. Herman Frick, a professor of religion at a German university who had located me through the National Geographic Society. He was studying religious customs of Mexicans and wanted me to be his guide into the country. The trip lasted eight days and, besides being his tour guide and instructor, I was his photographer. He bought, as research materials, 1,500 lantern slides and 1,000 7 x 11-inch enlargements of Mexican scenes from me. With Dr. Frick's research completed, I went back to Alpine to pursue my business interests seriously. I even got rid of my car to avoid the temptation to travel.

Since 1922 I had made "magic lantern slides," as I called them, for profit, and now, in 1936, I began to manufacture them in greater quantities and with much success. Color photography had not yet developed, and I made the lantern slides from black and white negatives on 3¼ x 4-inch glass plates, then colored each slide by hand. Most were of Mexican scenes—people, churches, historical sites—and I packaged one hundred of them to a wooden box. My customers were university professors throughout the country, who paid fifty dollars for the box. Mine was a rather bold direct-mail technique. I would send a box of slides to a professor for his or her viewing. I trusted the recipient to send payment if he liked the slides, otherwise to return the merchandise, express collect. Not a single order was ever returned.

Living in Alpine, I set myself up as a postcard manufacturer and became a booming regional success. Using pictures I had made in Texas, Mexico, New Mexico, and Arizona, I produced two thousand cards in an eighteen-hour period. Twenty cards, squeegeed onto an eighteen by twenty-four-inch ferrotype tin, dried in one hour. I had twenty of those tins, so my hourly rate was about four hundred cards. While I slept—for I had printed the cards into the late hours—the cards would dry and usually pop off the tins. When the noise woke me, I would gather up the dry cards and replace them with wet ones. My price to dealers was fifteen dollars per thousand.

Earlier, in San Antonio, I got the idea to make photo lamp shades —of translucent picture scenes. The first I made were from glass plates and they were cumbersome: weighty and stiff, requiring a tedious gluing job. It seemed that too much work was expended for too little reward.

But in the late thirties I wrote the Kodak and Defender film companies asking if they could not develop a film on the same order as the glass plates but more workable and lighter. Kodak said no; Defender soon had manufactured for me a film called Adalux, which I used until Kodak developed an improved version, many years later.

With this breakthrough I expanded my lamp-shade operation. The shades were printed in four sections onto a parchment-like material. Each section was colored by hand, then laced on a wire frame. Presto: a nifty lamp shade. Starting with two full-time assistants, I expanded until I had fourteen working for me. My work day began around three in the morning when my kitchen served as the darkroom. There I would print the panels I had cut and laid out with negatives the night before. When employees arrived at eight o'clock, materials for a hundred or more lamp shades were ready to be cut and stitched. We had trouble keeping up with orders, which came not only from around the country, but also from Europe. To meet the demand for the product, I trained interested persons to set up their own lamp-shade operations.

I never applied for a patent, but in 1955 some Arizona people did. They filed a suit against one of my "proteges," seeking to have every photo lamp-shade producer pay them royalties. When the case came up in Phoenix I was a surprise witness, and my testimony of how long I had been making the shades (I even produced a letter from Mrs. Franklin Roosevelt saying how much she liked the shades I had made for her and the President), and how I hadn't applied for a patent because the product was already on the market, caused the plaintiff to lose the case.

I kept my lamp-shade business going—interspersed with various free-lance writing assignments for the *El Paso Herald-Post*, mostly on the Big Bend—until I began the work of compiling my photographic collection for sale.

Even in the twenties, I was never at a loss for work, and Texas was certainly a real place of opportunity. The new movie industry was burgeoning and, as flying became a national interest, Texas grew into a major aviation center. Parts of the film "Wings" were filmed in Texas, and I was hired by the film company to make aerial photographs of the production, and publicity shots of its stars, Clara Bow and Buddy Rogers.

In July, 1926, the director of the film "Rough Riders," Victor Fleming, came to San Antonio to shoot some scenes and commissioned me as his guide and photographer. Camera in hand, I drove him all over: the old fair grounds, the railroad depot, the old market and Hay Plaza, Fort Sam Houston, streets of adobe houses, the hills near Leon Springs. In fact, a Leon Springs hill, stripped of its flora

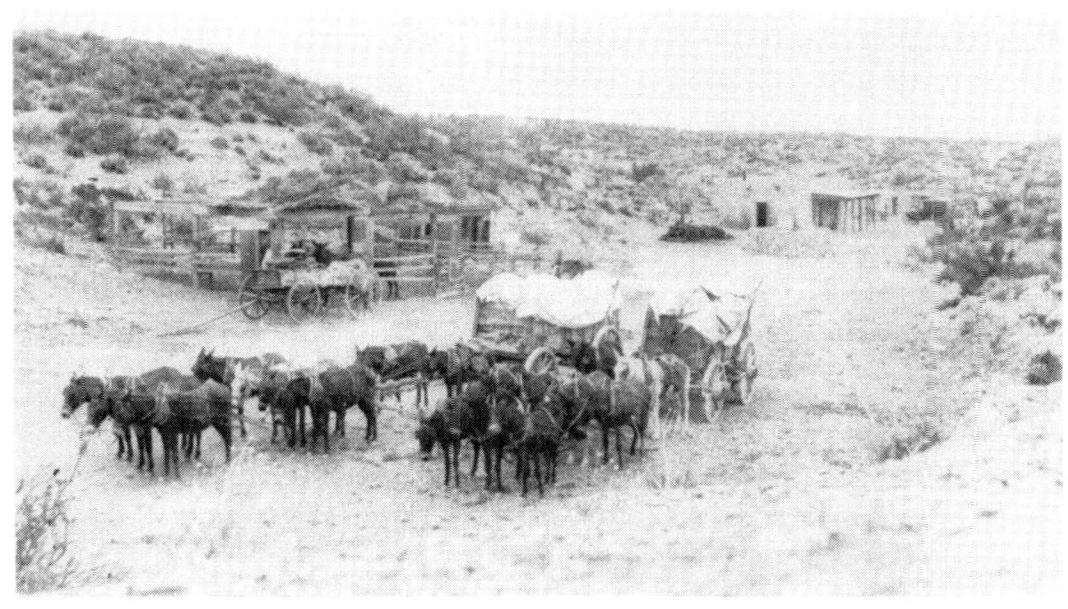

Wagons of supplies, above, arrive for freighters at Waldron Mines near Terlingua. Below, Howard Perry's Chisos quicksilver mine at Terlingua, the largest in the United States. Bottom, a view of Terlingua, showing the miners' homes and, at left, the jail, its door standing open. Most every Saturday night that jail was full.

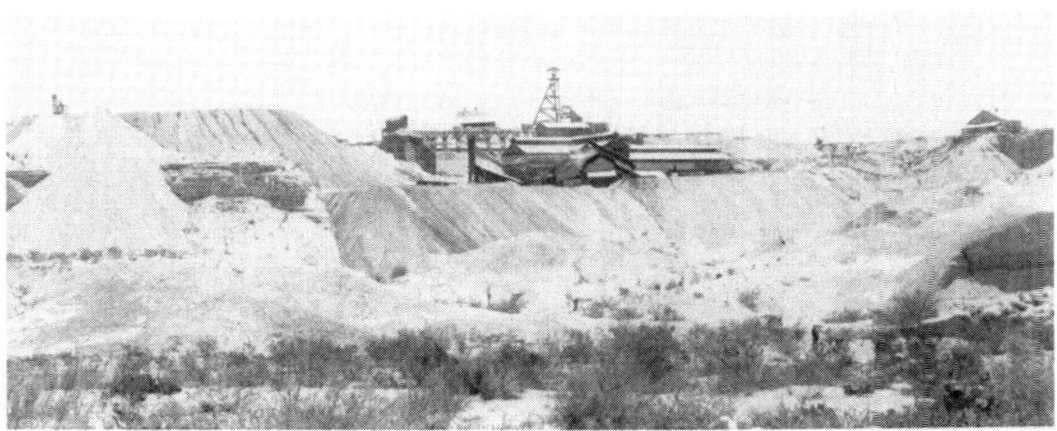

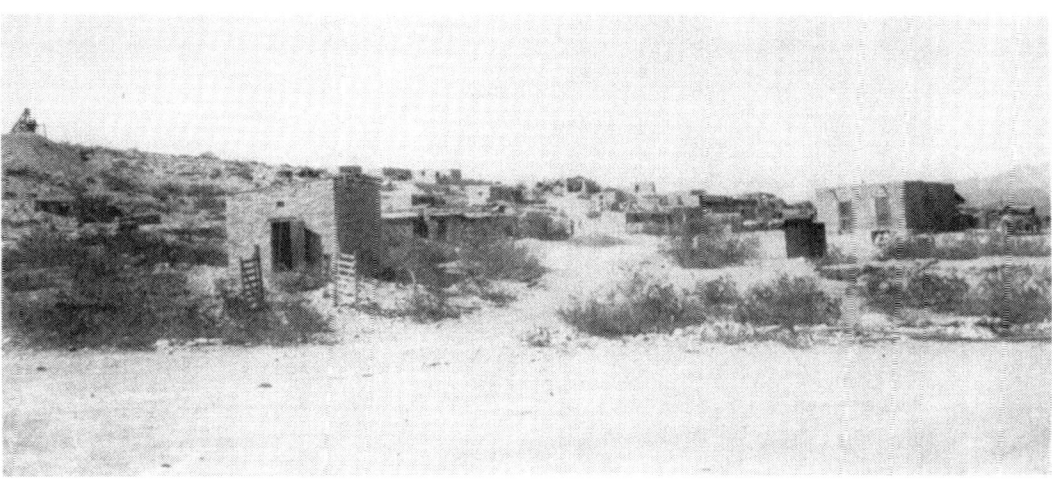

and replanted with banana and palm trees, was used as San Juan Hill in the film. The film starred Mary Astor, Noah Beary, Charles Farrell, and George Bancroft. The Fifth U. S. Cavalry played the Rough Riders.

During the early thirties I was a promoter for Fox News Films and a scout for Fox Movietone. I persuaded local film crews to sell my ideas for news features to their New York editors. I remember one in particular that tickled the editors. The story dealt with how some Texas ranchers were economizing in hard times by working in their formal attire rather than buying new work clothes. Since they could not afford to go to fancy places any more, it seemed thriftier to drive cattle in silks and frock-tail suits rather than in brand-new denims and flannels.

Traveling circuses were a great curiosity to me, and they offered much photographic opportunity. Training through Texas in the twenties were the circuses of Ringling Brothers, Barnum and Bailey, Sells-Floto, Clyde Beaty, the Gentry Brothers, and Hagenbeck Wallace. I followed the colorful, often bizarre circus people around Texas, taking photographs of the acrobats, jugglers, animal trainers, and high-wire artists. They were sure to pay the small prices I asked for large photographs of themselves doing what they did best.

When Mount Rushmore's future sculptor, Gutzon Borglum, moved

Above Mule Ear Mountain.

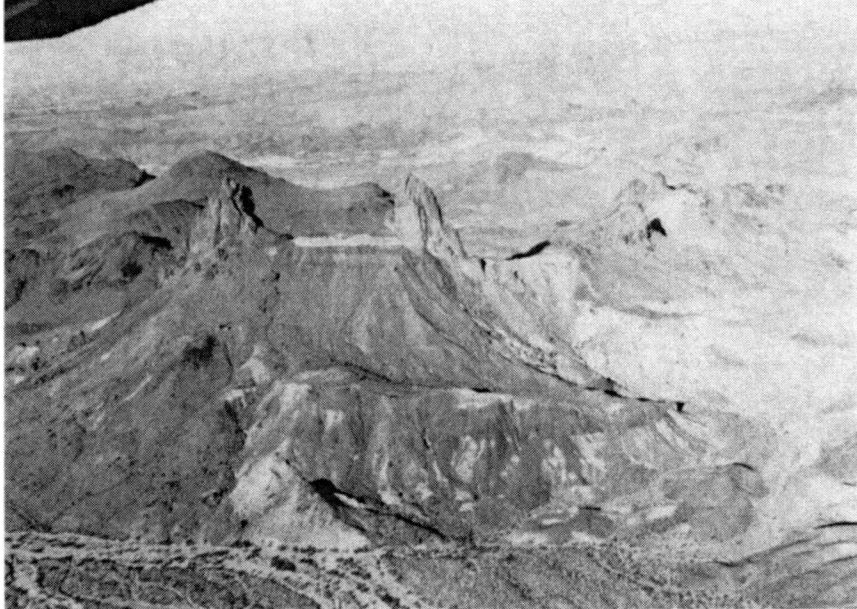

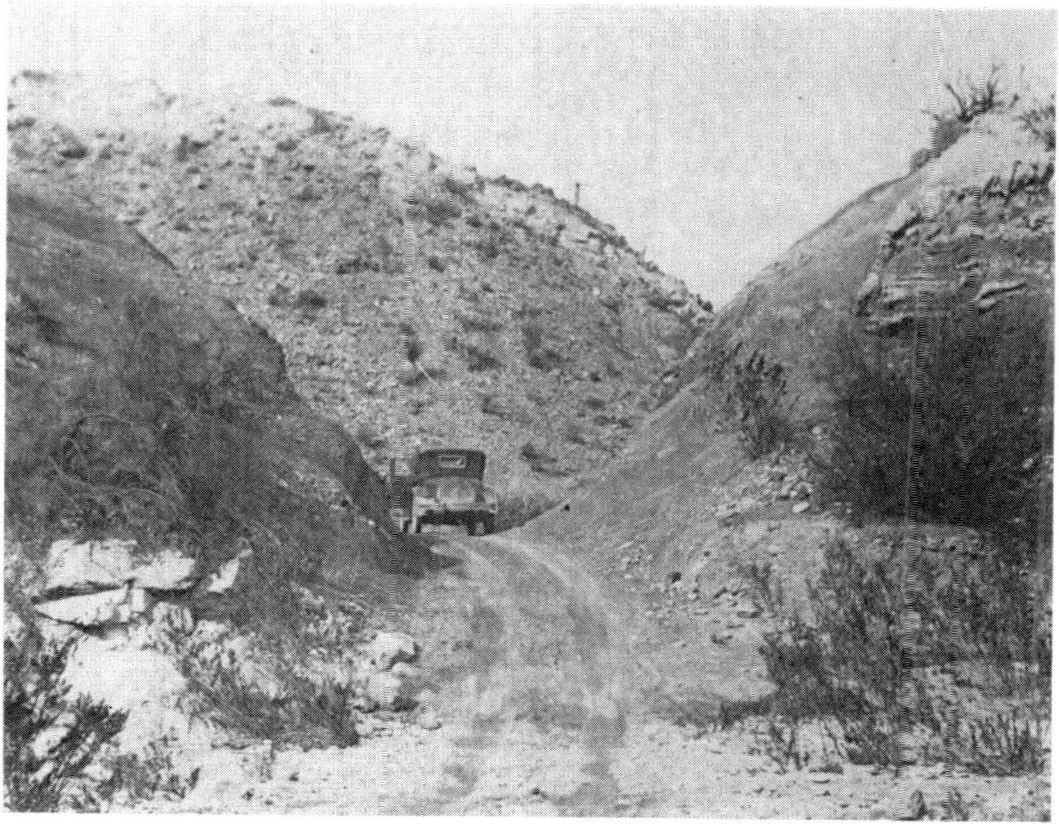

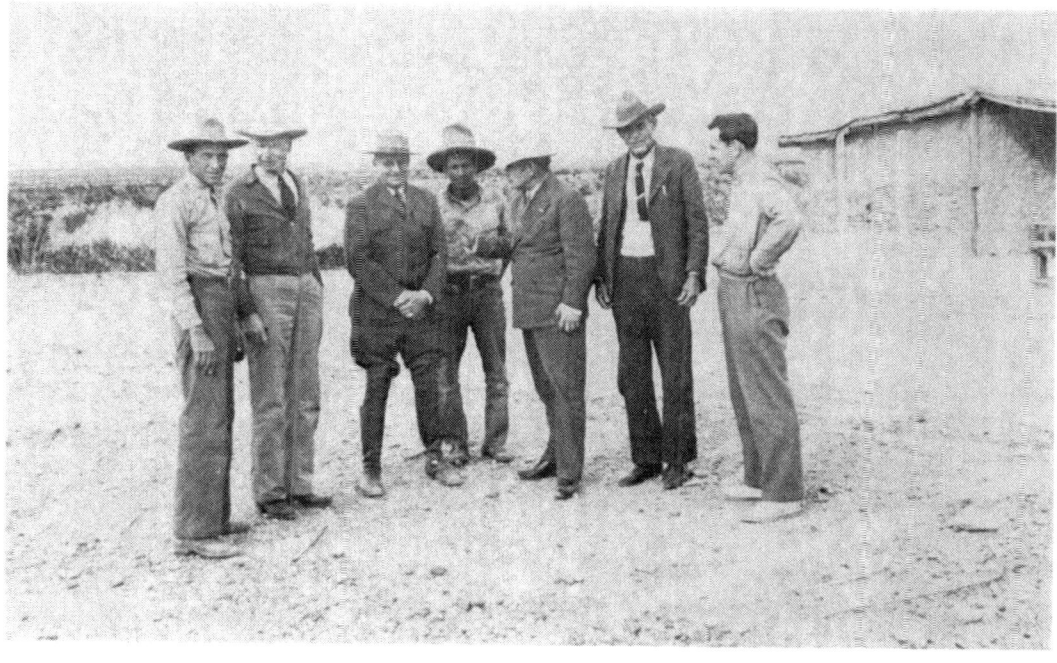

My Dodge roadster (above) near Terlingua, on one of its many trips to the Big Bend. Below, left to right: Elmo Johnson; Everett Townsend, exsheriff and U. S. Customs officer; National Park official Conrad Wirth; Earl Johnston, wax maker; Gutzon Borglum, famed sculptor; Uncle Tom Miller, pioneer; and Lincoln Borglum. The Borglums were touring the Big Bend with me. Wirth and Townsend were closing a deal with Johnson for the Big Bend National Park.

his studio to San Antonio in the early twenties, I became his personal photographer. While living at the Menger Hotel in 1927, he did the preliminary carvings for his massive South Dakota project in his studio on East Houston Street, and I photographed the progressive stages of his work on the Jefferson, Washington, Lincoln, and Roosevelt busts. In total, I made over òne hundred exposures. In the evening, when I took the last photograph, he would cover the clay with wet blankets until the next morning, when I brought finished prints for him, his wife, son, and daughter to see. Borglum believed the camera, and he studied my photographs of his work more than the sculpting itself.

He was delighted with the photos, knowing they would be invaluable during the years of the actual mountain sculpting. He ordered more than one thousand prints from the negatives. While Congress was considering the Mount Rushmore bill, Borglum wired me from Washington asking for five hundred eight by ten-inch prints of Washington's bust, apparently hoping to use them to gain support for his artistic venture. I received the telegram at four in the afternoon and worked all night to have his five hundred prints in the next morning's mail.

In 1935, during the ambitious, patriotic chiseling, Borglum and his son, Lincoln, visited me in the Big Bend, our first reunion in five years. He even took time to address students and townspeople at Sul Ross College on his work in South Dakota—using my lantern slides to illustrate his lecture. Borglum truly enjoyed the Big Bend. He spoke fluent Spanish to all the Mexican families we met, charming them all.

An artist on the watch for new media, he commented that magnificent results could come from carving the Casa Grande Mountain or one of the high walls of Santa Elena Canyon. He was interested in anything made of rock, so the Big Bend, with its petrified trees, canyons, mountains, and rocky terrain, was a real paradise for him. To him, all stone was potential sculpture.

His visit to the Bend, his first, was thorough. We went to the Rainbow Quicksilver Mine at Terlingua and the Castolon Trading Post; we visited Juana Ramirez, had dinner with Elmo and Ada Johnson, and spent the first night with Ray and Tom Miller at San Vicente, where our famed guest was toasted with sotol. The next morning, we traveled on to Boquillas, missing the colorful splash of afternoon sun on the Sierra del Carmen. But we did enjoy another of Boquillas's main events: Chata's tacos and beer!

From Boquillas, we went to Hanold's Fiber Factory, two miles north of Langford's Hot Springs. Mr. Hanold had unique handmade

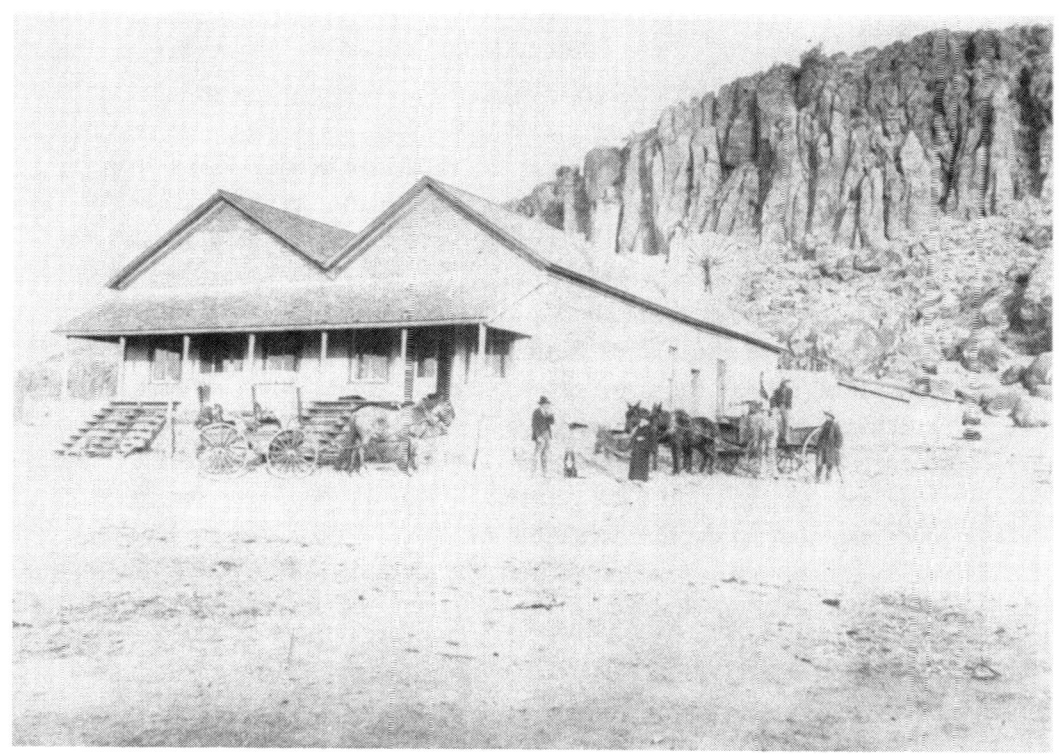

The Reverend Father Brockdus, Catholic priest serving the entire Big Bend, visited Nick Merfelder at his home as he was receiving three Fort Davis ranchmen in their covered wagon (above). Below, Merfelder in his Fort Davis home with his many antiques and musical instruments. Merfelder was Fort Davis justice of the peace for fifty years, and a fellow photographer.

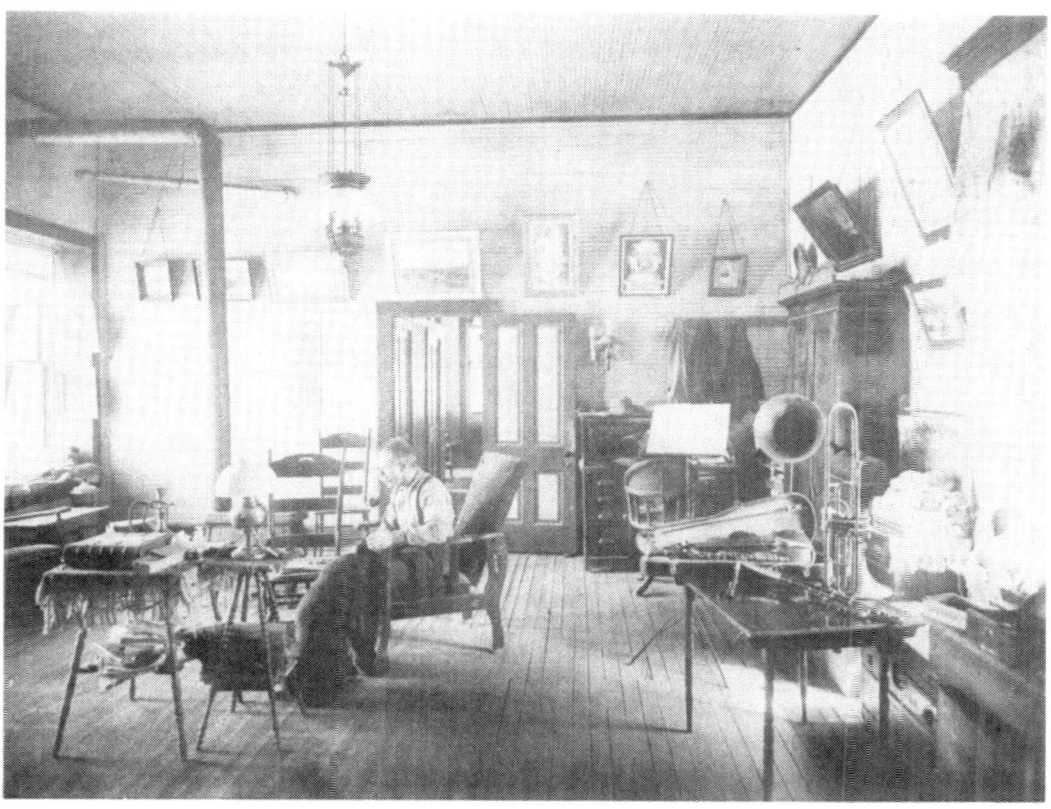

foot-and-hand-powered equipment to make numerous items from agave fibers. Ropes, cords, mats, bags, and brushes were his factory's major products, and he made them on a large scale, employing many workers. We visited him on a Sunday, so we didn't get to see the operation in action. From Mr. Hanold's, we returned to San Vicente, and went on to the Chisos Basin. After an excellent lunch at the Gage Hotel in Marathon, we drove back to Alpine, where he gave his speech at Sul Ross, culminating what he called an interesting, enjoyable trip through the picturesque Big Bend.

He was off to Rapid City, South Dakota, the next morning. With three presidential faces completed, he died before finishing Roosevelt's. Lincoln, his son, supervised the completion of his father's work.

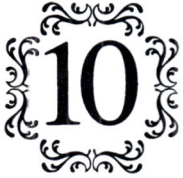

The Changing Big Bend

Before leaving Marathon, after our tour of the area, the famed sculptor Gutzon Borglum commented, "I am glad that we saw all the lower Big Bend before they destroy all those picturesque homes." Quite prophetic, for when the national park was created, all the Mexican homes and a few Anglo houses along the Rio Grande from below Castolon to Boquillas were torn down. Castolon was not included in the park until a few years later, and the buildings there were not demolished.

Only adobe walls remained of the Johnson ranch; Mexicans from Mexico were allowed to take all the lumber, doors, and windows from the ranch buildings. The historical village of Glenn Springs, which bandits had raided and burned, was bulldozed off the map. This action was unpopular and there were reports that the village was to be rebuilt. I was consulted by the Park Service about my photographs of Glenn Springs, but nothing was ever done to reconstruct the town. It was clear that the creation of Big Bend National Park would dissolve the community I had known.

Outside of razing the homes, and the subsequent desertion of the area, little was physically changed in the Big Bend. The Chisos Mountain Basin saw the most change. A park superintendent was stationed there to supervise extensive trail-making by the Civilian Conservation Corps, a federally funded organization designed to give employment to young men during the Depression of the 1930s.

The basin area, which today is the center of the national park, is of an entirely different formation, terrain, and vegetation from the rest of the Big Bend. Just twenty miles into the park, the basin seems a different world.

Even with the Big Bend's popularity and the evident tourist and park development, it remains a mysterious, isolated spot on the

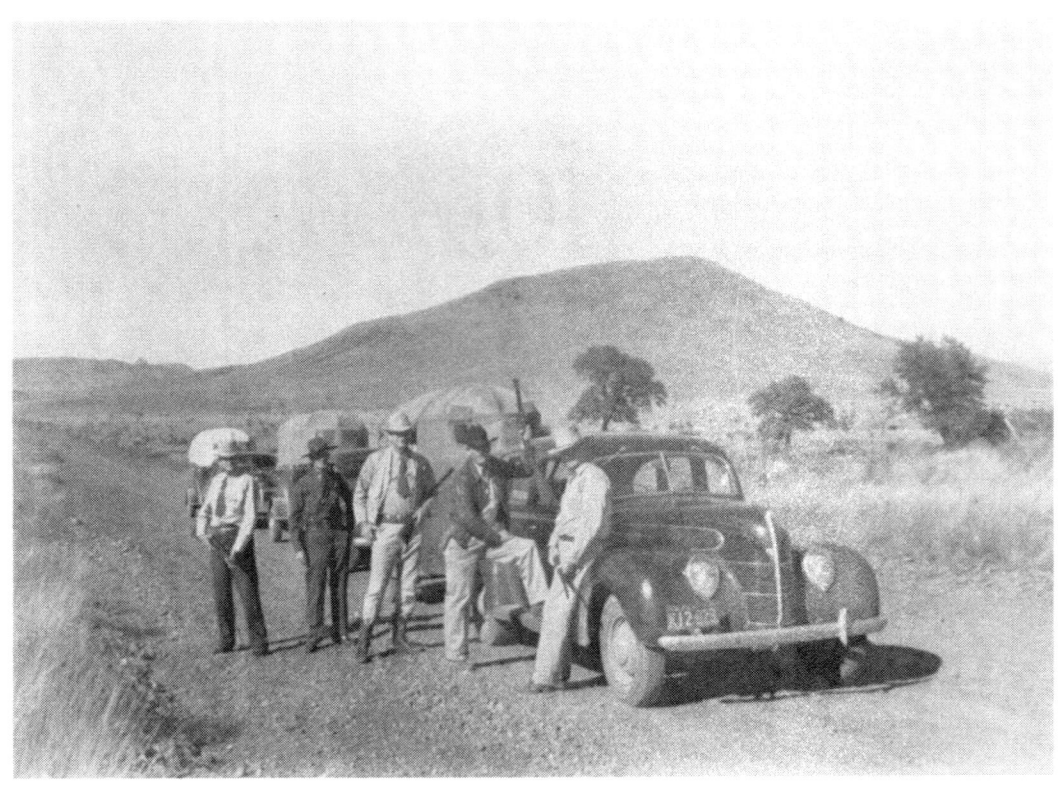

Left to right: Texas Ranger Captain Ernest Bert; Earl Fallis, chief of the U. S. Border Patrol, Alpine subdistrict; and Rangers Jim Flannery, Leo Bishop, and Pete Crawford. Near Alpine, 1941. Below, the adobe ruins of the Johnson ranch.

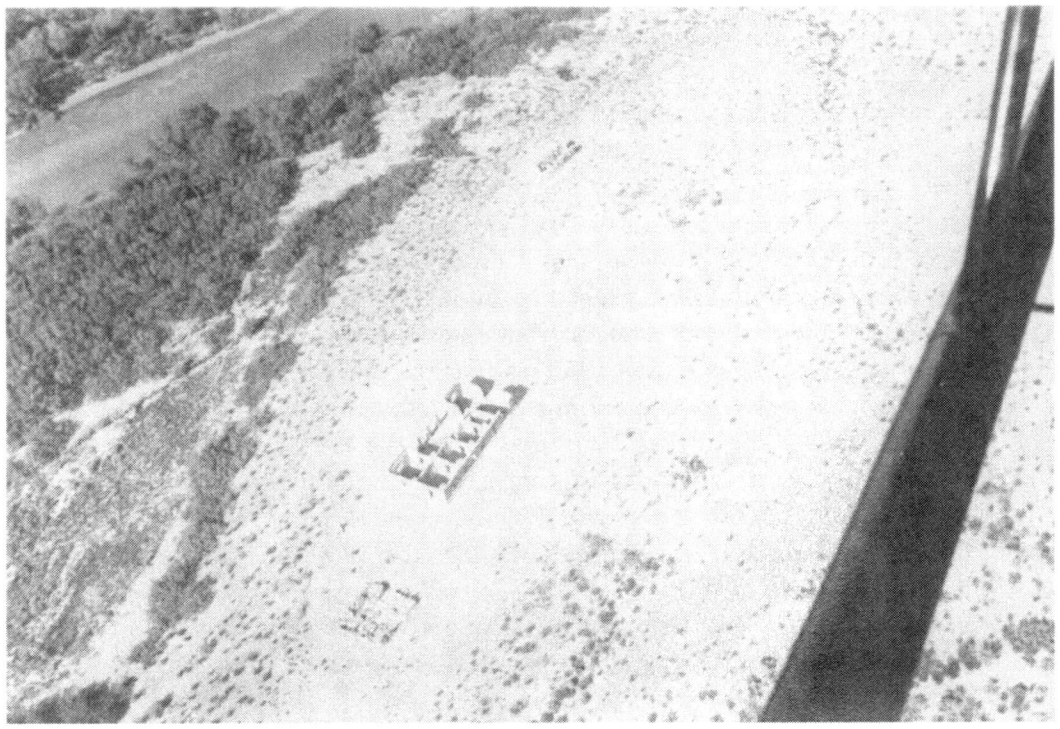

globe. At night, from June through September, "mystery lights" can be seen in the mountains. Merely the glowing effect of moisture on phosphate (from guano-rich caves), the lights are intense and haunting.

From time to time, a fossil discovery will remind one of the region's history and age. Remains of camels have been found, from the pre-Civil War times when the desert beasts were imported for use in army pack trains. But the discovery of the largest pterodactyl in 1975 multiplies the area's age many times. I think of the land as an ancient sea bed, today holding fossils of giant oysters; as the region where the pterodactyl soared above other terrifying reptiles; as the home of prehistoric terrier-sized horses and thirty-foot crocodiles. It also was a land of the Apache and the Comanche, and before them, stone-age cave dwellers. When I think of what life and change has passed over the Big Bend, I marvel at how truly little impact has been made on it by the National Park Service since 1944. And then I wonder if it can ever be tamed.

There is the harsh side of Big Bend life, noted by a cameraman in 1916, accompanying some reporters covering the Glenn Springs raid.

A Civilian Conservation Corps company surveyed a road into the Basin area while the Big Bend was still a state park; 1934.

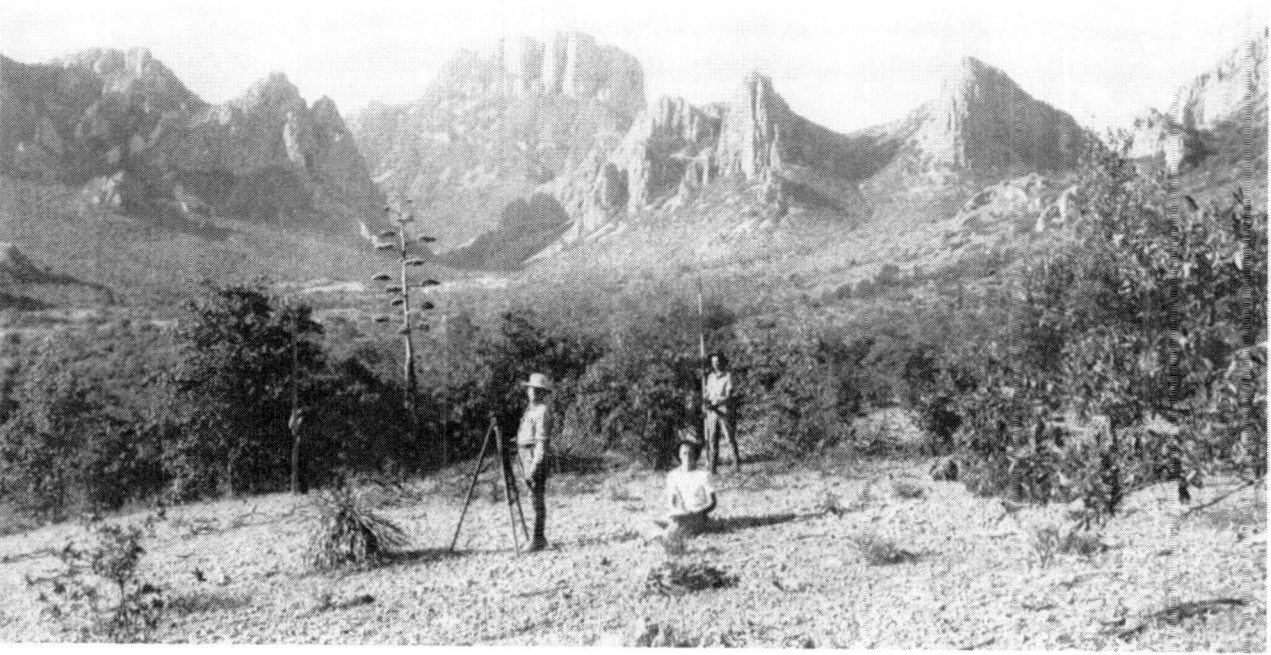

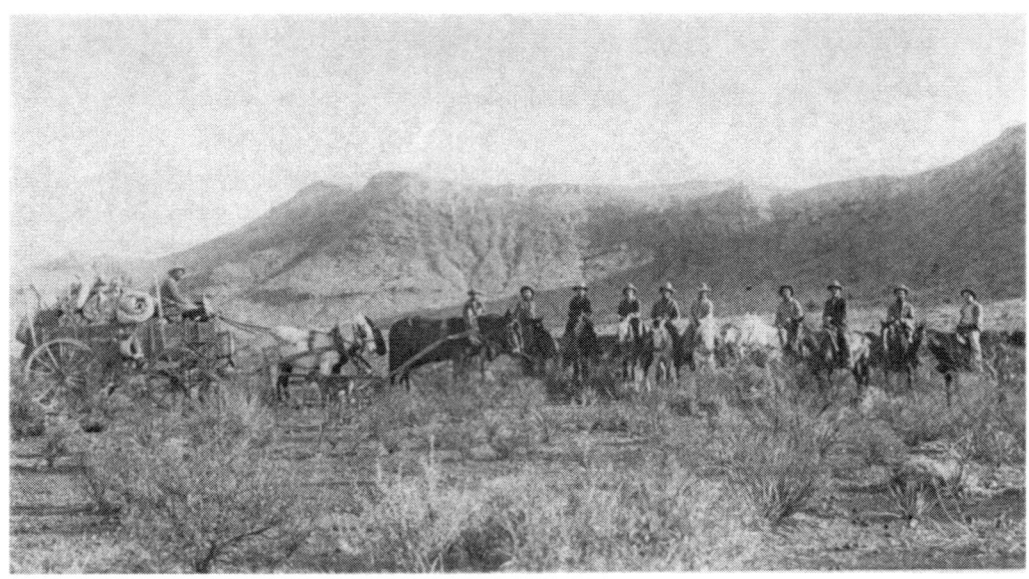

Above, Jim Stroud's outfit near Lajitas. Stroud, third from right, had just bought a large herd of Mexican cattle and was driving them to his ranch in the Rosilla Mountains south of Marathon. Below, four of Stroud's cowboys during the 1916 drive of Mexican cattle, most of which were bought for the low price of four to five dollars per head.

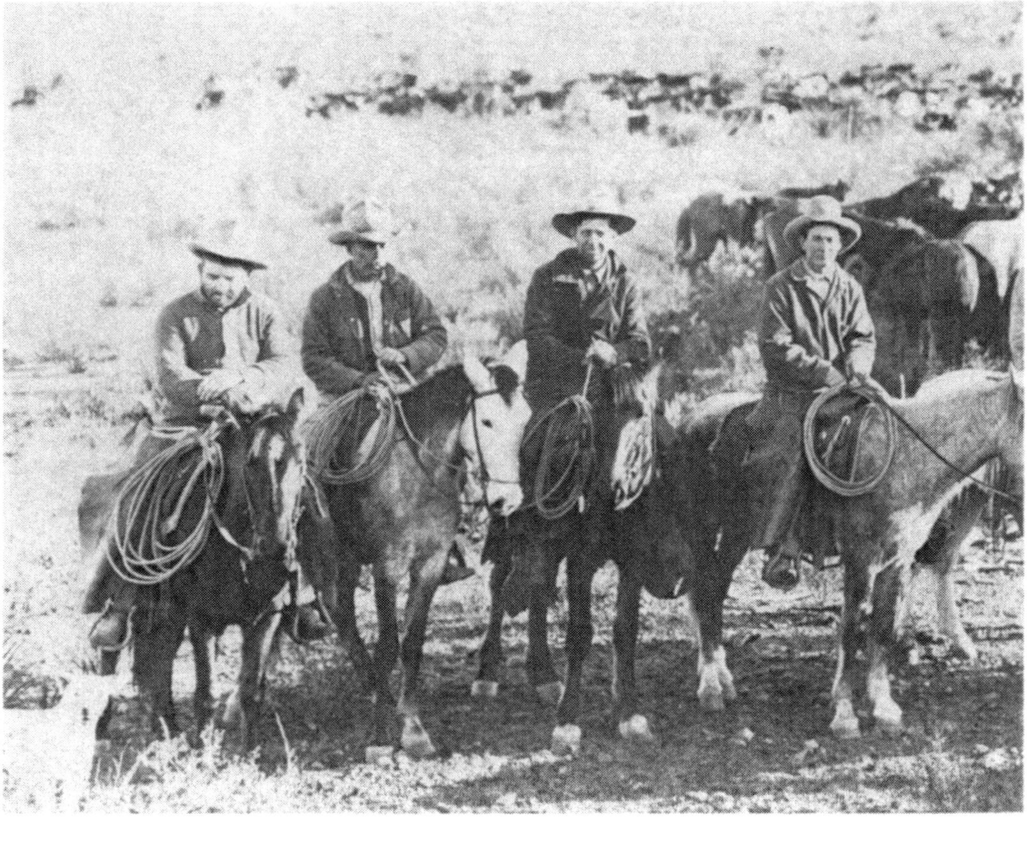

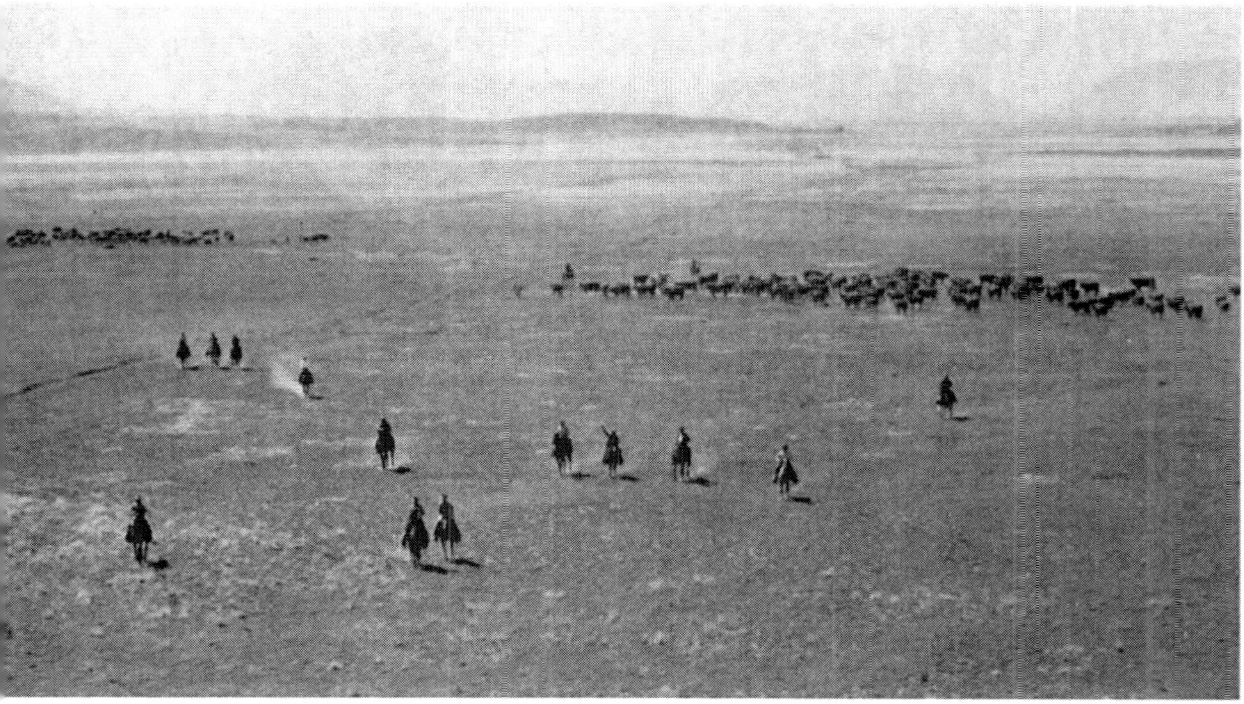

Cowboys above head for the chuckwagon after "cutting" the herd—separating calves from cows. Below, branding time on the J. W. Merrell ranch in the Davis Mountains.

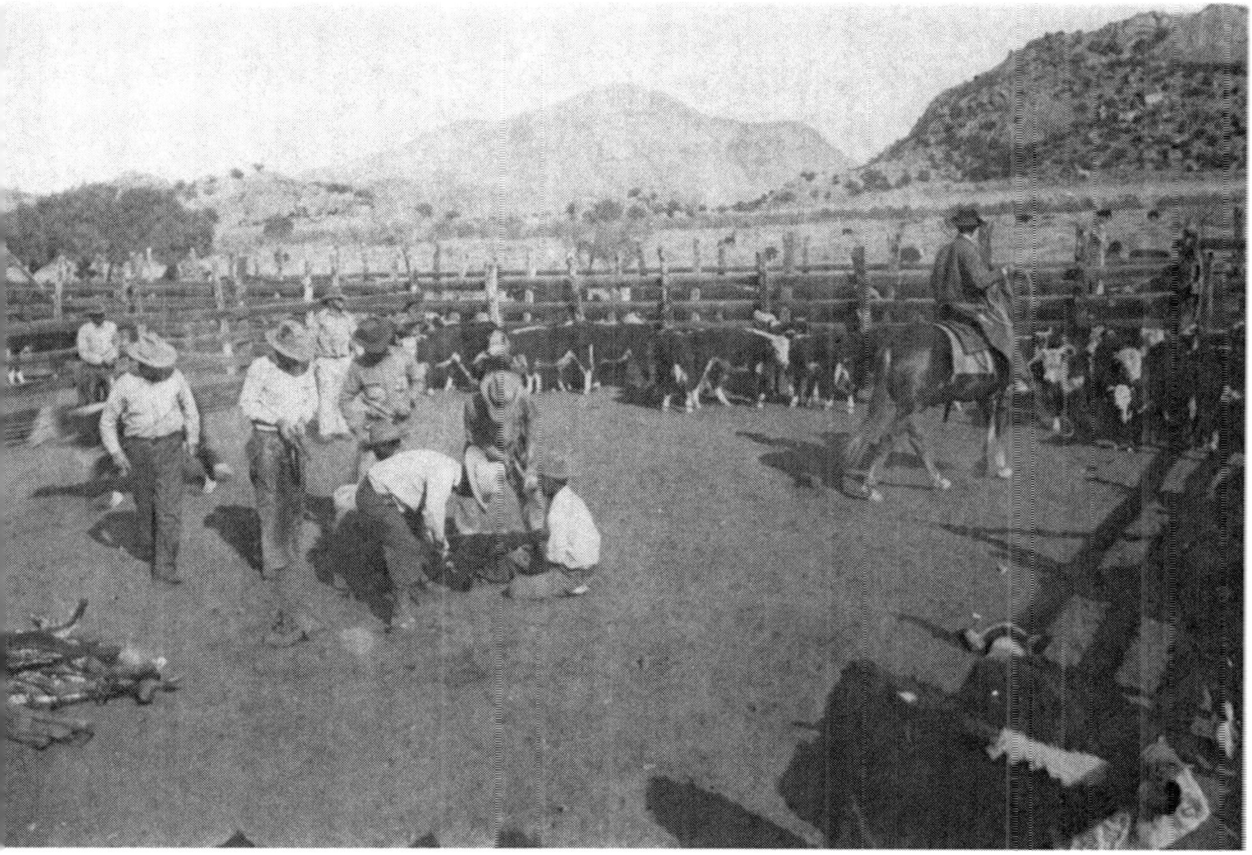

"The country isn't bad," he wrote. "It's just worse. Worse the moment you set foot from the train, and then, after that, just worser and worser."*

But then there is the gentle side of the Big Bend, the magical and beautiful land that I and my Mexican and American friends know. An old forgotten cowboy described it like this:

"You go south from Fort Davis until you come to the place where rainbows wait for rain, and the big river is kept in a stone box, and water runs uphill. And the mountains float in the air, except at night, when they go away to play with other mountains."**

*Ronnie C. Tyler, "The Little Punitive Expedition into the Big Bend, *Southwestern Historical Quarterly* 78, no. 3 (January, 1975), p. 284.

**Nathaniel T. Kenney, "Big Bend: Jewel in the Texas Desert," *National Geographic* 133, no. 1 (January, 1968), p. 133.

Index

CPSIA information can be obtained at www.ICGtesting.com
Printed in the USA
LVOW111018180113

316243LV00001B/1/P

9 781876 112615